SEVEN PLAYS OF KOFFI KWAHULÉ

AFRICAN PERSPECTIVES

Kelly Askew and Anne Pitcher
Series Editors

African Print Cultures: Newspapers and Their Publics in the Twentieth Century, edited by Derek R. Peterson, Emma Hunter, and Stephanie Newell

Unsettled History: Making South African Public Pasts, by Leslie Witz, Gary Minkley, and Ciraj Rassool

Seven Plays of Koffi Kwahulé: In and Out of Africa, translated by Chantal Bilodeau and Judith G. Miller edited with Introductions by Judith G. Miller

Seven Plays Of Koffi Kwahulé

In and Out of Africa

Translated by Chantal Bilodeau and Judith G. Miller

Edited with Introductions by Judith G. Miller

University of Michigan Press
Ann Arbor

Published in the United States of America by the
University of Michigan Press
Manufactured in the United States of America
♾ Printed on acid-free paper

2020 2019 2018 2017 4 3 2 1

A CIP catalog record for this book is available from the British Library.

Library of Congress Cataloging-in-Publication data has been applied for.

ISBN: 978-0-472-07349-8 [hardcover]
ISBN: 978-0-472-05349-0 [paper]
ISBN: 978-0-472-12280-6 [ebook]

We dedicate this volume to African theater artists wherever they carry on, in or off the African continent, to Nicole Bloom and the Cultural Services of the French Embassy in New York and to John Eisner and The Lark for all their help in the carrying we have done, and to John Conteh-Morgan, who should still be here carrying on with us.

ACKNOWLEDGMENTS

CHANTAL BILODEAU

Translating for the theater is a collaborative art. Just like a play cannot be fully realized until it has been staged, the translation of a play is not complete until the words have been spoken out loud and the intentions of the characters actualized in space. Six of the seven translations included in this anthology have gone through an extensive development process that included residencies with the playwright, workshops with actors and directors, and public presentations. I am therefore indebted to many organizations and individuals without whom this invaluable work would not have been possible.

Nicole Bloom and the Cultural Services of the French Embassy in New York championed this project from the beginning and were instrumental in supporting it through its thirteen years of unfolding. I am grateful for their generosity, enthusiasm, and trust.

John Eisner, Michael Robertson, and the entire staff of The Lark provided an artistic home for Koffi Kwahulé and me to work together, and precious support and guidance in the realization of the translations. I will be forever thankful for their loyalty, hospitality, and friendship. My thanks also go to Catherine Coray, director of the hotINK International Festival of Play Readings, formerly hosted at New York University's Tisch School of the Arts, who invited us twice to be part of the festival, giving us the rare opportunity to have the translations read in front of audiences and solicit feedback.

Several other organizations provided time and space, and a platform for encountering audiences: the Playwrights' Center in Minneapolis; the former Mark Taper Forum, now Center Theatre Group in Los Angeles; the Berkshires Theatre Festival in Stockbridge, Massachusetts; Howard University in Washington, DC; and New York Theatre Workshop. I feel lucky they opened their doors to us and welcomed us with such warmth.

Many talented dramaturgs, actors, directors, and musicians gave of their time to explore the worlds of these plays with me. Their questions, insights, and ability to breathe life into Koffi Kwahulé's words contributed to making the translations ever more specific and accurate. I am grateful for the willingness of the following people to tackle difficult material and for their unflinching dedication throughout the process:

That Old Black Magic: Chris Henry Coffey, Danyan Davis, Jonan Everett, Albert Jones, Angela Lewis, Robert Emmet Lunney, Chris McKinney, Jennifer Mudge, Chris Myers, Kevin O'Donnell, Postell Pringle, and Lucie Tiberghien.

Jaz: Dominic Duval, Zabryna Guevara, Michael Johnson-Chase, and Lynette Taylor.

Big Shoot: Michael Bakkensen, Brian Dykstra, Michael Johnson-Chase, Wayne Schroder, Lynette Taylor, and Sorab Wadia.

Misterioso-911: Stephanie Beatriz, Elba Sette-Camara, Amelia Campbell, Carmen M. Herlihy, Zainab Jah, Jessie Reagen, Shanessa Sweeney, and Liesl Tommy.

Blue-S-cat: Jamie Bock, Amelia Campbell, Marc Damon Johnson, Jacquelyn Landgraf, and Liesl Tommy.

Melancholy of Barbarians: Shiree Adkins, Charlie Barnett, Jocelyn Bioh, Carl Cofield, Aigner Corbitt, Treasure Davidson, Elizabeth Diamond, Asha Edwards, Lynnette Freeman, Joshua Gaddy, Candace Hale, Denise J. Hart, Frank Harts, Matt Holbert, Jabari Holder, Ameerah Legrande, Chris Myers, Yewande Odetoyinbo, Okwui Okpokwasili, Marita Phelps, Hubert Point du Jour, Tyshae Price, Shayna Nicole Small, Marcus Terrell Smith, William Sturdivant, Camille Thomas, John Douglas Thompson, Darius Vines, Samira Wiley, Kasaun Wilson, and Tamilla Woodard.

Judith G. Miller, my collaborator, was instrumental in getting this anthology together and offered precious editorial advice on the translations. She took on the translation of the seventh play, *Brewery*, the least lyrical and most grotesque of the lot, when difficulties with permissions made it impossible to include *Bintou,* and when time constraints prevented me from continuing with the translating. I thank her for taking this journey with me and making it so intellectually stimulating.

Finally, my deepest thanks go to Koffi Kwahulé, who trusted me with his beautiful words and allowed me to bring his work into the English language.

JUDITH G. MILLER

The work of bringing these texts together, commenting on them and on Koffi Kwahulé's theater in general would not have been possible without the friendship and cooperation of the author himself. I, too, am grateful to him for his theatrical gifts.

I would also like to thank Professor Sylvie Chalaye of the Institut d'Études Théâtrales of the University of Paris III and the members of SeFea, her research team, for many hours of stimulating discussions and workshops on African theater.

Nicole Bloom and the Cultural Services of the French Embassy based in New York City and The Lark have supported this project from the beginning. Professor Catherine Coray was there from before the beginning and her hotINK Festival will remain for me, as well as for many others, a model of international theatrical encounter.

My students from the Tisch School of the Arts, from the Department of French at NYU, and from the theater program at New York University Abu Dhabi, and Lydia Butt and Christiane Owuso-Sarpong (for the work in German) have taught me more about many of these plays than what I could have learned without their comments and enthusiasm.

The Department of French and La Maison Française at NYU have welcomed several events featuring readings and conversations about francophone theater, and especially about the work of Koffi Kwahulé. I am privileged to work in such a collegial intellectual environment.

Ellen Bauerle of the University of Michigan Press has made this publication possible despite many hurdles. I thank her and her team from the bottom of my heart.

And my dear friends Kate Turley and Judith Golden-Luck helped me remember to use commas and avoid the pitfalls of excessively academic writing.

Finally, Chantal Bilodeau has been an exemplary collaborator and inspiration. I thank her for the pleasure of thinking together.

The translation of *That Old Black Magic* was commissioned by and developed at The Lark, New York City, and was supported in part by an award from the National Endowment for the Arts. It was further developed and adapted at New York Theatre Workshop with support from the Cultural Services of the French Embassy in New York.

The translation of *Jaz* and *Big Shoot* was commissioned by and developed at The Lark, New York City.

The translation of *Misterioso-911* was commissioned by the Berkshire Theatre Festival and developed at the Berkshire Theatre Festival and The Lark, New York City.

The translation of *Blue-S-Cat* was supported in part by an award from the National Endowment for the Arts, and developed at the hotINK International Festival of Play Readings and The Lark, New York City.

The translation of *Melancholy of Barbarians* was supported in part by an award from the National Endowment for the Arts and developed at Howard University.

CONTENTS

Koffi Kwahulé at the White House, Washington, DC. Howard University workshop of Melancholy of Barbarians, 2010. Photo by Chantal Bilodeau.

Soundscapes, Mindscapes, and Escape

An Introduction to the Theater of Koffi Kwahulé

JUDITH G. MILLER

> Dispossessed of everything, blacks were in a better position to understand the world as it is, to better express the need for constructing something indestructible, something that can't be appropriated. They created jazz to express the black adventure, and it's finally become the human adventure.
>
> —Koffi Kwahulé, *Brothers in Sound*, 105[1]

In a series of 2007 conversations in Paris with musicologist Gilles Mouëllic, the Ivorian playwright Koffi Kwahulé spoke of the resonances between the theater he writes and the American jazz music that haunts so much of his writing. Kwahulé understands jazz as expressing the dispersion and disappearance of black peoples from Africa during the three-hundred-year tragedy of slavery. Jazz music, he believes, projects the absence of all those lost and exiled. Through their gifts, jazz musicians strive to build musical monuments to the disappeared. Speaking about jazz six years after September 11, 2001, and the destruction of the Twin Towers of New York's World Trade Center, Kwahulé asserts that jazz composition in fact encompasses the condition of every modern individual, or, as he puts it, today's "human adventure." Jazz, he contends, gives form and valence to both the volatilized bodies from the towers and the attacking planes and to the disarray and trauma that has followed. Like a jazz musician, Kwahulé intends his theater—with its stylistic nods to jazz, through its riffs, refrains, and repetitions, through references to composers and musical numbers—to capture both something of the pain of contemporary existential despair and the exuberant energy of improvisation. Kwahulé sees this as constructing a "suspended kingdom . . . more beautiful than what is there" (108).

In the impetus to capture both despair and beauty, he seeks to make work that speaks to "the universal," and this is not a universal that disguises imposed hierarchies of culture and an ideology of progress. Rather, his conceptualization enfolds human beings of all colors and genders while being based on the experience of blacks. As he further explains in *Brothers in Sound*: "In the symbolic tearing apart of the triangular trade, the black body is the first globalized space, foreseeing the fragmentation of the body of contemporary man" (98). This is how Africa grounds his work, providing the matrix from which emanates a modern sense of alienation and mourning but also the locus in which hope still lives.

Kwahulé's move to recenter how the human condition is figured in theater by infusing his plays with the felt experience of peoples of African origin echoes the playwriting philosophy of those francophone African writers whom Sylvie Chalaye calls "the new African playwrights"[2] and whom John Conteh-Morgan and Dominic Thomas name "the hybrid or crossroads generation." [3] Living across worlds and cultures, these writers are transnationalists, with subjectivities open to migratory inflections. They experiment with form and content but maintain a sense of Africa in their works through structures of feeling, specific cultural expressions, and allusions.[4] Theirs is the third and perhaps most rebellious iteration in a loose periodization of francophone African playwrights that traces the origin of francophone playwriting in Africa to colonial schools in the 1930s and 1940s. Under the tutelage of French teachers in the prestigious schools of Dakar and St. Louis, Senegal, meant to form "native" colonial administrators for what was then French West Africa, students learned to adapt the lessons of Corneille and Molière to their own expressive needs. One of these early playwrights, one of many from the 1950s and 1960s who were both politically astute and noted as fiction writers, was Ivorian Bernard Dadié whose caustic history play *Béatrice du Congo* (1970)[5] shows seventeenth-century Portuguese explorers being bested by the queenly woman warrior Beatrice—before they burned her at the stake. Another founding playwright, among the most performed in Africa and elsewhere, was Martinique's poet and statesman Aimé Césaire. Educated in the Caribbean and in Paris but similarly disposed to capturing historical figures in dramatic form, Césaire wrote the *Tragedy of King Christophe* (*La Tragédie du Roi Christophe*, 1963) in which the Haitian revolutionary leader confronts the limits of his own vision for a grandiose Haiti.[6] *The Tragedy of King Christophe*, an interrogation of leadership, has become a mainstay of the "African" repertory, produced regularly throughout West Africa.

This first generation of writers, reclaiming the history and myths of African peoples and producing plays that helped prepare and promote the ebullient independence period of the 1960s, eventually gave way to a second generation. In the 1970s and 1980s this next group proved itself more concerned with introducing African aesthetics to dramatic practice and with deriding the disappointing aftermath of decolonization than with celebrating Africa's historical or mythical past. Sony Labou- Tansi from Congo- Brazzaville and Werewere Liking from Cameroon, for example, theatricalized rituals from their respective Kongo and Bassa communities, crafting carnivalesque dancing and drumming spectacles and healing exorcisms to give shape to the devils of dictatorship (Labou-Tansi's *The Parenthesis of Blood*; *La Parenthèse de sang*, 1981) or communal strife (Liking's *Singuè Mura or Given That A Woman . . .*; *Singuè Mura ou Considérant que la femme . . .*, 1992).[7] The structure of their plays included their audiences in what can be seen as attempts at casting out evil and putting recovery in motion.

Reacting to what has come to be seen by some as the illusory pan-Africanism of the earlier generations and especially refusing the perceived expectation that African playwrights must produce plays in which the vision of Africa corresponds to a particular myth of Africa, to wit a culture of drums and dancing and themes of corruption and tribalism, the "hybrid" playwrights launched angry manifestoes in the early 1990s. Kossi Efoui, Caya Makhelé, José Pliya, Kangni Alem, to name a few, with Kwahulé among them—many of whom live outside of Africa—insisted on their right to critique the commodification of an "authentic Africa." They continue to write to wrench their theater away from comforting the Global North (Europe and North America) with the vision of Africa it has come to expect. By refusing to create portraits of the exotic other, they foil what they believe the North promotes as a one-dimensional image of the continent. Their plays depict a world in which themes of racism, exile, civil violence, cultural dislocation, and identity shifts can apply to all manner of people, not just the formerly colonized. They do not, on the whole, as does a comparable generation of black writers in the United Kingdom, attempt to capture onstage the lives of diasporic African communities, thus making people of color visible to "European" eyes.[8] Rather, through parables, mythic borrowings across cultures, and intensely lyrical dialogue, they establish mindscapes of fractured identities and violated psyches, states of being that capture the fate of millions of human beings on the move today or unable to escape from chaos and war.

Within this group of theater professionals, Kwahulé, now based in Paris but born in 1956 in central Côte d'Ivoire, is the most prolific, the best known internationally, and arguably the most intriguing experimenter. Having written some twenty-five plays,[9] having been translated into some seventeen languages and been produced in theaters from Abidjan to Djibouti, from Brussels to Budapest, from Montreal to Manhattan, and from Rome to Reunion Island, he brings his counsel and his aesthetic to theaters all over the world. Paradoxically, he garners more attention outside of France than on French stages, as French theatrical institutions still tend to compartmentalize what they consider to be "non-French" theater.[10] Hence, within France, Kwahulé's plays are especially featured in professional spaces subsidized to promote francophone (that is non-Metropolitan) work, theaters such as Le Tarmac or Le Lavoir Moderne in Paris; the Festival des Francophonies in Limoges; or the Avignon Chapelle du Verbe Incarné, active especially during the celebrated July theater festival. At the same time, French students auditioning for some of the best French theater schools, for example the Paris Conservatory or the Cours Florent, enthusiastically select excerpts from his plays as audition pieces. He is also called on frequently by French professionals in the social service sector—a call he willingly answers—to do theater workshops with prisoners, community groups, and adolescents of all stripes. This kind of mentoring has had a significant impact on his later theater pieces. Depending on the availability of performers and on the potential for metaphoricity of the play in question, young or amateur theater companies everywhere in Europe, and particularly in France, cast both actors of color and white actors in his plays.[11]

Kwahulé's theater has evolved from the kinds of political sketches he wrote as a student just out of theater school in Abidjan, the capital city of Côte d'Ivoire and in the 1980s and 1990s a thriving center for theatrical creation,[12] to the multilayered and polyvocal meditations that challenge readers and theater professionals today. Seven of the latter (*That Old Black Magic*, 1993; *Jaz*, 1998; *Big Shoot*, 2000; *Misterioso-911*, 2005; *Blue-S-Cat*, 2005; *Brewery*, 2006; and *Melancholy of Barbarians*, 2008) have been translated and collected in this volume.[13] These plays fold specific political commentaries into a larger concern about what it means to be a human being in postcolonial times. In his earlier works targeting avidity and the power structure in Côte d'Ivoire, Kwahulé lambasted both his countrymen and the Ivorian government, as in the nonpublished play *The Big Snake* (*Le Grand-Serpent*, 1982). The pointed critique behind these sketches, performed at his and his fellow actors' peril in the early 1980s, has taken a more indirect form in the works he has been writing since the mid-1990s and his permanent move to France.[14] He continues to attack materialism, but does so, for example, as in *Jaz* (a meditation on the effects of rape), in poetic riffs on lists of items to be buried with the dead. In *Brewery* (a biting satire of revolutionary action), the brewery itself becomes the locus of greed. And in *Melancholy of Barbarians* (a fantasy about dysfunctional communities and sick suburbs), centers of power, such as multinational firms, are attacked through the syncopated and desperate rants of specific characters.[15]

What was disgust in his early works with a fascination for the "bling-bling" factor so apparent in African media representations of the "good life" in the Global North becomes in his mature works, and particularly in those represented in the pages that follow, an insistent query about what really makes life worth living. He asks centrally a question that has stayed with him since his Christian upbringing among the Baoulé people of Côte d'Ivoire: Am I my brother's keeper? In all the plays found in this anthology, but most especially in *Big Shoot*, where the question forms the play's leitmotif, Kwahulé worries that the parable of Cain's violence toward his brother Abel, an act that marked him forever as murderer and outcast, may well be the common lot of humankind. How do we acknowledge and respect the place of the other, even if that other seems to benefit irrationally from life's gifts, while we are irrationally punished? How do we even see the other when we are so imprisoned, not only in our own narcissism and material desires but also in how others see us? Are we not, as Kwahulé would have it, often "killed" (that is, stopped in our tracks or frozen) by the identities imposed on us by others?[16]

Without definitive answers or resolutions, these queries reverberate through each of his plays like a series of unending, self-generating waves. Given form in stage images and actions, such questions result in a violent pummeling of the senses but also, if less frequently, in the tantalizing sensation that a soft flow of water can sometimes provoke. Kwahulé's musical partitions, less and less like conventional theatrical dialogue as his work progresses, communicate in high-fidelity carnal sounds something of the ineffable that affirms life. We might think of this process as a form of artistic redemption, and Kwahulé certainly hints that we should do so—from his positive treatment of the boxer character Shorty's love of Goethe's poetry (*That Old Black Magic*) to his sly appraisal of drug-dealing Baby Mo's unconquerable spirit of self-creation (*Melancholy of Barbarians*). Through the beauty of lyrical flights and the movement of exhilarating rhythmic invention, his plays register the possibility of resistance and survival.

Constant tension within themes and centers of interest, as well as in the overall structure of his plays, characterizes his aesthetic and philosophical vision. Thus, while American jazz provides a fertile model for self-expression (for characters in *That Old Black Magic*, *Jaz*, and *Misterioso-911*, indeed a model for the very articulation of most of his plays), the dream of America as a land of promise runs amok. In *Melancholy of Barbarians*, *Big Shoot*, *That Old Black Magic*, and *Brewery*, disconcerting and often mordant references to America give the lie to the land of opportunity. Kwahulé never simply opposes one measure of civilization or one set of values to another. Searching, not finding, is what he privileges. Whether the problem seems to be a clash of cultures (black American versus white American in *That Old Black Magic*), or styles of communication (the overdrive of the elevator-entrapped Woman, the indifference of the similarly entrapped Man in *Blue-S-Cat*), or positions of superiority and inferiority (the torturer Sir and the victim Stan in *Big Shoot*, the women inmates and the prison drama teacher in *Misterioso-911*), in the end or along the way each player or each perspective on the problem gets muddied, contaminated by other ways of seeing. Kwahulé never sides with the rightness or wrongness of a character's stance; he does not attempt to teach what must be done. By showing how damaged people struggle to keep their contours intact, he sends out questions to be grappled with by the public.

Images imposed by others or by media hype often hold his characters back from the ability to come to grips with their situation, imprisoning them in fantasies: White Magic, the German cabaret singer and beer entrepreneur in *Brewery*, for example, encases herself in the image of a Bavarian Josephine Baker. But in other instances the dogged quest for a self leads to wearing a mask or a veil: Baby Mo allows her head to be covered in *Melancholy of Barbarians*, prisoner Linda hides behind her fictional role in the embedded play in *Misterioso-911*. In Kwahulé's theater, having no boundaries or wishing to have no boundaries, refusing differentiation through, for instance, projections of incest or cannibalism (such as the inmates in *Misterioso-911* who ingest the drama teacher) keep the characters trembling in an endless and funereal deadlock. Obsession with no boundaries just like obsession with fixed ones highlights what theorist Edouard Glissant castigates as an unhealthy focus on the "Same" and thus a refusal of difference, a rejection of the other that leads to stagnation.[17] Kwahulé's plays paradoxically give shape and vibration to states of paralysis.

Horrendous, unpardonable, outrageous violence resides in the racism, exclusionary tactics, and misogyny spotlighted in so many of his works. In Kwahulé's plays, violence provides the only means of eliminating violence (such as the shooting of the rapist in *Jaz* or the dragging of psychotic supercop Komisari behind a truck in *Melancholy of Barbarians*). Brutality or, to be more accurate, dreams and fantasies of brutality, narrations of violence (rape, torture, beatings, mutilation) reveal the poisonous medicine used to assuage the suffering of being alive. Onstage projections of hurt and violated bodies become metaphors for both the dolorous African continent and the harsh experience of living anywhere in these postcolonial times.[18]

It is true that pastiches of Christ-like characters play a sacrificial and thus possibly redemptive role (the trapped Man expires when he attempts to reach out to the trapped Woman in *Blue-S-Cat*; Jaz loses herself to save herself in *Jaz*; drug lord Zachariah is killed trying to reestablish family in *Melancholy of Barbarians*). In almost every one of Kwahulé's plays, a character dies ritualistically in a quest for something greater than him- or herself. Nonetheless, for the characters transcendence remains out of reach and catharsis goes unrealized. No greater, purer, healthier community emerges at the end of the play, but rather, and most often, we are left with bodies stuck in suffocating spaces, set up to recommence yet again their painful, encaged hurtling.

In reading or staging Kwahulé's plays, we must take some distance from these mutilated bodies and tropes of violence. The author himself makes this known through self-conscious hyperbole and structuring devices. His is an uncomfortable real, situated somewhere between classical realism and surrealism, more a psychic state than a material one, often even cartoonish. The referential real hovers at several steps removed from what might happen on stage. We can even locate his theater in the realm of the hyper-real, taking our clue from Jean Baudrillard.[19] In Kwahulé's case, this means a heightened and intensified horror, so over the top that, paradoxically, it can also be laughable. We see this exaggeration, for instance, in the dope ring's porn fantasies in *Melancholy of Barbarians*, in the rapist's extolling of his manliness in *Jaz*, in the soldiers recounting their war escapades in *Brewery*. This kind of laughter, as in a Quentin Tarantino film, confronts the possibilities of human nature at its most extreme and calls for us to take a step back, hear what is being said, and judge it. Stepping back becomes easier in many of Kwahulé's plays for they indeed bracket the act of looking: *That Old Black Magic*, *Big Shoot*, *Brewery*, and *Jaz* all include implied audiences or interlocutors who silently interrogate the characters. Avatars of flesh and blood audiences, these staged audiences encourage a self-consciousness, a clairvoyance not only about what is happening on stage but also about the *mise-en-abyme* that queries the act of representation itself.[20]

Moreover, Kwahulé puts into motion a montage technique, borrowed from years as a child watching B-grade movies from the United States, India, and Egypt, that allows him to make meaning through juxtapositions and intersections, through alternating repetitive phrases with lengthy confessions. He thus multiplies the angles of vision, discounts the kind of suspense that sutures the audience to the play's articulation, and counts on the audience to find some sense in the story being told.[21] The roller coaster of registers (*Blue-S-Cat*'s tightly wound dramatic spring suddenly turning into a Hollywood dance number, *Jaz*'s storytelling interrupted by incessant bureaucratic voices) makes it impossible to ground the experience of the plays in anything that would permit a rigidly psychological interpretation.

In the more recent plays in this anthology (*Misterioso-911*, *Blue-S-Cat*, *Melancholy of Barbarians*), Kwahulé especially communicates meaning through the polyvocality (or choral groupings) that absorb the individual subjectivities of what we would more easily have called "characters" in earlier works. This constitutes the most startling difference with plays such as *That Old Black Magic* and *Brewery*, where there are clearly embodied characters. These circulating voices, nonattributed in the original French texts but separated out in the translations included here (with the exception of *Misterioso-911*) in order to make them easier to read, exist in a spatial limbo. (We are in a stuck elevator in *Blue-S-Cat*, in an exit-less glass cage in *Big Shoot*.) Such intercepting, crisscrossing voices, in such a suspended space, help preclude any specific identification with a character's particular plight. Rather, circulating voices and limbic space concentrate attention on the text and its music, and perhaps in doing so beckon toward an emotional exorcism operative for those listening and watching, even if there is no relief for the voices heard.

Kwahulé's focus on stage textuality would seem to place him within the current wave of nonmimetic avant-garde theater in France. Writers such as Valère Novarina and Noëlle Renaude also put pressure on the text, and thus on voices, in their case asking voices to do all the work of theater. Dispensing with "character," "plot," and "setting," Novarina and Renaude create crystallized language, concentrating on the theater text as a way of examining what writing, as speech, is and can do.[22] Kwahulé, on the contrary, still needs theater to say something about community, about marginalization, about the difficulty and the hope of creating a sense of self. The diasporic yearning in his plays, the references to and reverberations with contemporary black music, the predominance of violent encounters, and the background of postcolonial disarray align his work more with that of the much-lamented playwright Bernard-Marie Koltès, considered by many to be the last great international writer for the stage that France has produced.[23] Koltès's theater, like Kwahulé's, stages vocal concerts between ghostly characters strung out on images of themselves. Feeling hollow, they multiply attempts to ground an identity by weaving mythic stories, often interrupted. Koltès's real, much like Kwahulé's, does not differentiate between psychic truth and material reality. And as in Kwahulé's work, the pain contained in Koltès's recurring themes and images is offset by the incantatory formal aspects of his poetic prose: stops, repetitions, and interweaving of motifs and phrases. Perhaps we might see this resemblance as a sign that writers who still believe that theater should mirror the world will inevitably attempt to capture what was once thought of as the in-between and displaced. On the move themselves, living between cultures, refusing to celebrate the idea of nation, such writers broaden theatrical definitions of the human.

NOTES

1. Koffi Kwahulé and Gilles Mouëllic, *Frères de son: Koffi Kwahulé et le jazz, entretiens* (Paris: Éditions Théâtrales, 2007), trans. Judith Miller, "Brothers in Sound," *L'Esprit Créateur: Nouvelles dramaturgies d'Afrique et des diasporas* 48, no. 3 (Fall 2008): 97–108. Quotations from the translation will be indicated in parentheses in the text of the essay.

2. Sylvie Chalaye, *L'Afrique Noire et son théâtre au tournant du XXe Siècle* (Rennes: Presses Universitaires de Rennes, 2001), 38.

3. John Conteh-Morgan with Dominic Thomas, *New Francophone African and Caribbean Theatres* (Bloomington: Indiana University Press, 2010), xvii.

4. In Kwahulé's case, his sensitivity and sense of humor as a member of the Baoulé ethnic group from West Africa emerge through the presence of pigs in several of his plays. The pig is to him an emblematic animal, both good at cleaning up everybody else's messes and good to eat. Considered "dirty," even proscribed by certain religions, the sociable and sensual pig signals festivities for the Baoulé. Through its sacrifice, the pig brings the community together around the table.

5. Bernard Dadié, *Béatrice du Congo* (Paris: Présence Africaine, 1970).

6. Aimé Césaire, *La Tragédie du Roi Christophe* (Paris: Présence Africaine, 1963), trans. Paul Breslin and Rachel Ney, *The Tragedy of King Christophe* (Chicago: Northwestern University Press, 2015).

7. Sony Labou-Tansi, *Parenthèse du Sang* (Paris: Hatier, 1981), trans. Jill MacDougall, *Parentheses of Blood* (New York: Theatre Communications Group, 1986). Werewere Liking, *Singuè Mura: Considérant que la femme* (Abidjan: Édi-

tions Eyo Ki-Yi, 1990), trans. Judith Miller, "*Singuè Mura: Given That a Woman*," *Theatre Forum* 19 (2001): 11–32.

8. Awam Amkpa, *Theatre and Postcolonial Desire* (London: Routledge, 2004), 181.

9. Koffi Kwahulé's theater bibliography (major works) includes *Ave Maria* (Brussels: Éditions Lansman, 2008); *Big Shoot, P'tite-Souillure* (Paris: Éditions Théâtrales, 2000); *Bintou* (Brussels: Éditions Lansman, 1997); *Brasserie* (Paris: Éditions Théâtrales, 2006); *Cette vieille magie noire* (Brussels: Éditions Lansman, 1993); *Les Créanciers* in *25 Petites pièces d'auteurs* (Paris: Éditions Théâtrales, 2007); *La Dame du café d'en face, Jaz* (Paris: Éditions Théâtrales, 1998); *El Mona*, in *Liban, écrits nomades* (Brussels: Éditions Lansman, 2001); *Fama* (Brussels: Éditions Lansman, 1998); *Il nous faut l'Amérique!* (Paris: Éditions Acoria, 1997); *La Mélancholie des barbares* (Brussels: Éditions Lansman, 2009); *Le Masque boîteux: Histoires de soldats* (Paris: Éditions Théâtrales, 2003); *Misterioso-911, Blue-S-Cat* (Paris: Éditions Théâtrales, 2005); *Nema: Lento cantabile semplice* (Paris: Éditions théâtrales, 2011); L'Odeur des arbres et autres pieces (Paris: Éditions Théâtrales, 2016); *Les Recluses* (Paris: Éditions Théâtrales, 2010); *Le Sas, Jaz, André: Monologues pour femmes* (Paris: Éditions Théâtrales, 2008); *Village fou ou les déconnards* (Paris: Éditions Acoria, 2000).

10. In 2015–16, the Comédie Française, France's national theater, launched a reading series of new African plays at its annex, the Vieux Columbia. Four young playwrights from Guinea (Hakim Bah), Congo-Brazzaville (Julien Mabiala Bissila), Burkina Faso (Aristide Tarnagda), and Togo (Gustave Akakpo) had their works read by the prestigious and almost exclusively European actors of the "House of Molière."

11. The discussion of who can or should play which roles in a theater piece is somewhat different in Europe than in the United States. Categories of white and black or "of color" are not easily admitted in many European countries and especially not in France where a republican commitment to equality often masks the racialism operant there. Hence French theater, by not recognizing difference, can continue to cast only white actors in classical pieces, the tacit understanding being that only Europeans should play European roles. Cross-racial casting has been practiced for a number of years by directors Peter Brook and Ariane Mnouchkine, but, in the main, Euro-black actors are just now getting access to main-stage careers. Europeans do not have the same qualms about casting whites in roles of people of color that Americans do, and at this point in time there are also fewer black theater professionals in most European countries than in the United States. Kwahulé's plays offer rare opportunities for black actors in France, but because of the allegorical nature of many of them, they can be performed by nonblack actors without resorting to minstrelsy of any kind.

12. At the time that Kwahulé left his village to study in Abidjan (mid-1970s), the capital city boasted not only a fine university, the University of Abidjan at Cocody, but also a groundbreaking Institute for African Studies located within the university as well as an excellent theater school: l'Institut National des Arts d'Abidjan. Côte d'Ivoire had a very active Ministry of Culture, with a playwright, rather than a professional politician, serving as head. It is interesting to note that the recently deposed president of Côte D'Ivoire, Laurent Gbagbo, is himself a published playwright.

13. The version of *That Old Black Magic* in this anthology is an adaptation of the original play by the author who reduced the required number of actors from fourteen to seven. Since it is set in the United States, the play was further adapted by Chantal Bilodeau during the translation process to reflect an American sensibility. The translation was read at the New York Theatre Workshop in 2010.

14. Kwahulé went to France in 1979 to pursue further theater studies—acting and directing—at the Rue Blanche School (L'École Nationale Supérieure des Arts et Techniques du Théâtre de Paris). He matriculated into the well-known Institute of Theatre Studies at the University of Paris III–Sorbonne Nouvelle where he completed a doctorate in theater history and criticism in 1992. It was shortly after receiving his doctorate that he decided to stay in France.

15. Grotesque farce engenders a painfully funny Africa critiqued for its dictators for life and neocolonial economies in several of Kwahulé's plays written since the mid-1990s. In *Brewery*, 2006, represented in this anthology, a commando unit stages a coup at a tropical beer plant run by an expat German cabaret singer. Who owns the beer owns the country. Who owns the country exports the image of the country. In *Il nous faut l'Amérique* (We Need America), 1997, have-not Africans vie with each other to hook up with a countrywoman when she begins to birth oil rather than children. These satires offer up an idea of Africa as more obviously a specific geographical place than what we find in almost all of the plays collected in this anthology.

16. Koffi Kwahulé cited in Sylvie Chalaye, *Afrique Noire et dramaturgies contemporaines: Le Syndrôme Frankenstein* (Paris: Éditions Théâtrales, 2004), 44.

17. In almost all of his meditative essays, but especially in *Poetics of Relation*, trans. Betsy Wing (Ann Arbor: University of Michigan Press, 1997), Edouard Glissant, the Martinican writer and essayist, speaks to the need for a poetics and philosophy of relation, one in which definitions of self are never fixed but always moving in relation to others around oneself.

18. In many of Kwahulé's plays, he places a wounded or brutalized female character at the center. Representing for Kwahulé, on one level, the damaged African continent, this central female character is, in fact, a rarity in plays by African playwrights, most of whom focus on male characters.

19. The French sociologist Jean Baudrillard's complex notion of the hyper-real in *Simulacra and Simulations*, trans. Sheila Glaser (Ann Arbor: University of Michigan Press, 1994), posits a real so "hyped" that ultimately we cannot believe in it. Kwahulé's hyper-real catches more of what seems to be, unfortunately, all too real.

20. There is, nevertheless, despite the dizzying self-reflexivity of Kwahulé's plays, information to be had in all of them, for example, on how exiled communities live, on daily humiliations in marginalized housing, or on rules of behavior in circumscribed places.

21. In the short introductions that precede each of the anthologized plays, I have constructed a story for each one, a story that "develops on the surface of the language," as Jean-Pierre Ryngaert characterizes it, speaking of theaters of textuality in a 2009 article ("Speech in Tatters: The Interplay of Voices in Recent Dramatic Writing," *Yale French Studies: The Transparency of the Text: Contemporary Writing for the Stage* 112 (2007): 14–28, quote at 19.) There are clearly other ways of approaching these play texts and other stories to be found in them than those I outlined. Whatever the story found, it is crucial to pay attention to the music of the words.

22. See, for an illuminating analysis of this theater, Jean-Pierre Ryngaert's article.

23. Bernard-Marie Koltès died at age forty-one in 1989 after having created a body of works casting the nightmarish climate at the end of the twentieth century as a series of louche transactions, or "deals," notably in *Combat de Nègre et de chiens* (Paris: Minuit, 1989), trans. David Bradby and Maria Delgado, *Black Battles with Dogs*, in *Bernard-Marie Koltès Plays: 1* (London: Methuen, 1997), 1–71; and in *Dans la solitude des champs de coton* (Paris: Minuit, 1986), trans. Jeffrey Wainwright, *In The Solitude of the Cotton Fields* (London: Methuen, 2001).

SELECTIONS FOR FURTHER READING

Amkpa, Awam. *Theatre and Postcolonial Desires*. London: Routledge, 2004.

Barrière, Caroline. *Le Théâtre de Koffi Kwahulé: Une nouvelle mythologie urbaine*. Paris: l'Harmattan, 2012.

Chalaye, Sylvie. *Afrique noire et dramaturgies contemporaines: Le syndrôme Frankenstein*. Paris: Éditions Théâtrales, 2004.

Chalaye, Sylvie. *L'Afrique noire et son théâtre au tournant du XXe siècle*. Rennes: Presses universitaires de Rennes, 2001.

Chalaye, Sylvie. *Dramaturgies africaines d'aujourd'hui en dix parcours*. Brussels: Éditions Lansman, 2001.

Chalaye, Sylvie, ed. *L'Esprit créateur: Nouvelles dramaturgies d'Afrique et des diasporas: Cantate des corps, sonate des voix* 48, no. 3 (Fall 2008).
Chalaye, Sylvie, ed. *Nouvelles dramaturgies d'Afrique noire francophone*. Rennes: Presses universitaires de Rennes, 2004.
Chalaye, Sylvie, and Virginie Soubrier, eds. *Africultures: Fratries Kwahulé/Scènes contemporaine choeur à corps* 77–78 (July 2009).
Conteh-Morgan, John. *Theatre and Drama in Francophone Africa*. Cambridge: Cambridge University Press, 1994.
Conteh-Morgan, John, and Tejumola Olaniyan. *African Drama and Performance*. Bloomington: Indiana University Press, 2004.
Conteh-Moran, John, and Dominic Thomas. *New Francophone African and Caribbean Theatres*. Bloomington: Indiana University Press, 2010.
Irele, Abiola. *The African Experience in Literature and Ideology*. London: Heinemann, 1981.
Jeyifo, Biodun, ed. *Modern African Drama*. New York: W. W. Norton, 2002.
Kwahulé, Koffi. *Pour une critique du théâtre ivoirien contemporain*. Paris: l'Harmattan, 1996.
Kwahulé, Koffi, and Gilles Mouëllic. *Frères de son: Koffi Kwahulé et le jazz, entretiens*. Paris: Éditions Théâtrales, 2007.
Mossetto, Anna Paola, ed. *Théâtre et histoires: Dramaturgies Francophones extra-européennes*. Paris: l'Harmattan, 2003.
Mounsef, Dounia, and Josette Féral, eds. *Yale French Studies: The Transparency of the Text/Contemporary Writing for the Stage* 112 (2007).
Prieto, Eric. "Koffi Kwahulé's Coltranean Theatre of Cruelty." *Modernist Cultures* 8, no. 1 (2013): 138–56.
Soubrier, Virginie. *Le Théâtre de Koffi Kwahulé: L'utopie d'une écriture jazz*. Amsterdam: Rodopi, 2014.
Soyinka, Wole. *Myth, Literature and the African World*. Cambridge: Cambridge University Press, 1982.

A Word about the Translation

CHANTAL BILODEAU

My introduction to Koffi Kwahulé's writing was through his play *Jaz*. After a brief e-mail exchange in 2002 where I explained that I was looking for plays from the African diaspora to translate into English, Kwahulé sent me his two latest publications. Immediately, *Jaz* captured my imagination. Though I could not have articulated why at the time, I knew this play was important and needed to be heard on this side of the Atlantic. And so our collaboration was born.

What began as one translation soon evolved into two and three and four. In getting to know Kwahulé's work, I discovered that in addition to the stories being told in each individual play, there was a bigger, equally compelling story unfolding throughout his entire body of work. This was the story of an aesthetic—more specifically, a jazz aesthetic—taking shape over a twenty-year period. It was also the story of a writer's exploration of form, of his gradual shift from traditional narrative to creative storytelling, and of his increasingly sophisticated exploration of the concept of identity. This bigger story is what compelled me to spend the next seven years translating six of the seven plays included in this anthology. Along the way, I also translated his 1997 play *Bintou*, which could not be included because of rights issues, and adapted my original translation of *That Old Black Magic* into a tighter and more focused piece. The latter is, indeed, the version we have chosen to include here.

In the process of translating these plays I faced a number of challenges, which led me to sometimes depart from the original French. The most significant of these departures was to assign dialogue to specific characters in four of the five plays where, in the original, that assignment is left open to interpretation. Starting with *Jaz* and continuing with *Big Shoot*, *Misterioso-911*, *Blue-S-Cat*, and *Melancholy of Barbarians*, Kwahulé removes the markers normally used to define a character's identity: race, family history, profession, age, and even name. Like musical instruments, his characters exist as pure sound (or pure dialogue), only recognizable by the music of their voice or the pattern of their speech. In *Jaz*, the first play where this obscuring of identity happens, the reading of the play is not affected; since there is only one character, it is always clear who is speaking. But in *Big Shoot*, *Blue-S-Cat*, and especially *Melancholy of Barbarians*, it is easy to get lost. Arguably, the reader's reconstruction of the characters' identity is part of the experience of the play, and by making clear to whom each line of dialogue belongs, I am hiding an important aspect of Kwahulé's formal exploration. Nonetheless, I felt it was necessary to make that choice in order to facilitate the reading of these unfamiliar and dense texts.

In *Big Shoot* and *Blue-S-Cat*, both two-character plays, assigning the dialogue was easy. With two characters speaking alternately, and with very distinct rhythms (and layouts on the page) to differentiate them, there was little room left to interpretation. However, in *Melancholy of Barbarians*, which has a much larger cast and a number of polyvocal scenes, distributing the lines (and determining the number of characters) was less obvious. While I used the many clues offered in the text and consulted with Kwahulé, the character distribution is ultimately only one out of many possible ways of constructing this story. Anyone working on the play should feel free to create their own version.

Misterioso-911 presented a slightly different challenge. In contrast with *Melancholy of Barbarians*, where most of the characters are addressed by name in the dialogue, only two characters (Linda and the drama teacher) are clearly identified. And while the text offers clues as to who the other characters might be—through the manner in which they speak or the stories they tell—their identities are so loose, so amorphous, and so dependent on how we, the readers, perceive them that I felt assigning lines would have pushed the translation into the realm of an adaptation. Therefore, the text appears as it does in the original French, with the lines of dialogue following one after another without any character indications; it is up to each reader or artist to structure the play.

Another translating challenge, evident in slightly different ways in *That Old Black Magic* and *Melancholy of Barbarians*, was finding a level of language in English that mirrored the level of language in the original French and rang true to the English ear. *That Old Black Magic* in particular presented a unique problem: the story takes place in New York City, the characters are Americans, but the play is written in a French that mimics the French dubbing of 1950s American films noirs, one of Kwahulé's sources of inspiration. Because the text of origin is a French writer's impression of America, translating directly from the French would have resulted in an English translation that sounded foreign—not what Kwahulé intended. So I had to look beyond Kwahulé's text and, in a sense, "reconstruct" the sounds and rhythms of 1950s American film noir English. By doing that, the experience of an English-speaking audience hearing the translation would be the same as the experience of a French-speaking audience hearing the original, which is to say that both would feel like they were in New York encountering American characters.

In *Melancholy of Barbarians*, the central characters are teenagers who express themselves in a language that flirts with slang. They pepper their speech with curse words, and use a rhythm that is youthful and in contrast with the rhythm of the adults around them. By definition, slang is local. It is a language shared by a small group of people, generally from a small geographic area. In translation, this becomes problematic because the use of slang automatically locates the play in a specific time and place that may have nothing to do with the original. One possible choice to address this problem is to set the play in a new location—for example, in a small town in North America—and to use the slang spoken by that particular group. But Kwahulé remains intentionally vague about the setting of *Melancholy*, using a mix of French slang, American and Middle Eastern cultural references, and Eastern European–sounding words throughout the text. So to respect that choice, I let the play exist, as in the French version, in an unnamed town, and gave the teenagers a language that has the flavor of American slang but is not so specific as to make it impossible to believe they may be from somewhere else.

What happens when language itself is used as a weapon? In the original French version of *Big Shoot*, the character Sir, who speaks French, uses English (and more specifically American English) to intimidate his victim. In that play, Kwahulé uses English as a language of dominance and those who are fluent in it become imbued with the qualities of strength and power attributed to America. In translating the play into English, I had to decide how the passages that were originally in English in the French text should appear in the English text. As the dominant language of globalization, English has no equivalent. However, in America, French is equated with sophistication. It is the language of choice for many of the good and more refined things in life: cuisine, fashion, art. So even though Sir can't bully his victim with French in the English text the way he does with English in the French text, he can at least position himself as more sophisticated, and therefore superior. (The character Schmeckel in *Brewery* similarly uses language, again in our translation in French rather than in English, to demonstrate a certain superiority.)

Thirteen years and seven translations after my first contact with Kwahulé, I can better articulate what first drew me to his work and compelled me to translate it. There is, in every one of his plays, an intense, if at times disturbingly primal and visceral, craving for love. No matter how dire the situation or desperate the circumstances, ultimately Shorty, Jaz, Sir, Linda, The Man, and Baby Mo want to be loved. And it is this most human of feelings that elevates them above the mess of their lives, above the violence and questionable choices, and into the realm of the mythic and the spiritual. What Kwahulé does, perhaps better than any other playwright I know, is give us a taste of the transcendent. Braver than we are, his characters take on our most elemental quest and lead us, buoyed by the poetry of his language and the rhythms of jazz music, to a place that is beyond family history, race, profession, age, or name; a place where true identity is found. That is what captured my imagination all those years ago. And it is what I have tried to bring to the English-speaking world.

Virgile Mfouilou (Shorty) in *That Old Black Magic*, directed by Claude Bokhobza at l'Atelier du Plateau de Paris, France, 2007. Photo by Andréa Florès.

That Old Black Magic

1993

TRANSLATED BY CHANTAL BILODEAU

INTRODUCTION TO THAT OLD BLACK MAGIC

The most "realistic" of Kwahulé's plays—in that the characters have a good deal of psychological depth, the story arcs and concludes, and the setting ostensibly mimics the entwined and fraught African diasporic worlds of boxing rings and jazz clubs—*That Old Black Magic* can also be understood as a dream play. As in dreams, one space morphs into and overlaps with another: here a boxing ring becomes both theater space and jazz club and later insane asylum. These overlapping spaces make it impossible to locate exactly where or when the action takes place. Rather, we might think of this as an exploded universe or layers of consciousness in which the main character Shorty, the reluctant protagonist, tries to work out his identity as an African American in the professional sports world of New York City. Shorty is torn between being a race hero or following his more high-brow artistic ambitions.

Likened to a jazz composition and even nicknamed "Li'l Jazz," Shorty, whose "jab is as thrilling as Monk's piano," feints and dodges, trying to fulfill both his sister Angie's ambitions for him to be someone black children can look up to and his own sense of himself as a quester, seeking to grab life through practicing theater and great literature. An accomplished jazz singer, Angie does her best to help him realize both goals. She would even save Shorty from his inner demons if she could. However, Shorty has made a pact in blood with the character Shadow, an enigmatic manager who guarantees unending success in the ring in exchange for Shorty's total submission. Shadow thus constructs Shorty as a black avenger, and like Goethe's Mephistopheles tempts the Faustian Shorty to his doom. Shadow's dichotomous worldview, in which "black" always has to face off with "white," orients the central plotline leading to the culminating fight between Shorty and his childhood friend and former "Great White Hope," Todd Ketchel. Fallen into alcoholism, delusions of grandeur, and hypocritical jingoism, Ketchel provides the bait for Shadow's disastrous manipulations.

His control ends up sacrificing not only Todd but Shorty as well, who really does not want to set up Ketchel to be killed. He, like Todd's wife Susie, seeks forgiveness and reconciliation, skirting the racialized rift promoted by Shadow, the bearer of death. Shorty ultimately refuses the role Shadow would have him play, but as a consequence he is reduced to a "shadow" himself. He cannot live free or be creative in a world in which he is governed by the fury of his manager and the bloodthirstiness of a crazed boxing crowd. Nevertheless, something of elusive freedom, of sublime striving, makes itself felt in Shorty's final pantomime. Boxing to a rap about loss and pain, Shorty hints at a realm beyond Shadow's and society's reach. Maybe this is a nod to the Africa from which his ancestors have been torn. Maybe this is simply the pure pleasure of finding within himself his own special music.

Notes for reading and production:

1. *That Old Black Magic*, the first play that Kwahulé wrote after immigrating to France, won Radio France International's highly competitive best play prize in 1992. It was the first African play to win that did not take Africa as subject and the first time Kwahulé dealt in a theater piece with the racial question outside of Africa. To create the tone of the play, Kwahulé was inspired by the ambience of a classic Hollywood *film noir.*

2. *That Old Black Magic* is also a 1942 jazz song by Harold Arlen and Johnny Mercer, in which the protagonist finds himself spinning and falling as a result of love's bedevilment. What makes Shorty spin and fall is the temptation of unyielding triumph, a different version of the devil's black magic. Jazz pieces frame and introduce many of the twelve tableaux, like the twelve rounds of a boxing match, that make up this play. Kwahulé would have music resonate with different moments of his piece. He suggests a range of songs, from jazz standards to gospel to Gabriel Fauré's richly layered *Requiem.* John Coltrane's musical spirit is behind many of the most intense moments in the play. A major American saxophonist and composer, at the forefront of modal and free jazz, Coltrane played with Miles Davis and Thelonious Monk in the 1950s before forming his own groups in the 1960s. He is known for altered and rapid chord progressions and improvised harmonies that in his late work take on a searching, spiritual, and rhythmically driven quality, as in his signature piece *A Love Supreme.*

3. Goethe's *Faust* (c. 1831) is one of Europe's most renowned Romantic verse plays, based on the age-old myth of a scholar (Faust) who sells his soul to Mephistopheles in exchange for having his every wish fulfilled. In part I, he obtains the love of young, innocent Gretchen (also called Margarete), only to lose her to her own increasingly insane acts: matricide and infanticide, and eventually death. In part II, less directly an intertext in Kwahulé's play, Faust earns redemption.

4. The passage in German in Kwahulé's play (tableau 8), from *Faust*: Part I "Martha's Garden," reads as follows in English:

> Margarete:
> That man who hangs round you so,
> I hate him in my innermost soul.
> Nothing in my life has ever
> Given my heart such pain, no, never,
> As his repulsive face has done.
>
> Faust:
> Don't be afraid of him, sweet one!
>
> (English translation by A. S. Kline, www.poetryintranslation.com)

SETTING

New York City.

CHARACTERS

SHORTY: African American. In his thirties. A boxer.
SHADOW: African American. In his forties. Shorty's manager. Puts on the intellectual airs of a dandy.
ANGIE: African American. Late twenties. Shorty's sister and a jazz singer.
MICKY: Caucasian. In his forties. A journalist.
TODD KETCHEL: Caucasian. Same age as Shorty. Boxer and former "Great White Hope."
SUSIE: Caucasian. Late twenties. Ketchel's wife.
CHUCK: African American. In his forties. Ketchel's manager.
A JAZZ QUARTET

AUTHOR'S NOTE

The passages in *italics* in scenes 1, 2 and 5 indicate moments when Shorty is doing theater. They are paraphrased excerpts from Goethe's *Faust*.

The musical pieces are mentioned as guides only. However, it would be appropriate to stay within the realm of the Coltrane universe.

TRANSLATOR'S NOTE

This is an adaptation of the original play by the same title.

1

A boxing ring. In the center, standing in a pool of light: Shorty, a fighter. Shadowboxing. Shorty is not happy with himself—with his jabs, his bobs and weaves, his legwork, his hooks, his uppercuts . . . Shorty is simply not happy with his boxing. Yet he keeps working, accompanied by jazz music with Coltrane inflections (played by a jazz quartet we will discover later). Shorty fights tirelessly until, out of breath, he collapses on a corner stool and undoes the wraps around his left hand with infinite grace. Following the movement of the wraps, the light expands to reveal Shadow, at the foot of the ring, holding a red robe and a pair of red gloves. He climbs slowly up to the ring, signals the quartet (which we discover now that the light has expanded) and the music stops.

SHADOW *(to Shorty)*: *Stop playing with your sorrow; it is a vulture that gnaws at your mind. Even in the worst company, you should feel a man among men. Not that I mean to count you among the common herd. I am not one of the greats, but if you make your path through life by my side, I will happily help you as we go. I shall be your companion and, if it suits you, your servant and your valet.*

SHORTY: *And what must I do in return?*

SHADOW: *There will be plenty of time to repay your debt.*

SHORTY: *No, the devil is selfish. He does nothing solely for Heaven's sake. State your conditions clearly. Servants such as you are dangerous in one's home.*

SHADOW: *In this world, I want to be of service to you, obey your every desire without rest or delay. But when we meet again on the other side, you shall do the same for me.*

SHORTY: *The other side does not worry me. Once this world is shattered and destroyed, the next one can replace it. From this earth springs my joy; this sun shines upon my sorrows. Once I am free from them, let come what may! It does not matter in the future whether men hate or love. Whether there is a below or an above, I do not care to know.*

SHADOW: *In that case, you may accept my offer. Commit yourself and you will immediately reap the benefits of my art. I will give you what no man has seen.*

SHORTY: *Foolish devil, what can you give me? Has the human spirit in its highest aspirations ever been understood by one such as you? Perhaps yours is food that satisfies no hunger, red gold that slips through fingers like quicksilver, a game that can never be won, a girl who from my arms flirts with the neighbor, the divine pleasure of fame which disappears like a meteor? Show me the fruit that rots before being ready and the tree that grows green again every day!*

SHADOW: *Such a request does not frighten me. I am prepared to provide all those treasures. So it is time, dear friend, to sink our teeth into life's pleasures.*

SHORTY: *I accept your bargain. But I do not take this commitment lightly. As I am, am I not a slave? No matter whose! Yours or someone else's!*

SHADOW: *From this very day, I will carry out my duties as a valet. But one more word! Just in case, I ask for a signature from your hand.*

SHORTY: *You stickler! You demand this in writing? Do you not know the value of a man and of a man's word? Is the word that binds me forever not good enough?*

SHADOW: *Why this anger? Any scrap of paper will do. You will sign with a drop of blood.*

SHORTY: *Very well then. If that satisfies you.*

Shadow pulls out a piece of paper and a needle. He pricks Shorty. Shorty marks the paper with his blood.

Lights up on Micky. While the quartet plays a Webster-like ballad, he speaks directly to the audience in a low, confidential tone.

MICKY: Good evening and welcome to our network's special presentation: "The Strange Destiny of Shorty." Shorty! Just the name . . . No doubt the oldest among you will remember him, but for our young viewers, Shorty is the man we just saw in the role of the fighter. In reality, Shorty was a fighter . . . Or rather, he became a fighter because he didn't think he could make it as an actor. The ring was for him a sort of purgatory where he was waiting for the gates of heaven . . . or hell to open before him. Yes, Shorty wanted to be an actor but he became a fighter. And what a fighter! The greatest of all times! They say his legwork was as sensual as Billie Holiday's voice and his jab as thrilling as Monk's piano. They say he was as fast as Charlie Parker's sax and his fists were as powerful as Dizzy Gillespie's horn. They say he would dance very fast around his opponent sometimes, sticking jabs—only jabs—for three or four rounds then abruptly change rhythm and dance in slow motion. They say in those moments, he was floating. His jabs would slow to a crawl and the whole fight would become imbued with a kind of languorous joy typical of Lester Young's choruses. Then without warning, straights, hooks and uppercuts would erupt from up, down, left, right, front and sides like a big band of ten thousand Coltranes. Fast fists full of nightmares. Angie, his sister, had nicknamed him— . . . Angie is that woman over there, see? The singer in the band? That's Angie. Angie was a jazz singer who owned a club in Spanish Harlem. She and Shorty were very close. And Angie had nicknamed him Li'l Jazz . . .

Rumor has it that to fight this well, Shorty had sold his soul to the Devil . . . Speaking of the Devil . . . Shadow! His name was Buster McCauley but very few people knew. Shadow was Shorty's manager. They say he was his shadow. They also say he had dubious habits; that before meeting Shorty, he was rotting in a Kansas prison, a sex crime of course, little boys. They say at six, he killed his father: he slashed his throat with a razor blade when he discovered he wasn't really his father. The same people also claim that after that crime he became a minister. They say— . . . but what don't they say about Shadow? In reality, we only know one thing: other than the fact that his name was Buster McCauley, we know nothing . . .

Ah, Susie Ketchel, as elegant as ever. And her husband Todd Ketchel, "The Hammer," a fearsome puncher as well. One of Shorty's childhood friends and the only fighter to ever beat him. As an amateur. Long considered "The Great White Hope," Todd Ketchel didn't live up to his promise. Haste, career mistakes, rumors of fixed fights, all of that made his star decline. But anyway . . . You'll have a chance to get to know everyone better before the evening is out . . .

The music stops. The scene shifts to a press conference.

Tell us, Shorty. Is it true you're considering giving up the ring for the stage? You're not going to do that to us, are you?

SHORTY: I'm strictly a fighter.

MICKY: Then why is it that lately we've seen you more on the stage than in the ring?

SHORTY: I like it. For me, it's a childhood dream.

MICKY: What's more frightening? Acting or fighting?

SHORTY: I'm not— . . . I don't really think about these things. Yeah, you're always scared before a fight or a performance but during, never. It's like you've thrown the dice and are waiting for them to stop rolling. 'Cause above all, actors and fighters are . . . gamblers. Actors gamble their most intimate secrets for the love and recognition of others, while fighters—and that's the difference—fighters gamble everything, even their own lives, to earn the right not to be scared . . .

SHADOW: And that's why, I'm sure you'll agree with me, that's why a fighter is first and foremost a black man. But let's talk about his next fight against Eddie Jones.

MICKY: Yes, let's talk about that fight. Don't you think your age might be a handicap against his 27 wins out of 27 fights? And to be clear, 25 of those were by knockout.

SHORTY: That's what they all say. Against Ronnie, too, they said the same thing. But I laid Ronnie flat exactly when and how I chose to. It'll be the same with Jones. I'm gonna play with him until the sixth—'cause people should get their money's worth—and in the seventh, I'll beat him to a pulp . . .

MICKEY: But Jones claims that he won't make the same mistakes as Ronnie. That he has a strategy.

SHADOW: They've all got a strategy. Until they find themselves standing in front of him, between the twelve ropes, and realize with terror that if Shorty's ever beaten, it won't be in a ring . . .

Todd Ketchel, who wasn't part of the conference, rushes in. He grabs a mike and throws himself in front of the camera.

KETCHEL: I've had enough of this bullshit! You all know—everyone in America knows—that Eddie's never gonna beat Shorty, that the only one who can beat him is me. 'Cause I've beaten him before and if I did it once, I can do it again. The whole world's waiting for that fight—everyone but Shorty and Shadow. Why do they boycott white fighters? Why does Shorty refuse to take on white fighters?

MICKY: Ladies & Gentlemen, Todd Ketchel. *(to Shorty)* It's true, we've noticed there hasn't been a single white fighter in your last fifteen fights.

KETCHEL: If they weren't black, Eddie Jones and all the others would never have been challengers. Shorty will fight any phony or journeyman as long as he's black.

SHADOW *(whispering between his teeth)*: I'm gonna kill you, Todd. One day I'm gonna kill you, I swear.

KETCHEL *(screaming)*: Now it's threats! Bluffs! Intimidation! He's threatening to kill me! He threatened to kill me!

SHADOW: Not at all. I was just trying to explain to him that his attitude before the press is harmful to the boxing world.

MICKY: But Shadow, wouldn't a fight between Shorty and Ketchel be a spectacular event? "The Revenge of the Century" . . .

KETCHEL: Of course, it would be a spectacular event. But this fight's never gonna happen 'cause Shadow's a racist.

Susie intervenes.

SUSIE: Todd, that's enough!

SHADOW: It's OK, Mrs. Ketchel. Isn't it common nowadays for people to justify their own racism by referring to some kind of black racism? . . . But I won't be dragged into that polemic. Let's simply consider the facts. The boxing world may very well be a jungle but it's a jungle that has rules. Ask Todd Ketchel his current ranking . . .

KETCHEL: Cut the crap, Shadow. You know very well that rankings don't count for the title, that you—Buster McCauley—and you alone are holding all the cards and that if you want it, that fight will take place. But you've always been against it. You've always tried to discredit me with accusations of fixed fights, doping, or whatever.

SHADOW: As I was saying, if we look at the world rankings, we can see Todd Ketchel isn't in the top ten. And rules are rules . . .

KETCHEL: It's not the rules, it's you.

SHADOW: Sorry, Todd. As things stand, this fight cannot take place.

KETCHEL: Let's get out of here, Susie . . . Ladies and gentlemen and viewers at home, good night. Come on, Susie.

He exits.

MICKY: Well, at least that has the merit of being clear. I think we've covered everything. Thank you for being with us tonight. This is Micky Abraham for Network Sports.

Lights shift.

SHADOW: Little jerk! Sooner or later, I'll crush him. I'll crush him like a cigarette butt!

ANGIE: Come on, Shadow. Let the damn fight happen.

SHADOW: If you throw a bone to hit a dog, it doesn't offend the dog. Don't you see that's exactly what he's after? Winner or not, he wants that fight.

ANGIE: So what's it to you? This is the sixth press conference that this fool's wrecked for us. Shorty and I have talked about it and he's completely up for it. So why not?

SHADOW: Because I said so. What Ketchel wants is to fill up his pockets before he retires. He wants the jackpot and only a fight against Shorty can get him the jackpot. But Shorty's no jackpot. The day Todd's ranking allows him to be an official contender, the fight will take place. We're not the Salvation Army. Have we ever been handed anything? We've always had to prove something, including the fact that we're men—us, the forefathers of civilization! So let Ketchel prove himself! Let him prove that he's strong enough, agile enough and smart enough to have the right to fight for the world title!

ANGIE: Then do something so he stops badmouthing us every time he finds a mike!

She storms out.

SHADOW: If you want to bite someone, don't show him your teeth first. Right, Shorty? . . . Don't show him your teeth first.

2

Spotlight on the ring. Angie is chained to it. She sings a spiritual in the style of "Sometimes I Feel Like a Motherless Child," accompanied by the jazz quartet. At the end of the song, we hear Shorty's voice.

SHORTY *(in the dark)*: *A lover is at your feet. He will free you from this hideous captivity.*

ANGIE *(kneeling)*: *Oh yes, let us kneel and call on the saints! See under these steps, under this threshold, hell is seething! The Devil's awful brawling makes an unbearable din!*

SHORTY *(still in the dark)*: *Gretchen! Gretchen!*

ANGIE: *It is the voice of my beloved!*

She springs up. Her chains fall from her.

Where is he? I heard him calling. I am free! No one shall stop me. I will fly to his arms, lay in his embrace! He called out Gretchen! He stood on the threshold. Amidst the howl and clatter of hell . . .

SHADOW: OK, hold! Angie, let's do this again 'cause you're falling into the same old patterns. I've told you a hundred times not to go around in circles, wringing your hands like a Broadway actress. As soon as you hear his voice, you run to each corner of the ring to look for him. Tell yourself that this ring's hanging in the sky, that it's floating over the world like a blimp and that Shorty's voice is rising from the darkness below. So look down as if into a well . . . Come on, let's do it again.

ANGIE: Take it from *Gretchen! Gretchen!*, Shorty.

SHORTY *(in the dark)*: *Gretchen! Gretchen!*

ANGIE: *It is the voice of my beloved! Where is he? I heard him calling. I am free! No one shall stop me. I will fly to his arms, lay in his embrace. He called out Gretchen! He stood on the threshold. Amidst the howl and clatter of hell, amidst the devil's infernal laughter, I recognized his voice, so sweet and loving.*

SHORTY: *It is I!*

ANGIE: *It is you! Oh, say that again!*

Shorty climbs in the ring. She kisses him furiously.

It is he! It is he! Where is the torture now? The anguish of imprisonment? . . .

SHADOW: Keep kissing him . . . It's good but keep kissing him. *It is you! Oh, say that again!* You kiss. *It is he! It is he!* You kiss. *Where is the torture now?* You kiss. *The anguish of imprisonment? Of the chains?* You kiss again. *It is you! You have come to save me.* There you kiss for a long time, very tenderly. And while you kiss, the light will slowly expand until the entire stage is lit. Come on, let's do it again.

ANGIE: *It is you! Oh, say that again!*

They kiss.

It is he! It is he!

They kiss.

Where is the torture now?

They kiss.

SHADOW: For God's sake, are you doing it on purpose? Listen, Champ, this kiss is very important, you know that. So I don't understand why you're playing some character when you know perfectly well that there is no character. It's your lips that Angie's lips are seeking. The pleasure you'll get from her lips, from her body, her hands, her breasts against your chest, her breath, the smell of her longing for you—only you will feel it. I've told you a hundred times: an actor's not someone who plays a role or tries to embody a character. Those are lies you learn on Broadway. An actor's someone who tries to break a pact with himself, to betray a secret about himself so he can offer it to others. Everything else is fluff. I know you've desired Angie before and Angie's desired you. That's the moment the audience wants to see. So don't act as if you're being subjected to the kiss. Grab your sister and kiss her. From your line, Angie.

ANGIE: *It is you! Oh, say that again!*

They kiss.

It is he! It is he! Where is the torture now?

They kiss.

The anguish of imprisonment? Of the chains?

They kiss.

It is you! You have come to save me.

A long and deep kiss. The light gradually expands. The entire stage is lit.

I am saved! Yes, here is the street where I saw you for the first time and the lovely garden where neighbor Martha and I awaited you.

SHORTY *(pulling her)*: *Come! Follow me!*

ANGIE: *Oh, linger! I am happy wherever you are.*

SHADOW: There you go. Isn't this better?

ANGIE: Yeah, it's good. It's like we're doing a different play . . .

SHADOW: All right. Same time tomorrow.

He exits. Shorty, laying in the ropes, suddenly bursts out laughing.

ANGIE: What's so funny?

SHORTY: I'm quitting.

ANGIE: What?

SHORTY: I'm fed up. I get no pleasure out of being in the ring. After the fight against Jones, I'm giving up boxing.

ANGIE: Why?

SHORTY: I'm not afraid anymore.

ANGIE: What are you talking about?

SHORTY: I'm not afraid. I even wonder if I ever was. When I first started maybe . . . But not anymore. Otherwise, why would I be here pretending to be an actor when I've got a fight coming up? Why isn't everyone busy training? 'Cause not only am I not afraid, people around me aren't afraid either. Everyone knows I'll beat Eddie Jones just like I beat everyone else before . . . and will beat everyone after. There's no more danger.

ANGIE: Don't be stupid. Yes, you'll beat Jones, even without training. Because you're an exception or, at least, you've become one. But you had to work hard to earn the right not to be afraid anymore. Remember, at first you were just a journeyman, a third-rate fighter.

SHORTY: Maybe, but the bottom line is, I'm not afraid anymore. I know that I'll win no matter what. Plus, I'm sick of Shadow. I'm sick of all his games.

ANGIE: What games?

SHORTY: It's taken me a while but I get it now. From the very beginning, everything was in place. Everything was doomed.

ANGIE: Li'l Jazz, what's going on?

SHORTY: What's going on is, I'm done. I'm not gonna fight for Shadow or for anyone else.

ANGIE: Who says you fight for Shadow? You fight for yourself and for the community. You may not be aware of it but for kids, every one of your fights restores hope. Forget Shadow, forget me even . . . but think about the kids . . .

SHORTY: Yeah, I know. I know . . .

He starts to dance.

Fight, Shorty, fight
Fight for the kids
Whose dreams have been wrecked
Whose dreams have been trampled
Whose dreams have been stolen
Fight, Shorty, fight
Fight for the kids
Who are cold
Who are hungry
Who are thirsty

Fight, Shorty, fight
Fight for the kids
Who are blown up in smoke
Who are crushed like cigarette butts
Who are swept into a common grave
Like ashes into an ashtray
Fight, Shorty, fight

He stops dancing.

I know, Angie . . . I know. But I'm a fighter and I wanna feel what every fighter feels: doubt, fear and even defeat.

ANGIE: But Shorty, you've been defeated before! When you started, you had doubts. You lost to Todd!

SHORTY: I'm talking about the fear of tumbling down from the top. They say the closer a fighter is to the top, the crazier he becomes. Crazy with fear. And I'm the champion, so in theory I should be at the very height of fear. Yet, before, during and after each fight, I feel like a woman who can't climax. I often tell journalists that a fighter gambles his life . . . Well, I don't gamble anything. I know I'm gonna win.

Silence.

ANGIE: How do you know you're always gonna win?

SHORTY: Do you really wanna know?

A beat. She looks him in the eye.

ANGIE: No, don't say anything. Don't explain. It's good that you're the best. Everyone can afford to lose in this country but not us; only the winners will make it. Don't forget that we come from a place where hope is suffering. Don't ever forget that. We're black. It's good that you're the strongest. And it's even better if you stay that way . . . Whatever the price, Li'l Jazz. Whatever the price. *(beat)* And if you've had enough of Shadow, leave him; find yourself another manager.

SHORTY: I can't.

ANGIE: What do you mean, you can't?

SHORTY: There's a contract.

ANGIE: What contract? A contract can be negotiated. It can be broken.

SHORTY: Not this one.

ANGIE: Why, it's carved out in stone? Listen Shorty, I gotta go to the club.

We'll talk about this some other time, when you've come back to your senses.

Angie exits. He follows after her.

3

At Angie's club. Soft lights. At the bar, knocked out by alcohol: Todd Ketchel. Susie sits alone at a table, listening to the band. Shorty enters. Charlie Chuck—half businessman, half pimp—waves him over to his table.

CHUCK: Come, sit. Your sister's wonderful. Her voice is so exquisite! I mean, to put it simply, she's an absolute treat. But I don't know what's going on with Todd; he's interrupted her at least three times. Not that I let that spoil my pleasure. 'Cause for a treat, she's a treat . . . What would you like?

SHORTY: Nothing. I've got a fight soon so now's not the time for booze and all that jazz.

CHUCK: Oh yeah, that fight against Jones . . . Then this is no place for you, big guy!

SHORTY: I'm just here to pick up Angie.

Angie enters.

CHUCK: Angie, Angie, Angie . . . I was just telling your brother what a treat you are . . . It's true. I mean, to put it simply, your voice is life.

ANGIE: Thanks, Charlie. You're very sweet. But jazz is life, not my voice.

CHUCK: I'm sticking to my guns! You're life itself, you're . . . You're pure oxygen! I mean, to put it simply, your voice, I don't hear it; I breathe it. When that fool Todd was misbehaving, your voice alone saved me from the spectacle of his decline.

SHORTY: He was really misbehaving?

ANGIE: I think he had one too many. I'm gonna get changed. See you in a bit.

She exits.

CHUCK: So I heard you're thinking of leaving us . . . Is it true? You're thinking of leaving us? . . . It's Shadow, isn't it? I heard you two don't get along anymore. I mean, to put it simply, I expected it. I knew that sooner or later you'd end up feeling trapped with him. The guy's not a manager, he's a pimp. Remember, Shorty . . . Remember, Chuck warned you. But nobody ever listens to Chuck. So for once, open your ears, Champ. You can't quit boxing because of a pimp! Boxing's in your blood . . . And if you feel trapped with Shadow, there's room with Chuck. And I'm not saying this for the money; it's for the art, strictly for the art. I mean, to put it simply, name your price. I'll do anything to see art triumph. I'll drop all my fighters to take you alone. *(indicating Todd)* See that drunk splayed out on the counter? I've got thirty-five percent in him. I've got fifty-five in Mateo, forty-five in The Grave-Digger, seventeen in Shoji Mugurama and listen to this: eighty-five in Carlos Zapata . . . I've got stocks everywhere. But I'll sell everything in order to have you. What do you say, huh?

SHORTY: Shadow and I are getting along fine, Charlie.

SUSIE: Todd, let's go.

CHUCK: 'Cause you're still in the game, Shorty. You still have it. I'm telling you . . .

SUSIE: Todd.

CHUCK: . . . Chuck's telling you, you'll be at the top for another ten years. At least!

Todd wakes up and sees Shorty.

KETCHEL: Ah! Shorty! There you are!

Susie tries to stear Todd toward the exit.

SUSIE: No, come on. We're going home.

He breaks free from her.

KETCHEL: I heard you decided to quit. You're bailing out. You're throwing in the towel. You're abandoning me, Todd, your childhood friend.

SUSIE *(to Shorty)*: I'm sorry.

KETCHEL: We played in the sand together, Shorty. We grew up together. Didn't we?

SUSIE: I'm so sorry.

KETCHEL: And here you are abandoning me, without so much as a compassionate look for good old Todd, without giving Todd his chance . . .

SUSIE: Todd—

KETCHEL *(to Susie)*: Let me finish. *(to the last patrons)* I'm the reason this guy's quitting boxing! I'm who he's running away from! 'Cause he knows that I, alone, can beat the shit out of him . . .

SUSIE *(to Shorty)*: Don't say anything back. Please don't say anything back.

KETCHEL: You're not a friend, Shorty. A friend would never do what you did to me . . .

SUSIE *(trying to hold him back)*: Can you help me?

CHUCK: All right, Todd. We've heard enough from you tonight.

Chuck helps Susie drag Ketchel away.

KETCHEL: This isn't the last you'll hear from me, Shorty!

CHUCK: What a waste! That guy had everything going for him: color, talent . . . What a terrible waste!

SHORTY: Good night, Chuck.

CHUCK: Wait, Shorty, I've got something else to ask you . . . I read that for your fight against Jones, you wanna drop him in the first. That's what you said, right? It's not just journalists' talk?

SHORTY: Yeah, I might have said that.

CHUCK: 'Cause the thing is, if you don't come with me, it's no big deal. You do what you want. But for this last fight, I'd like you to do me a favor. Everyone's convinced that you'll do exactly as you said. So they're all gonna bet on the first. But to put it simply, I've got a little stash I'd like to put on the third.

Shorty smiles.

What? What you can do in the first, you can do in the third, right?

SHORTY: Charlie, what I said to the journalists was just prefight talk. It was just for show.

CHUCK: Just for show, just for show . . . But you always do what you say.

SHORTY: Pure coincidence, Charlie. A fight's like a journey. You never know how it's gonna end.

Angie enters.

ANGIE: Shall we go, Shorty?

CHUCK: Listen, Shorty. For me, it's the third! I'm putting everything on the third!

SHORTY: You do as you want, Charlie.

ANGIE: Good night, Charlie.

He chases after them.

CHUCK: Wait, Shorty . . . Listen . . . I've got a better offer . . . Shorty!

4

At Shadow's place. Micky, in his underwear, reads from a pile of newspapers. Shadow collects clothes scattered around the room.

MICKY: Wow, they're not letting him off easy. Basil Brand talks about "a fight unworthy of a world title." Arthur Jansen writes that "Shorty disregarded the crowd at the Madison Square Garden." And do you know what conclusion Mathews comes to? "It's time for the boxing world to kill Shorty before Shorty kills the boxing world!" Can you believe it?

Shadow hands Micky his clothes.

SHADOW: Put your clothes on.

MICKY: Then again, his last seven fights were won by decision. If you want my opinion, the theater's taking too much of his time.

SHADOW: Put your clothes on. Shorty and his sister are on their way.

Micky starts to get dressed.

MICKY: Either that or he's getting old.

SHADOW: He seems old to you?

MICKY: No, I wouldn't say that. But theater is for old guys . . . It's like a Latin mass, a language nobody speaks anymore. He may look young on the outside but inside, he's old. That thing he did in the tenth? When he dropped his guard and took a barrage of punches without punching back? It's like he wanted to taunt Jones the way Muhammad Ali used to do. Given the kind of puncher Jones is, it's a miracle Shorty didn't go down. If you ask me, Shorty went blank in the tenth . . . And going blank, that's an old guy's thing . . .

SHADOW: The old guy's the one who goes down, the one who grovels in his own sweat and blood while the crowd mocks him. The old guy's the one whose arm isn't raised, the one we look at with pity or don't look at at all. The old guy's the one to whom you say: "Don't worry, man, you weren't bad, but that's boxing." The old guy's that one, Micky. So don't tell me about going blank in the tenth. For all you know, Shorty did it on purpose so he could get the thrill of coming within an inch of defeat. That's why he's in the theater . . .'Cause in the theater, you don't get hit in the face, you get hit in the soul. It's more painful.

MICKY: Then do something! You said you were gonna provide the press with interesting fights, make boxing the first sport in the nation again, "restore the legend." Where are those fights?

SHADOW: Patience, Micky. Patience.

MICKY: Patience, patience . . . The man's gonna kill boxing! Shorty used to be confident, arrogant, have a mouth full of insults. But what do we see now? An old guy who bends himself out of shape to avoid saying dirty words so he can come up with stupidities that pass as wisdom. He's not a fighter anymore, he's a fucking clown! What's going on between you two?

SHADOW: There's nothing going on other than what goes on between a fighter and his manager.

MICKY: Fine.

Micky storms out, bumping into Angie and Shorty on his way out.

SHORTY: What's up with Micky?

SHADOW: Oh, you know how he is . . . *(to Shorty)* So, easy fight, huh?

SHORTY: That's what people think. But Jones is not that easy to take out. In the early rounds, he was brawling so I had to take the fight to him. You have to admit those first five rounds were spectacular.

SHADOW: Yeah, but after the fifth, what the hell?

SHORTY: That's Jones's fault. He changed tactics. It threw me for a while 'cause a one-punch fighter never lets a fight go stale . . .

SHADOW: Result: a boring fight, a booing audience and a hysterical press.

SHORTY: What the hell do they expect? That I'll slit my opponent's throat? I'm not a butcher; I'm a fighter . . .

SHADOW: You're not a fighter, you're The Fighter, The Champ. I've told you before, a fight is a dream in which the fighter makes love to the audience . . . It's sex . . .

ANGIE: Actually, Shadow, we're here to talk about something else.

SHADOW: I know, Angie. I know. *(to Shorty)* People pay a lot of money to see you fight 'cause they want you to turn them on. But what do they get instead? Two men pawing each other as if they were lovers . . . Two sweaty bodies slipping against one another . . . But people don't give a shit about that, just like they don't give a shit about you and your feelings. They didn't pay to watch other people make love; they paid to be made love to. They're the ones who wanna come. And what makes them come, huh? What makes the audience come?

SHORTY: The knockout!

SHADOW: There you go. The knockout.

SHORTY: Well, it's over; I'm quitting. I won't knock anyone out or make anyone come anymore. And if you insist I keep fighting, I'll fight . . . but I'll throw all my fights. I'll fuck with people. I'll keep them on the edge of their seats and leave them high and dry with nothing but bitterness between their legs. I'm gonna kill boxing, Shadow.

ANGIE: If you don't kill yourself first. What was the tenth if not a suicide attempt?

SHADOW: Not at all, not at all . . . *(to Angie)* Didn't your brother tell you that it's impossible to commit suicide? . . . *(Angie turns to Shorty)* No? . . . We never commit suicide; we die, that's all. Suicide's just another choice that death imposes on us. In fact, the contract anticipates that possibility.

ANGIE: We'd like to break the contract.

SHADOW *(to Shorty)*: You don't tell your sister anything, do you? *(to Angie)* There's a small problem: This contract cannot be broken.

ANGIE: All contracts can be broken.

SHADOW: Not this one.

ANGIE: What kind of contract is that?

SHADOW: A very good contract.

Shadow pulls out the contract and hands it to Angie. She examines it.

ANGIE: This is the contract? *(Shorty nods)* This piece of paper's worth nothing. You can't even see when it was made and there's no signature . . .

SHADOW: At the bottom, on the left.

ANGIE: I don't see anything . . . Only a stain . . . A— . . .

SHADOW: A blood stain, yeah.

She's suddenly horrified.

ANGIE: Oh my God! *(to Shadow)* Who are you?

SHADOW: My name's Buster McCauley. I was born in Topeka, Kansas. My father was a lumberjack and sang the blues . . .

ANGIE *(almost hysterical)*: Shadow, who are you?

SHADOW: I wish I could say I was the devil but we all know the devil doesn't exist.

ANGIE: And why him? Why Li'l Jazz?

SHADOW: He chose me. He called and I came. So many souls call out for help . . . but only those who want it really bad are heard. Shorty wanted it really bad.

ANGIE: But he doesn't want it anymore.

SHADOW: Too bad. I've fulfilled my part of the contract—to make the third-rate fighter Shorty was then, the renowned champion he is today. In return, he needs to fight for the community, be a source of pride, rebuild its dreams, help it to its feet again so it can believe that everything's possible . . . Can you think of a better deal? Not only did I give him the title, I also gave meaning to his fists, to his life . . .

SHORTY: Shadow, I've been giving myself body and soul to the community for years! No one can find fault with me about that. But now I've had enough.

SHADOW: The contract, nothing but the contract.

SHORTY: So many fighters would do anything to take my place. For God's sake, why me?

SHADOW: You can teach a fighter to move, to stick the jab, to work his hooks and his uppercuts, to get off the ropes or use them. You can teach him everything, but not elegance, or grace, or the poetry of the steps, or that little something that makes Angie call you Li'l Jazz. You're magic, Shorty. In the entire history of boxing, only a few fighters—Sugar Ray Robinson, Muhammad Ali and Sugar Ray Leonard—have been able to remind us that boxing's the noble art. Like them, you're destined to rebuild our dreams, to lift our chins up and put us back where we truly belong: as the forefathers of civilization.

SHORTY: Here we go again!

SHADOW: From generation to generation, that's the story our champions tell so we can be reminded that the cycle won't be complete until we've regained our rightful place in History. Every generation has its champion. You're ours. So we can't encourage you to fail. We can't let our generation be the weak link . . .

SHORTY: You keep spewing out the same insanities.

SHADOW: You're the guardian of our memory . . .

SHORTY: Save your breath, Shadow. I'm telling you, I can't fight anymore. What the soul refuses to do, the body cannot accomplish.

SHADOW: The body will do what the soul refuses to do. You're gonna fight. You're gonna fight a lot longer than you think and your longevity will defy their understanding. And then one day someone will come, he'll beat you, he'll grab the torch and we'll give you back your freedom . . .

ANGIE: We?

SHADOW: Yeah, I'm just a middleman . . . But that's another story. So that day, you'll realize that you fought more for the IRS than for me. But you'll still have enough money to get yourself a wife and a house in a white suburb—one of those clean and quiet towns only white folks know how to build—so you can fade back into the oblivion you pulled yourself from when you signed with your blood. See, I can be reasonable: money, a white suburb where from time to time you'll perform a play in the community hall, and a nice wife and kids. You couldn't ask for a more anonymous life! A clean and quiet life as smooth as a white tombstone.

SHORTY: I'll never climb back in—

SHADOW: Never say never.

SHORTY: Let's go, Angie.

SHADOW: You'll see. You'll fight again soon.

They start to leave.

By the way, Angie, a little piece of advice: If I were you, I wouldn't mention the contract. No one would believe you and you'd run the risk of ending up in the insane asylum . . . You know how people are. Oh, and one more thing . . . We're still on for the theater?

SHORTY: The theater's got nothing to do with this. We're still on.

SHADOW: Well, that's at least one thing we all agree on. Better than nothing. So, to the theater.

Shorty and Angie exit.

5

A performance of the same scene as earlier.

ANGIE: *I am free! No one shall stop me. I will fly to his arms, lay in his embrace! He called out Gretchen! He stood on the threshold. Amidst the howl and clatter of hell, amidst the devil's infernal laughter, I recognized his voice, so soft and loving.*

SHORTY: *It is I!*

Shorty joins Angie in the ring. We hear increasingly loud laughter, which eventually drowns out the actors' voices.

ANGIE: *It is you! Oh, say that again!*

She kisses him furiously.

It is he! It is he! Where is the torture now? The anguish of imprisonment? Of the chains?

They kiss.

It is you! . . .

They kiss. Suddenly, Angie bursts into tears and runs off stage. Ketchel, who was hiding in the audience, steps forward.

KETCHEL: Now come out here, Shorty, you limp dick. Come out so I can kick your ass . . .

Shorty throws himself at Ketchel but is immediately restrained by Shadow.

SHORTY: Let go of me! Let go of me so I can kill this bastard!
KETCHEL: Come on! Come over here, you fucking showgirl! If you're the real Champ, come on over.
SHADOW: Ladies and gentlemen—
SHORTY: The only thing you know how to do is run off at the mouth!
SHADOW:—we regret to inform you that we cannot go on with the show.
KETCHEL: You're so afraid of me that you wanna quit! You're bailing out! You're throwing in the towel!
SHADOW: On behalf of the entire company—
SHORTY: I should take you on right here with just my own two fists! I should whip your ass for—
KETCHEL: Oh, yeah? Well, bring it on!
SHORTY: I should—
KETCHEL: What are you waiting for?
SHORTY: I'm gonna give you what you want, Ketchel. I'm gonna give you that fight.

Shadow suddenly lets go of Shorty, as if petrified by what he's just heard.

I'm gonna put you off boxing forever.

Ketchel is stunned. A beat.

KETCHEL: You said it, Shorty! Everybody's a witness!
SHORTY: I'm gonna destroy you!

Ketchel goes to Shadow, a smile on the corner of his lips.

KETCHEL: See? I won.

He exits.

SHADOW *(to Shorty)*: Have you lost your mind?
SHORTY: Get out of my face, Shadow!
SHADOW: Ketchel is egging you on! *(out)* Drop the curtain!
SHORTY: And mind your own fucking business!
SHADOW: Well, it so happens that my business is you. You're gonna allow this guy to make a fortune off your back, as if the hissing of whips and the buzzing of flies vying for our wounds were nothing but a footnote in History. As if the moaning and lamenting of the cotton fields had already faded in your memory . . . *(out)* Would you drop the fucking curtain? . . . As if—
SHORTY: I said get out of my face!
SHADOW: Ketchel's your friend. And your friend needs a little boost . . . But we're not a soup kitchen. This fight will not happen.
SHORTY: Who are you to decide what will or will not happen? I told you it was over between us.
SHADOW: You and I are not old lovers . . . There's a contract. A contract that states that it cannot end between us, that you can't do anything without my consent . . . *(out)* Would you drop the fucking curtain? . . . *(to Shorty)* Remember this, Shorty. For as long as I'm alive, this fight won't take place.
SHORTY: Whether you're dead or alive, this fight will take place. I'll stake my connections, the connections of my connections, my fortune, my name, everything. I'll fight without a penny if I have to, I'll back the fight myself if I have to but it will take place.
SHADOW: The Great Mystery is even darker than you imagine, Shorty. This everything is very little compared to the power of the pact that binds us. Soon, very soon, you'll have a chance to understand how everything is contained in that mystery.

He exits.

6

Shorty's gym. Angie enters.

SHORTY: So?
ANGIE: It's tough . . .
SHORTY: Why?
ANGIE: There's a lot of resistance out there . . .
SHORTY: You talked to Alvaro . . . Duff . . . Dixon . . . ?

Angie nods after each name.

How about Chuck? You talked to Chuck?
ANGIE: I talked to everyone.
SHORTY: And?
ANGIE: No one wants to cough up a single penny. They all say if Shadow doesn't back this fight, it means something isn't right. Even Charlie Chuck said this fight doesn't feel right. You need to forget about—
SHORTY: No.

Shorty goes to the ring where the light is now focused. Replay of the beginning of the play. Shadowboxing to the same jazz music. Then, out of breath, Shorty collapses on a corner stool and undoes the wraps around his left hand with infinite grace. Following the movement of the wraps, the light expands to reveal Shadow, at the foot of the ring. He slowly climbs up.

OK, I thought about it . . . I'd like to—
SHADOW: No. From now on I'm gonna do the thinking. 'Cause when you do, look what kind of mess you get yourself into! *(beat)* The fight against Ketchel will be in three months.
SHORTY: Three months!
SHADOW: Take it or leave it. We have three months to make Ketchel a credible challenger. If we want the networks and the public to follow, he has to become the Great White Hope again. So I've set up two warm-up fights against Bill Randall and Jim Skelly . . .
SHORTY: Randall and Skelly?
SHADOW: Yes. To be the Great White Hope, he needs to measure up against guys like Randall and Skelly.
SHORTY: But they'll kill him!
SHADOW: Leave it to me. Ketchel will win both fights. Randall's gonna "lie down" in the fifth and Skelly in the third. They've already pocketed half of the money.
SHORTY: And in return?
SHADOW: Nothing. Absolutely nothing. Except the ring on the night of

the fight has to be to Ketchel what the hawk's game bag is to the newly hatched chick.

SHORTY: I don't understand.

SHADOW: Of course, you understand, Shorty. Other than the chick, no one knows what's in the hawk's game bag. 'Cause once the chick goes in, it never comes out.

SHORTY: You're not asking me to—

SHADOW: Yes, you have to kill Ketchel. It'll happen in the third. In the first two, you'll play possum and let him do his thing to lull him. Then as soon as you hear the bell for the third, you'll step out as calm as before and throw the fatal uppercut.

SHORTY: That's murder!

SHADOW: You want this fight or not? *(beat)* I've always been against it so you're not gonna act like a diva now that I've said yes! I've had it up to here with your bullshit. There are no murders in the ring, only tragic accidents.

SHORTY: But why kill him?

SHADOW: You have to kill Ketchel like one kills hope. You won't be killing him; you'll be killing white folks' overblown hope of one day seeing one of theirs in your place . . . The hope of every person for whom boxing will only be honorable again the day champions are white.

SHORTY: But didn't you always tell me white "Hope" was necessary because the crowds are mostly white?

SHADOW: We'll always find white "Hopes" . . . We can make them from scratch if we have to.

SHORTY: But why me? Why not Randall . . . or Skelly? . . . Since they're gonna fight him first?

SHADOW: Because those will be small-time fights, without significant media coverage. But a fight between Shorty and Ketchel, who'll have just whipped Randall and Skelly's asses—that's sure to bring in the crowds. You'll commit this unpunished crime with all of America as witness.

SHORTY: For God's sake! Why should Todd be the sacrificial lamb?

SHADOW: Because a sacrificial lamb is always, by definition, innocent. And Ketchel's not that innocent anyway. He had it coming, that piece of shit.

SHORTY: What do Todd and I have to do with this? We're just fighters!

SHADOW: You're not a fighter; you're a failed actor. And Ketchel's not a fighter either. Hell, don't you understand anything? What he wants, I'll tell you once again, is to make some good hard cash off your Negro back; he doesn't give a shit about boxing.

SHORTY: Look, I'm willing to humiliate him, to kick his ass like never before, to beat the shit out of him in front of all of America . . . I'm willing to do everything . . . But not that!

SHADOW: What is everything to you, Shorty?

SHORTY: Everything! *(silence)* I'll do everything you want me to do. I'll continue to fight; there won't be any talk about quitting anymore. I'll give twenty percent of my salary to the community instead of fifteen. I'll do everything but not that! This fight's between Todd and me. I wanna fight it alone. I wanna be alone in the ring, alone in front of Todd, with no one helping me. For once, I wanna know what I'm capable of.

Shadow examines Shorty as if to see into him.

SHADOW: All right. You can have your fight. See, I'm not a monster. All your conditions are accepted. You'll fight Ketchel exactly the way you want to—alone, without my help, like a big boy. Then, you'll fight Jimmy Fauley from New Mexico. The fight's already set up, it'll be in Santa Fe. The networks have signed; everything is in place.

He goes to exit then stops.

You know, I've often dreamt about that third round when you throw the fatal uppercut to Ketchel's chin . . . I've often dreamt about those white faces staring in disbelief at Ketchel's lifeless body. But oh, well . . . you've decided otherwise. The devil proposes; man disposes! See you later, Champ.

He exits.

7

Todd Ketchel's gym. Ketchel is training. Charlie Chuck watches from the ropes.

CHUCK: The jab, Todd, the jab! Keep him away with your jab. That's it. Don't rush it. Good . . . Good . . . Keep going . . . Combinations . . . Work the combinations! That's it, pow, pow, pow, pow! Back up! . . . Pow, pow, pow, pow! . . . Stay away from the ropes! The ropes, Todd! . . . Shorty's gonna kill you if you stay on the ropes!

Micky enters.

CHUCK: Ah, there you are! I thought you'd never show up. *(to Ketchel)* I said stay away from the ropes! Nice and easy, yeah, nice and easy! . . . Don't back up. No! Don't give him an inch. That's good. Work the body, Todd! That's good . . . All right, take a break. *(to Micky)* So? How's he training?

MICKY: Hard. Real hard.

KETCHEL: He's scared. I'm telling you, Shorty's pissing his pants.

CHUCK *(to Ketchel)*: Cut it out, Ketchel. No one's pissing their pants.

MICKY: Something's changed though. Shorty's always made people believe that to be a champion you just gotta have the gift. But not this time.

CHUCK: Is he not as fast? Not hitting as hard?

MICKY: No. His speed, his legwork, his combinations, his punching power—everything's the same.

CHUCK: Don't bullshit us, Micky. After so many years in the ring, he can't still be as strong.

MICKY: By the way, Todd . . . You should talk to your wife. She was at Shorty's the other day. It wouldn't be good, a few days before the fight, for people to start thinking the challenger's wife's knocking around with his opponent, you know what I mean?

Ketchel makes a move toward Micky. Charlie Chuck stops him.

CHUCK: Easy now. *(to Micky)* What's his strategy?

MICKY: Shadow's convinced that Todd's gonna go for a knockout early on. He thinks the longer the fight, the weaker he'll get. So he's gonna force Todd to chase him to tire him out. In other words, Shorty's game is to stay away until Todd starts to lose his cool . . .

KETCHEL: What if I don't?

MICKY: If you don't, Shorty's gonna let himself be dominated in the fifth. He might even hit the floor to let you believe you've got the upper hand. And he's gonna look for a moment when you make a mistake to pounce on you.

CHUCK: *(to Todd)* So, to put it simply, your only chance is to cut the ring off.

MICKY: Yes, he's gotta take advantage of Shorty's letting his hands down when he's on the ropes. Shorty has a tendency to drop his guard while he sticks the jab; it's a bad habit years of training never fixed. Todd, you gotta watch for that moment to throw your right.

CHUCK: Good. Now tell me . . . Shorty . . . Women . . . How's that working?

MICKY: Well . . . He's not queer if that's what you mean.

CHUCK: How about his sister? What's going on between them?

KETCHEL: Chuck, let's not get into that. This is about boxing.

CHUCK: And I say we need to intensify our campaign against Shorty. For God's sake, do you wanna remain a Great White Hope for the rest of your life? Enough with the Great White fucking Hopes! You're gonna win this fight. Just like you won against Randall and Skelly. You're gonna be the greatest sensation in the entire history of boxing. But when the press comes, I want you to insist on the relationship between Shorty and his sister . . .

KETCHEL: I just told you. I won't talk about that.

CHUCK: Let me tell you something, Todd. Boxing's a fairy tale. It's the eternal struggle between the hero and the villain. That's why it's an American sport. Black and white.

MICKY: Except this time, things aren't that simple; Shorty's not like other black fighters. Sure, he took a stand on racial issues but he never got as outrageous as Ali. And he doesn't mess around with white women like that old pervert Jack Johnson. No, Shorty's the modest, polite and mysterious champion that all of America admires. And that's the danger! He's the perfect American hero. So you gotta confuse the issue. You gotta force white America to take sides—your side. You gotta probe the depths of America's consciousness so the silt that fertilized this nation can rise to the surface again. You need to provoke white America so it realizes that behind the perfect American hero is a Negro mocking them . . .

KETCHEL: Do you realize what you're saying? Not all of us here are white.

CHUCK: That's the business, Todd. We have to do whatever it takes to weaken Shorty before the fight.

Chuck helps Todd put on his red, star-spangled robe.

We have to hit where it hurts. So when you talk to the press, I want you to say "I'm going to bring the title back to America."

KETCHEL: That's ridiculous.

CHUCK: You know what Floyd Patterson said before his fight against Ali? *(to Micky)* Tell him, Micky.

MICKY: "I'm going to bring the title back to America."

CHUCK: And Floyd Patterson's black. But he knew about heroes and villains. And he knew it's always best to be the hero . . . Now I'm counting on you, Todd.

Lights isolate Ketchel. Mickey points a mike at him.

MICKY: Can you be more specific with regards to your statement about the relationship between Shorty and his sister?

KETCHEL: It's true that I mentioned— . . . I did talk about that but those things have nothing to do with boxing. I talked about it, it's true . . . but only as a civilian . . . not as a fighter . . . I know Shorty well. We played in the sand together. We started fighting together . . . So I'd hate to cause him and Angie any harm. And anyway, it's their business. But as a Christian and as an American, I do find these things shocking just like the men and women of this country must find it shocking to learn that their great American hero indulges in . . . practices . . . which constitute a danger for the American people and upset our Christian sensibilities. What they've done is not American. You and I know where the real America stands. But those who have their hopes pinned on America, who admire America from afar—how can they understand that these people are not the real America, the America of the pioneers, of hard work, courage, democracy, freedom and love? No doubt Shorty's a great champion but he's not America's champion. Through these practices—as God is my witness, I say this with no hatred—these practices that take us back to the worst barbarians, I know there's a clear and conscious desire to soil America. He's hurting you, he's hurting us, he's hurting America. So this fight against him is your fight, it's America's fight, it's God's fight. Let's ask God to help me finally bring this title back to America. And may God bless America.

8

Shorty is alone, shadowboxing. Susie enters.

SUSIE: Good morning.

SHORTY: Good morning. *(silence)* You can come up.

She climbs in the ring and examines it as if she were entering a church for the first time.

SUSIE: It feels strange to be up here . . . It's like slipping into a man's bed for the first time . . . Like when I used to climb in my parents' bed as a kid. My father enjoyed it when I pulled his mustache . . . I don't know why I'm telling you this . . . I've been by twice already—yesterday and the day before. Did someone tell you?

SHORTY: Yeah, I heard.

SUSIE: Even at Todd's gym, I've never climbed up. He's never let me. So it's led me to believe things. Like when you're young and you start thinking your parents' bed is nicer than yours . . . The way Todd talks about it! . . . But here I am and there's nothing unusual. There's you, there's me and here are the–– . . . *(she counts the ring ropes)* There really are twelve ropes. I've always heard about "the twelve ropes" without ever giving it much thought, but it's true, there are twelve ropes . . . Am I boring you?

SHORTY: No.

SUSIE: If I am, please tell me.

SHORTY: You're not boring me.

SUSIE: In my dreams, you're always furious as a beast . . . Did I tell you I came by yesterday and the day before?

SHORTY: Yeah, but that's OK.

SUSIE: I wanted to ask forgiveness for everything that's been said about you in the papers. You know, it's not Todd's fault. It's the people around him who—

SHORTY: Don't worry, that's boxing.

SUSIE: I also wanted to thank you for agreeing to this fight. The closer we get to the day, the more I dream about it. The same dream for an entire week now. You climb in the ring and here I am facing you. I hit you. You collapse. The referee starts counting you out but you get up and throw yourself at me. You punch me everywhere as if you've gone crazy. Your fists smash my jaw, my ribs, my breasts, everything. I collapse. The referee counts. I get up and you hurl yourself at me again. You look even meaner and your fists are like stone. Blows rain down, faster and faster, more and more violent, to my stomach, the sides of my head, my forehead, my jaw, my breasts. I try to hold you but sweat makes our bodies slippery so I have no grip. You push me away. Then the blows again . . . How long is a round? Three minutes, right?

SHORTY: Yeah.

SUSIE: Well, in the dream it's endless; those three minutes seem as long as my entire life. Every blow ripples through my body in search of a place that pain hasn't reached yet. I collapse, exhausted. I see your feet come toward me. You're wearing silver boots. With a rage I didn't think you capable of, you kick me with your silver boots. And then all of a sudden, nothing. No more blows. The crowd is silent. The referee counts 1-2-3 . . . I'm a wound . . . 4-5-6 . . . my teeth hurt . . . 7-8 . . . my breasts are heavy with pain . . . He starts counting again 1-2-3 . . . He counts several times to 8. I want to get up, be the little girl who used to climb in bed to pull her father's mustache.

She starts to laugh.

Then just as you get ready to leave the ring, the referee tells you that the fight's not over.

Her whole body is now shaking with laughter.

You turn around and who do you see? Todd, still fresh in his pretty red robe.

Shorty smiles.

Your fists make him laugh because you've used up all your strength against me. Todd gives you a little tap on the jaw and you fall flat on your face. The referee raises Todd's arm. He's the winner . . . You think I'm ridiculous, right?

SHORTY: We're never ridiculous when it comes to love.

SUSIE: For an entire week, this dream's been haunting me. But the day I came by, I didn't dream. And I haven't dreamt since. So I feel like I've been abandoned by someone I like very much . . .

A beat. She pulls out an old book.

Here. I came to give you this. It's the play you're in. This edition dates back to when the author was still alive. I thought you would enjoy it.

He leafs through the book.

SHORTY: For me?

SUSIE: I wanted to thank you for giving Todd a chance. He's calmer now. He doesn't drink. And even if he loses, we'll make it! He's gotten offers from Hollywood and journalists actually pay to hear him talk. I know it's not nice to say this but if Todd wins, he could become mayor . . .

SHORTY *(who wasn't listening, engrossed in the book)*: Do you speak German?

SUSIE: My mother is German. Why?

SHORTY: Can you read me a few sentences?

SUSIE: What do you want me to read?

SHORTY: Whatever you want . . . Just read. I wanna know how it sounds in German.

SUSIE: Margarete: Der Mensch, den du da bei dir hast,
Ist mir in tiefer inner Seele verhasst:
Es hat mir in meinem Leben
So nichts einen Stich ins Herz gegeben,

Als des Menschen widrig Gesicht.
Faust: Liebe Puppe, fürcht' ihn nicht!
More?

SHORTY: No, thank you. That's what I thought. This story could only have been conceived in a language like German. Thank you very much. It's a beautiful gift.

SUSIE: I'm glad you like it. *(beat)* I also wanted to tell you I'm going to have a child. Todd doesn't know. I'll tell him after the fight to make up for his loss. Because I know he's going to lose. The fact that this dream is not coming to me is a sign. Dreams never lie. They're always the first to let you down . . . I wanted you to know before Todd . . . I don't know how to thank you . . . I'm so ashamed of what these people make Todd say about you and your sister . . .

SHORTY: Don't worry, that's boxing.

SUSIE: Well, I think I've wasted enough of your time. Please offer my apologies to your sister.

She starts to leave then stops.

Can I ask you one more thing?

SHORTY: Yes?

SUSIE: Who is Shadow?

SHORTY: . . . Shadow?

SUSIE: Yes. How did you two meet?

A beat.

SHORTY: Oh, you know . . . In this business, people come and go . . . All sorts of people . . . That's boxing.

Angie barges in. She's fuming.

ANGIE: These people are completely out of line!

SUSIE: Good morning.

ANGIE *(ignoring Susie)*: Did you hear the latest?

Susie slips away.

Because of what Todd and the media are saying about us, the Commission doesn't want me to sing the National Anthem. Can you believe it?

SHORTY: Don't worry, you'll sing the National Anthem. Shadow will take care of it . . .

ANGIE: They said I was going to defile it!

SHORTY: I'm telling you, Shadow will take care of it.

He shows her the book.

Look. Susie gave it to me . . . She wanted to thank me for agreeing to this fight . . . And apologize for what the papers are saying . . . She said she's ashamed . . . You know, she told me about a crazy dream . . . She's expecting a child . . . She's gonna tell Todd after the fight so he— . . . The child's Todd's . . .

ANGIE: I didn't ask.

SHORTY: You should've said hello when you came in.

Angie storms out. Shorty opens the book and examines it like a strange object while the stage turns to black.

9

In the ring. The quartet starts improvising on Fauré's Requiem *while Ketchel, lit by a spotlight, makes his entrance. Once he reaches the ring, the spotlight expands to the edge of the ring. The entire sequence happens in a deep silence underlined by the* Requiem. *We then see Shorty's entrance. Same spotlight, same* Requiem.

The two camps are in the ring. It seems overcrowded after the previous emptiness. The quartet stops. Total silence. The light moves from the ring to the quartet to Angie. She walks to the center of the ring and starts singing the national anthem, a cappella.

The two fighters move to the center of the ring. Drum roll. The fight begins. The quartet will play during the entire fight, starting with Fauré's Requiem *and shifting, as the fight unfolds, to something increasingly more violent that eventually reaches the explosive exuberance of Coltrane's* A Love Supreme.

In the first two rounds, Ketchel has a slight advantage. But in the third, after a flurry of punches from Shorty, he collapses. He gets up before the count but has clearly not recovered. After another flurry, he goes to the floor again. He gets back up. Another flurry, again the floor. The quartet stops except for the sax which, like a car horn stuck after an accident, stretches the same note indefinitely. Shadow exits while Ketchel is counted out.

The quartet takes up the Requiem *again. Following its rhythm, the count is endless, eight . . . fifteen . . . twenty . . . in slow motion. But Ketchel is still down. Susie rushes up. Ketchel's body is taken away.*

Shorty looks dazed, as if coming out of a bad dream. He realizes that he's alone in the ring. Suddenly, appearing out of nowhere, three crows fly into the room.

SHORTY *(screaming at the crows)*: Shadow!!!

He collapses into tears.

Oh, my God . . .

Angie joins him in the ring.

As they exit, the cawing fades and the stage turns to black. The Requiem *continues.*

10

At the cemetery. Susie stands by a freshly dug grave. Shorty enters. He respectfully waits to the side.

A few steps away from them, Micky talks to a camera.

MICKY: But Todd Ketchel—God bless his soul—was not only a brave and talented fighter; he was a generous and caring husband. No doubt he would have made an exemplary father for the child that the unfortunate Susie, who is dignified in her sorrow and her love, wanted to offer him at the end of the fight. We, who were privileged to feel the power of his love, know how loyal he was in friendship. Exemplary husband, faithful friend, Todd Ketchel was most of all Christian. Profoundly Christian and profoundly American. We will miss him dearly. This is Micky Abraham for Network Sports.

Micky exits. After a beat, Shadow appears with a bouquet of flowers. He steps in front of Shorty.

SHADOW: My condolences, Mrs. Ketchel.

SUSIE: I knew you would come. The assassin rarely misses his victim's burial.
SHADOW: I have no idea what you're talking about.
SUSIE: Not true. You know very well what I'm talking about . . .

Shorty pulls out the book Susie gave him.

SHORTY: I'm here to ask forgiveness. And to give you back the book.
SUSIE *(to Shadow as if she hasn't heard Shorty)*: What did Todd do to you? From the very beginning, you spun your web around him. You made him believe that Shorty was afraid of him and that even you were afraid. And Todd fell for it. We all fell for it. From the very beginning, it was rotten to the core. His fights against Randall and Skelly were fixed, right?
SHORTY: I'm here to give you back the book.
SUSIE: You managed to lure us with the idea that Todd was back to his former self while the evidence was right in front of our eyes. Todd was worn-out, broken, finished . . . And someone was slowly pushing him into the grave.
SHADOW: You're flattering me, Mrs. Ketchel. To do what you're describing, one has to be damn intelligent!
SUSIE: I don't know if one has to be damn intelligent but one has to be diabolically patient.
SHADOW: Possibly. But can you be black without being patient?
SUSIE: I don't know how you did it but I know you killed Todd.
SHADOW: I understand the extent of your grief, Mrs. Ketchel. But it doesn't give you the right to make such an accusation. You have no proof.
SHORTY: I'm here to ask forgiveness.
SUSIE *(to Shorty)*: What did you do to have to ask forgiveness and who am I to forgive you? If you did wrong, I know God has forgiven you. Isn't it written that much will be forgiven to those who have suffered much? And you have suffered a lot, Shorty. And . . . that's boxing. Keep the book, it's yours. See? Dreams are always the first to let you down.

She turns to Shadow and examines him from head to toe.

Who are you?
SHADOW: My name's Buster McCauley. I was born in Topeka, Kansas. My father was a lumberjack and sang the blues. Mom used to work for white folks as a cleaning lady. Every Sunday— . . .

Susie is gone.

It's strange, everybody wants to know who I am but nobody cares enough to listen to the whole story. *(pause)* So, Shorty . . . You came to wrap your big black muscles around the white chick? You came to comfort her over her husband's freshly dug grave?

SHORTY: If you don't respect the living, at least respect the dead.

SHADOW: I can see why. For a white chick—

SHORTY: I forbid you to call her that.

SHADOW *(parodying)*: My, oh my! If no one holds him back, he's gonna rip my eyes out. He's gonna hit me with his great big fighter hands. Big brute. It's lucky he doesn't dare do that among the dead. He respects them too much. *(addressing the dead)* Thank you, all!

SHORTY: You're not funny.

SHADOW: Already giving each other gifts, bringing them back, forgiving each other, even quoting the Bible. Good old Shorty! You've got good taste, you know. She's an attractive woman.

SHORTY: Why do you always see evil behind everything?

SHADOW: 'Cause behind everything, there's evil. Young, attractive, white and a widow. God, that's exciting! This woman's the erotic embodiment of the devil. And God knows I know a thing or two about the devil.

SHORTY: You dirty everything you touch.

SHADOW: Oh, and you don't? Who's rummaging under the widow's skirt right over her husband's freshly dug grave?

SHORTY: You didn't keep your word.

SHADOW: I wanted to teach you a lesson, remind you that I make the decisions. 'Cause the moment I got you the title, you became mine body and soul. "You didn't keep your word." You make me laugh! My only word was to make you the Champion. Plus, I had to step in. I learned at the last minute that Micky had ratted on you.

SHORTY: Micky?

SHADOW: That piece of shit tried to screw us up. Todd and his people knew everything about your training. And I was told Ketchel's wife came by the gym a few days before the fight. Where's your head, Shorty? That woman wanted to milk you of your venom!

SHORTY: You don't get it.

SHADOW: Sometimes I wonder what would become of you if I wasn't here keeping watch. That woman knows that deep inside, you're just a softy.

But you need hatred in your eyes and death in your fists to win a fight like that. So I had to do something. Otherwise it'd be you lying in the grave. But against Fauley, you'll be on your own. You have my word.

SHORTY: It's no use. I can't fight anymore.

SHADOW: You're starting again.

Shorty shows his hands. They're shaking.

SHORTY: I'm ill, Shadow.

SHADOW: You're not ill. Your hands are shaking from remorse.

SHORTY: No, I'm ill. I need rest.

SHADOW: It's all in your head, Shorty. You didn't kill anyone. Tell yourself that's boxing. That woman was right: Much will be forgiven to those who have suffered much. You, me—we've been steeped in suffering. It's our most precious asset. It's an investment in everybody else's conscience . . .

SHORTY: She wasn't talking about that!

SHADOW: Look, I'm not asking you to share my ideas, I'm asking you to fight for me.

SHORTY: Then cure me.

SHADOW: How can I cure you when you're not even ill?

SHORTY: I'll take some time off then.

SHADOW: We can't back out of the fight against Fauley. It's sold out, the networks are ready . . . It's all in motion.

SHORTY: If you force me, I'll talk about my illness to the press . . .

SHADOW: No, you won't. You know why? 'Cause you love Angie too much. You wouldn't want anything to happen to her, would you?

SHORTY: You wouldn't.

SHADOW: I wouldn't hesitate for a second. Respect the contract, that's all I ask.

Shorty exits.

For the widow, I can put her in your bed anytime, as a bonus for what you did to Todd. In your bed anytime.

Shorty has disappeared. Shadow approaches Ketchel's grave. He throws the flowers on the grave.

See, Todd. I always keep my promises.

He exits.

11

Angie and Micky in Angie's club, after hours.

ANGIE: They say my brother doesn't train anymore. They say he doesn't even go to the gym. They say he spends most of his time with Ketchel's widow. They say that ever since the accident, he's been seeking forgiveness. So he visits her, keeps her company, tries to make himself useful. I think he feels the need to atone for his sin. But people are talking . . . When you spend your days with a pregnant woman whose husband just died, of course there's gonna be gossip. They say my brother is sick. That he doesn't have good coordination anymore and that his reaction time is getting slower and slower. Still, if he climbed in a ring tomorrow, he'd win . . . I know it. I know he'll win against Fauley, even with his hands cut off. My brother was hungry. He was hungry for money, fame, love . . . everything. So he signed a terrible contract. A contract that obliges him to fight forever. People don't understand. All they see is the pomp, the bright lights, the glamour . . . They don't see how miserable he is in a ring. My brother is dying a slow death . . .

A beat.

Please help me help him . . . What if the Commission suspended his license?

MICKY: For what reason?

ANGIE: Couldn't someone arrange for my brother to test positive after the fight against Fauley? If it becomes known publicly that Li'l Jazz is doping, his career will be over.

MICKY: It's not the only thing that will be over, everything will be over. His name, his reputation, his legend . . . Everything he's built since the beginning. He won't even be able to do theater.

ANGIE: Everything will be over but there'll still be Li'l Jazz.

MICKY: Actually, no. There'll be no Li'l Jazz. Because Li'l Jazz is the legend.

Behind her, newspaper headlines from around the world flash across the stage: "Shorty Charged with Doping" . . . "The Fall of a Myth!" . . . "World Champion Doped Up" . . . "Scandal!" . . .

ANGIE: Please. I know you have the right connections. I'll testify. I'll say that Li'l Jazz was already into it.

MICKY: I'll think about it.

ANGIE: Thank you.
MICKY: I only said I would think about it.
ANGIE: I know. But thank you anyway.

12

Projected on stage is a crowd of photographers, cameramen and curious onlookers. They become increasingly hysterical and violent. Shorty throws himself in the ring as if in a safe haven.

We now see images of joyful daily life in an African village. We hear the cheerful sounds of women pounding grain, masks dancing, children playing in a river. The last images show mostly children.

Soon, the images disappear but the light from the projector still illuminates the stage, which is obscured by a huge shadow. A man is standing, motionless, as if behind a door.

SHORTY *(waking up)*: Angie? Angie, is that you?

Shadow appears in a white lab coat.

SHADOW: No, it's just me.
SHORTY: Oh, Shadow. It's you.
SHADOW: How are you?
SHORTY: Fine . . . I'm fine . . . I was so happy I thought I was dead . . . God, they were so mean!
SHADOW: Forget it, it's over. Here, look what I brought.
SHORTY: Thank you.

He hands him a red robe, hand wraps and a pair of boxing shoes. Shorty begins to get dressed.

They stole everything . . .

A beat.

It's clean here. Everything's clean and tidy. Even the people are clean but they're thieves. They steal everything you bring . . . But they're clean . . .
SHADOW: You need anything else?
SHORTY *(as if he hasn't heard)*: How about Angie?

SHADOW: Angie? I told you yesterday . . . She's resting . . . She's got some problems. During her testimony in court, she screamed that I was after your soul but that I was wasting my time 'cause your soul had crawled up her vagina to hide in her belly. Then she took off her clothes, right there, in the middle of the court, and hit me with her panties . . . She kept hitting me with those bloodstained panties, screaming that I was the devil and that I was after your soul . . . God, it was terrible! The white folks said that she— . . . that she needed rest. They put her in a hospital.

SHORTY *(who didn't really listen)*: Ah . . . It's clean here! Everything's tidy. Even the people are clean and they're polite but they steal. Did you see the cafeteria? Everything shines! The napkins, the plates, the forks, the knives . . . everything . . . But the food's crap . . . I like clean things . . . Oh yeah, look!

He shows his hands. They don't shake anymore.

SHADOW: See? I told you they were shaking from remorse. You like it here?

SHORTY: Yeah, I think so . . . I don't know . . . Maybe . . . Yeah, I'm more or less happy but—

SHADOW: Don't judge happiness, it's bad luck. Look where it got us. All those people who kept trying to turn you against me, who told you I was selling illusions, utopias and damnation . . . Where are they now? Where are those who know where happiness begins and where it ends? And what do they know about happiness other than the words that disguise it? Does it matter whether you're loved by the Devil or by God? Isn't the most important thing to be loved? And I love you, Champ. I love you despite them and despite yourself. You'll see, everything will be just like before. I'll get you out of here. You'll serve your suspension and then you'll climb back in the ring and dazzle the world with your magic again.

SHORTY: There's a nurse who keeps hitting on me. Every time she sees me, she asks for an autograph. Today, she waited for me by the cafeteria. She smiled at me. Her mouth looks like a carnation. I like her perfume. We had lentils. The food's crap. Lentils are only good if they're cooked right. But they make you fart anyway. Look.

He shows his hands again.

They don't shake anymore.

SHADOW: That's good.

SHORTY: Tonight I'm gonna cut my nails . . .

He bursts into tears.

God, they were so mean . . . so mean! At least, you stayed. Here I was thinking that—

SHADOW: Abandoning you would be like abandoning myself. I'm your servant, you forget it too often. Even if you decided to never see me again, I'd still be by your side.

SHORTY: Tell me, Shadow, what did I do to deserve so much love?

SHADOW: Don't judge happiness, Champ. It's bad luck. The people here are gonna take care of you. Your soul got frightened by the recent events and escaped. But they're gonna bring it back . . .

SHORTY: Tonight I'm gonna cut my nails. How about Angie? . . . Oh yeah, you told me, she's pregnant.

SHADOW: She's not pregnant; she thinks she's pregnant . . . Anyway, it doesn't matter.

He takes out Susie's gift.

Look, I brought your book . . .

SHORTY: No, keep it. I'm afraid they're gonna steal it. You know, they're clean but they're thieves . . .

Shorty is now fully dressed. He makes a few moves to see if his robe fits, if his hand wraps are not too tight, if his shoes are comfortable. Then spurred on by Shadow's voice, his movements become more coherent, more fluid and gradually shift into wild shadowboxing accompanied by fiery Coltrane-inspired music.

SHADOW: That's it. Go ahead, Champ, nice and easy, nice and easy . . .
Dance, Shorty, dance
Dance for the kids
Whose dreams have been wrecked
Whose dreams have been trampled
Whose dreams have been stolen
Dance, Shorty, dance
Dance for the kids
Who are cold
Who are thirsty
Who are hungry

Dance, Shorty, dance
Dance for the kids
Who are blown up in smoke
Who are crushed like cigarette butts
Who are swept into a common grave
Like ashes into an ashtray
Dance . . .

Little by little, his voice is drowned out by the intensity of the quartet. The music stops. Shorty falls to his knees as if the music alone had held him up. He looks at his wrapped hands.

SHORTY: Yeah, tonight I'm gonna cut my nails.

END OF PLAY

Nicaise Wegang (Jaz) in *Jaz*, directed by Yaya Mbilé at the Centre Culturel Français in Douala, Cameroon, 2008. Photo by Fabrice Ngon.

Jaz

1998

TRANSLATED BY CHANTAL BILODEAU

INTRODUCTION TO JAZ

Jaz puts the fragmented consciousness of a rape victim on stage in the form of a musical incantation interrupted by "improvisations." We might also think of this piece as a nonchronological narrative poem in which the character Jaz plays out in her mind in a question and answer format (that could also be a police interrogation) the circumstances of her existence and her rape. The setting is a highly metaphorized urban project located on Golden Yellow Street. Other names of buildings and squares in Jaz's physical universe also bespeak bright colors, but Jaz's experience has taken her out of the rainbow. She has no more contact with hope, with joy, with the possibility of a future, and with the luminosity that had marked her trajectory up until the rape. She seems to be contemplating suicide, or perhaps murder, but in any case she is locked in a death-focused mind trip, nourished by the Egyptian *Book of the Dead*. Her rapist, a control freak with Christ's eyes—who is afraid of anything smacking of otherness (hence his negative references to the "Tower of Babel")—identifies only with his masculine weapon, what he calls his "scorpion's tail." To exist, he needs to wound, to shame, to destroy women, and he couches this need in a sick vision of purity. Unlike Jaz, he could never work his way out of the excrement that surrounds them.

Perhaps the rapist stands for all the misery that has thrown Jaz into her strange death ritual, she who is a kind of beautiful lotus miraculously sprung to life from mud and muck. Jaz fights back against her wounding by telling her own story. But this is a story she tells as though not herself, as though out of her body. And with her own story, she also tells that of her friend Oridé, Oridé being another version of the same fate. For Oridé has already committed suicide by putting on a mask to hide her beauty, a way of recognizing and concretizing the painful revelation that the world only desires easy money and exchanges based on hard cash. Such a world refuses the gift that does not take, the gift that instead gives: the gift of intimacy, tenderness, and art itself.

Another voice, that of the soulless bureaucracy that has abandoned the project to its broken plumbing and unhinged mailboxes, courses through the play (in italics in the text) and through Jaz's mind. This petty, virtual superego condemns Jaz to a hollow life without comfort or community. The only voice providing some respite lives in the musical instrument meant by Kwahulé to dialogue with and punctuate Jaz's complex polyvocal monologue. Its notes contain something of her secret, untouchable self, a reserve of freedom that lets her fly. And the flight is figured in the layout of the text when in the last part of the play the lyrical riff on her name becomes a *calligramme*, a typographic image of Jaz as a bird.

Notes for reading and for production:

1. Kwahulé wrote this play after the 1992–95 genocide in Bosnia in which systematic rape was used as a weapon against Bosnian women. He learned from a UNESCO official how these women always disguised their own stories as those of friends. This is the first play in which he begins to replace characters by the notion of voices, including, in this play, using a musical instrument as a voice. Jaz, who has lost a letter from her name, is also like those Africans taken into slavery and amputated of their identity.

2. *The Book of the Dead* is an ancient Egyptian funerary text with instructions for magical spells and incantations that help prepare the voyage through the underworld to the afterlife.

3. The Tower of Babel is an Old Testament reference to a tower being built by a monolingual people in order to reach the heavens. God is said to have punished their pridefulness by causing these people to speak in different languages; and it is this multilingual tower that the rapist character hates.

4. The Valley of Jehosaphat: interpretations vary about this Old Testament reference but most agree that this is a valley where God's judgment will be heard; it is perhaps even the location of the Last Judgment. Jaz wanders there, her beauty perhaps a connection to God.

5. Other names could easily be substituted by a director for the names listed by "the bureaucratic voice" as belonging to residents of Jaz's building. In Kwahulé's text, these names comprise a random compilation of invented people and people Kwahulé knows and admires. In the same spirit of allowing interpretive freedom to directors, the character Jaz could be played by one or multiple actors.

In light of the multiple voices she embodies, a chorus of Jaz figures might prove very effective.

CHARACTERS

JAZ: A woman
A jazz instrument

A woman.
Her head shaved perhaps.
Naked perhaps.
A gun.
Bullets.
A mug shot ID board.
Jazz (a single instrument)
which, from time to time,
pierces/is pierced
embraces/is embraced
by the woman's voice.

Jaz.
Yes Jaz.
She has always been called Jaz.
Jaz.
She doesn't know anymore.
Simply Jaz.

No.
No.
No.

Earlier.
This morning.
In a public bathroom.
China Blue Square.

My girlfriend.
My friend.
I'm not here to talk about myself but to talk about Jaz.

No.
Jaz didn't want to.
But we see each other often.
Mostly at my place.
Not really.
Some temp work.

It's not easy to talk about that yourself.
Shame and guilt I suppose.
In a public bathroom in China Blue Square.

A maid's room on the sixth floor.
Due to the difficulties encountered
in delivering the mail
to the building listed above
Because there's no toilet in her room.
The one in the hall is out of order.
Everything is falling apart even the—
In consequence we ask that you make
the following improvements.

No janitor.
On the corner of Golden Yellow Street.

The first time
Jaz unclogged it.
The second time too.
The third time she didn't do anything.
Let someone else unclog it.

Since this morning Jaz wonders too.
No one took it upon themselves to unclog it.
No she left it alone.

But they kept going.
Until the bowl was full and overflowed.
The neighbors kept going anyway.
All shitting wherever they could.
It then overflowed from the bowl
plastered the entire hall
tumbled down the stairs.
From bottom to top.

For more than two weeks.
From first floor to sixth floor
no one was complaining.
Yet from the street and
the buildings nearby
the smell was unbearable.

Very odd.
A sort of no man's land in the middle of the City
clear and standardized labeling
of all the mailboxes
using block letters the mayor and the police and
those who keep the records of the Book of the Dead
everyone is waiting for
everything to rot and collapse on its own.

But they are mistaken.
For as long as Jaz lives there
the building will keep standing.
I know.

Crazy things.

One summer
someone shot killed
somebody in the building across the street.
The shot came from Jaz's building.
Nobody ever figured out who or why.

No.
She doesn't think about moving.
I suggested it but she refused.

About her.
Very little in fact.
Jaz almost never talks about herself.
Very little.
I even wonder
if Jaz is her real name.

She owns her room.
Like everyone else in that building.

An inheritance.
An aunt.

The bare minimum.
A room almost empty.
Jaz doesn't own anything
doesn't hold on to anything.

Nothing in any case that
could be locked in a coffin.
By choice.
Because of what happened
at the death of Oridé's grandfather.

Oridé.
A friend of Jaz.
Jaz's friend.
So beautiful she could wake the dead.
They lived together for a while.
At Jaz's place.
Jaz has always lived on Golden Yellow Street.

The custom of the City.
That the dead be buried
with one of their objects.

Anything.
A lipstick
a nail file
a credit card.
There are some who have been
buried with their bank.

Their coffeepots
their saucepans
their vacuum cleaners.
Some had their kitchens
rebuilt in their graves.

Their pens
their books
their paintings.
The worst are those

who get incinerated with
rare masterpieces.

Their cars
their helicopters
their planes.
From there the idea of building
an airport in the cemetery.
For the dead.

Their houses
their private suites
their buildings.
For some time now
in the circles where
it is decided who is going to die
there are rumors that
one of the accountants of
the Book of the Dead
wants to be put into the ground with the City.
Cemetery included.

At the death of Oridé's grandfather
everyone realized
that he didn't own anything.
No lighter
no cane
no eyeglass
not even an ID card.
Nothing.

It was the first time
and to this day the last
that such a case was seen in the City.
Everything that had helped him in his life
from the buttons of his shirt
to the laces of his shoes
everything had been rented or borrowed.

Oridé suggested that they bury
her grandfather with her.
But the police and

the mayor and
those who keep the records
of the Book of the Dead
refused.

The grandfather was thrown to the fish
in the river that surrounds the City.
As dictated by custom.

Jaz was inspired by these things
and set out to make her life a challenge.
To live with no future no past.

Perhaps.
Yes.
But the Board *new locks*
on all the mailboxes to ensure
the security of the mail quit a long time ago.

A total mess.
The approved and completed work hadn't been paid for.
Jaz showed them to me laughing one day.
Minutes from the General Board Meeting.
Like for example:

ARBÉ Management Company reminds shareholders that a detailed statement of expenses incurred by the Board for the period closing on 12/31/199 . . . was sent to everyone prior to the convocation of the present meeting. Please note that there are seven outstanding balances. MR. KOABLÉ: (15 178.13 francs), MR. BARLET: (19 735.51 francs), MR. and MRS. XINGJIAN: (15 117.90 francs), MR. LÉKÉMA: (18 000.05 francs), MRS. de KERMABON: (13 131.31 francs), MISS ZAMBONI: (23 791.94 francs), MR. and MRS. LANSMAN: (19 003 francs), and many others above 5000 francs: MR. WITTORSKI, MR. MEUNIER, MR. BENGUETTAF, MR. and MRS. COHEN, MRS. CÉSAIRE, MR. ISHERWOOD, MRS. BLIN, MR. and MRS. MATSHUMOTO, the Countess of ROUGEMONT, Guru MAHARAJI, MR. and MRS. DIABATÉ, MISS YLACHA. Shareholders give the Property Agent the power to recover any amounts due to the Board, including the authority to appeal to the justice system.

But justice never entered this building.

Jaz has always paid.
Until the Board abandoned the building.
Jaz is like that.

From now on Jaz goes down to
the public bathroom in China Blue Square.
Not necessarily.
She disciplines herself and
her body finally understands
that there are things
it cannot ask of her.
On a newspaper.
She throws it in the garbage in the morning.

A diarrhea after midnight.
Never.
No.
She goes down only
when absolutely necessary.

Except on Sundays.
In the mornings.
Religiously yes.
Her body has developed the habit that's all.

Because afterwards she wanders.
Jaz likes to wander on Sunday mornings.
When the City sleeps the hours away
and the streets are still empty and peaceful.

He must have noticed that.
A week perhaps.
Or a month.
Probably.
Maybe ever since
the day the toilet clogged up.
That's why he came to wait for her this morning.

Once.
On the stairs.
I was going up to Jaz's room.
I can't say he does.

At first glance nothing whatsoever.

Rather ordinary.
Thirty-three-years old I would say.
No more.
A little boy.
Six seven years old.
Jaz told me he was married but I've never seen her.

No.
No.
No.
I'm not here to talk about myself but to talk about Jaz.

In fact she should have.
Because of what happened on the stairs.
Of their building.

Jaz was coming back from the grocer's shop.
He was waiting for her on the stairs.
Jaz thinks he was waiting for her.
Because of his eyes.
They were imploring her and defying her at the same time.
Perhaps.
Given the circumstances she felt
he could only look at her
the way he did.
Possible.
But there's no doubt he was waiting for her
that he had rushed there
after seeing her come out of the grocer's shop.

I don't know.
Probably because of her beauty.
It's obscene how beautiful Jaz is.

A lotus.
Jaz is a lotus.
In that building *new directory*
with all renters and shareholders listed in alphabetical order where
people wade in their own shit
Jaz rises like a lotus.

Her presence illuminates it
and maintains it in a semblance of humanity.
Is it why she refuses to leave.
It's more for Oridé I think.

Oridé.
Jaz's friend.
So beautiful she could wake the dead.

Not anymore.
Oridé died from knowing she was beautiful.

On the Boulevard of Burning Incense.
A stretched hand
open like a prayer
under a closed sky.

Oridé stops in front of the hand
who sings psalms for a coin.
Oridé looks at the hand.
Attentively.

A hand used to being stretched.
Filth lies in a bed of creases.
Being dirty the nails lower their eyes.
Plague thoroughly consumes the index.

A few passersby stop
dazzled by the sight of
the girl so beautiful she could wake the dead
frozen in front of the expecting hand.

Already the first drops of rain
crash on the Boulevard of Burning Incense.

"A coin" sings the hand.
Oridé unbuttons her blouse.
Two buttons.
Oridé takes the hand kisses it
then rolls it
between her blouse and the hills of her breasts.
With her right breast she caresses the hand
with her left breast she caresses the hand.

Oridé slides the hand
on her stomach
around her navel
down to the moist intimacy of her offering
to this source
where no other man's hand
has ever drunk.

It had to be.
To respect the pleasure of the other.
It had to be.
Above all a gift is dialogue.
It had to be.

The crowd grows
around what in the rain
the girl so beautiful she could wake the dead
offers to the plagued hand.

Oridé buttons up her blouse.
Expectation stretched again in front of her.
But the hand doesn't beg anymore
it demands.

Oridé walks away.
The hand cries out.
Oridé comes back.
"Now my coin" says the hand.
"But I've already given you everything" says Oridé.
"My coin."

Oridé is crushed.
She runs down the Boulevard of Burning Incense
her mind clouded with shame
runs across
the rainy City
all the way into Jaz's arms.

The coin.
That's what killed her.
The coin killed Oridé.

The next morning
Oridé wore a mask.
As one takes the veil.
Something most ordinary.
A white mask bought in a store.

At first to see her
walk around with this mask
the City smiled *this directory*
being essential for the delivery
of registered parcels
money orders and telegrams
later no.
Because Oridé didn't wear it
one two or three days
she wore it until the end.

Every night
Oridé removed the mask
to offer her beauty to Jaz.
To Jaz alone.

One night however
the mask resisted.
Oridé fought.
To no avail.
Jaz hung on to the mask.
To no avail.
Oridé and Jaz circled the mask.
To no avail.

Oridé died as the clock struck twelve
asphyxiated by the white mask.

The next day Jaz shaved her head.
A custom long fallen into oblivion.
The lover shaves her head at the death of the loved one.

Every year
on the day of Oridé's death
Jaz shaves her head.

A lotus.
Jaz is a lotus.
Often on the street
people stop us to
thank her for being so beautiful.
One day
in the valley of Jehosaphat
a man threw himself at her feet
covered them with kisses and
trembling said to her
"Don't be afraid."
A little.
"Don't be afraid.
I want to thank you.
You are God's erotic testimony.
For such beauty is only possible through Him."

I who've often had the privilege of seeing her naked
know the amazement of
the man in the valley of Jehosaphat.

She's my friend.
That's not important.
It's not important.
No relevance.
I'm not here to talk about myself but to talk about Jaz.

Yes.
His pants were down.
Around his ankles.

He was stroking it.
Probably.
Jaz didn't tell me.
She mostly talked about
this thing both tensed and relaxed
in the man's eyes.
Like Christ's face
on the stained-glass windows of churches.
Those are Jaz's words.

He said nothing.

He only looked at Jaz while
between his legs
his fingers kneaded his desire.

No nothing
no swear words.
Not even.
No insults.
Only this vertical look
while his hand was moving up and down
his erected insolence.

His eyes were imploring Jaz
to watch him do that
to embrace him with her admiration
or even her disgust.
Especially her disgust.
In a way.
Jaz's presence was an endorsement of his pleasure.

But it's an aggression.
It's always an aggression.

I think so.
She mumbled something like
"You should be ashamed of yourself."
I can't imagine Jaz yelling at him.
Jaz is very calm.
Too calm.
I now realize that
I've never seen her angry.
As if
nothing is worth getting angry over.

At a loss.
He suddenly seemed at a loss.
To hear Jaz react like that no doubt.
He got scared.
Quite the opposite.
He needed this urgency this cold panic.
Fear had ripened his pleasure.

In moments like those
one doesn't glance at a watch.
Jaz doesn't wear a watch.
No more than five seconds
even if talking about it gives the impression
that she was sitting back on the balcony
watching him do that.

Especially since the groceries
fell from her hands
and the Starking apples
rolled all the way to *the installation of a communal mailbox*
of large dimensions
(600 X 500 X 110 minimum)
that can be locked and where the bottom of the stairs
the Starkings rolled all the way to the bottom.
Jaz went down to retrieve them.

He wasn't there anymore.
He had disappeared.

On the fourth floor.
Jaz lives on the sixth floor.
It's the top floor.
He does too.
No relevance.
I don't.
I'm not here to talk about myself but to talk about Jaz.

A flash.

Once.
Six months ago.

A few days before
what happened on the stairs.
He had offered his toilet to Jaz just in case.
On that floor
he's the only one with a toilet . . .
I guess since he offered it to her.
Jaz refused.
Because she couldn't imagine

knocking on the door of the man and his family
every time.

Why should she have talked about it with his wife.
Jaz had refused to give
any importance to this incident.
Besides the man didn't bother her again.
He wouldn't even greet her
if they happened to pass each other on the stairs.
As for her
Jaz had wiped from her memory
the man with Christ's eyes
waiting on the stairs
his pants down around his ankles.

Until this morning.

Jaz went down
like every Sunday morning.
He was waiting.
The man.
Jaz.
She thought the bathroom was occupied.

It didn't occur to her.
They are public bathrooms after all.
The sign indicated vacant.
He didn't either.
Since the incident on the stairs
they had stopped greeting each other.
Or saying anything at all.
Why should she have suspected him.
She had erased him from her memory.
One or two days after.

No eye contact.
Jaz is like that.
Because she didn't expect
to see him or not to see him.
Erased.

She put a coin
in the slot
the door opened
and she felt brutally pushed inside.
By the man.
He immediately closed the door behind them.

No.
She didn't scream either.
Because she didn't understand what was happening.
The mind stalls in moments like those.

"Get undressed" he said to Jaz.
The voice was soft
and the tone a bit obsequious.
He all but added please.
Strangely.

A knife.
A kitchen knife.

At first yes.
Obviously.
To be addressed politely in a public bathroom
a knife between the thighs
can't be reassuring for anyone.

Jaz got undressed.

"Your underwear."

Because Jaz was afraid of the man's fear.

Very.

He was shaking like a leaf.
Not of being caught.
More as if witnessing a blasphemy.
The more frantic he was the more
Jaz was drawn into his hysteria.
She told herself that a man that frightened
is capable of anything.
To the point of losing his mind.

Anyway on the stairs he hadn't said anything.

With the tips of his fingers
he brushed Jaz's nipples.
As if he were afraid of being struck down.
It wasn't about having a choice or not.
In moments like those one hopes that
every concession will prevent the worst.

Unlike on the stairs.

While his fingers grown more assertive
were caressing her breasts
he whispered to Jaz
how beautiful she was.

"You're exactly how
God imagined
woman
for the first time
just before the Tower of Babel.
Naked
you're even more beautiful."

"Most people are hideous once naked.
It's on a beach that is revealed
in the most shameless manner
the disgrace of the flesh."

"How could the Eternal"
I must inform you that
if these improvements are not made
within "How could God
have tolerated" *the mail addressed*
to the occupants of the building
will be held—
"How could God have tolerated
such ugliness."

"Clothes help to conceal
the immorality of their bodies.
The more people dress the uglier they are.

Physically.
No don't cross your arms."

Jaz understood that the Inquisitor
that's what Jaz calls him
wasn't shaking from fear but from insanity.

Yes.
"Let my eyes be filled with the caresses
of your breasts
of your lips
of your eyes.
Allow my eyes to find peace in your eyes.
What are they saying?"
That she didn't know.

"My eyes have followed you all the way here
to watch you refuse to give birth to the shit
out of which they build their Tower of Babel."

"Shit
shit
shit
that's all they have left to share."

"Shit in the earth
shit in the sky
shit in the air
shit
shit
shit."

"Shit in the 'good mornings'
shit in the 'good evenings'
shit in the smiles
shit
shit
shit."

"Shit in death
shit in life
shit in mankind.
This century reeks of defecation."

"While man is putrefying
here
on the bare ground
in the middle of swarming maggots
and processions of vultures
they build Pharaonic burials
to throw away their shit
while man is putrefying
here."

"But you
oh look at me.
Smile.
Just one smile.
I beg you smile for me.
Sanctify me 'man' with
the ripe sun of your smile.
What a desert life must be
for those who haven't been held by your eyes."

Jaz doesn't remember.
Maybe she smiled but she doesn't remember.

If she had ever given birth to shame.
Jaz said yes.
He got angry.
Screamed.
The Inquisitor was shaking all over.

That it's not true
that it's not possible for
beauty to give birth to ugliness
that Jaz must stop toying with
his patience and his tolerance.

Otherwise he would slit her throat.

Just what he wanted to convince himself of.
To buy some time.
Indeed what time.

That in all her life
she had never stooped so low as to give birth to that.

He gloated “I knew it I knew it.”
Crazy. He was crazy.

Jaz believed him.
Without hesitation.
He would have slit her throat.

No.
I don’t see the connection.
I don’t.
I’m not here to talk about myself but to talk about Jaz.

Incoherent things.
The same old story.
Marriage honeymoon children.
Jaz was created for him he for Jaz.
She was his delicate music
his archangel sent to wash with her urine
the stains of the earth.
Jaz was his redemption.

So let Jaz piss on the world.

She couldn’t.
She wasn’t in the right mood anymore.

He slapped her.

He forced her
to sit
on the bowl
and yelled
“Now piss
piss or I stick the knife in it
to extract the purifying sap.”

Yes he was cursing.
Terribly.
Of suddenly being cursed at.

She still couldn’t urinate.
He didn’t do it but he threw himself at her.

Yes.

"On all fours.
You're just like all the others.
On all fours.
Don't ever forget that from now on
you are my wife
On all fours."

Finally.
But by force.

Insults.
"You're just like the others.
It's you who are forcing me to.
Just like there are faces asking to be slapped
there are women asking to be raped."

For the first time
since the man with Christ's eyes
had pushed her in the bathroom
Jaz felt guilty.
Because of what Oridé had told her one day.

Oridé.
The one for whom Jaz shaves her head
once a year.

Oridé was a stripper
in a club full of wandering hands
The Café of the Angels
on Moldy Green Street
formerly Apple Green Street
in the Curb-Your-Joy neighborhood.

Curb-Your-Joy.
Shady I would say.
Impossible.
It's funny to say but
Curb-Your-Joy carries misery well.
One doesn't live in Curb-Your-Joy
one waits for death.

But still it's there that
Oridé
the girl who knew she was beautiful
so beautiful she could wake the dead
Oridé for whom any
accountant of the Book of the Dead
would have ruined himself to watch her undress
it's there
at the Café of the Angels that
Oridé had decided to share
every night
the gift of her beauty.

"Because" Oridé would say
"It's there
in this pestilence rotting under the open sky
that man is in most dire need of beauty."

Out of love but also as a challenge.
Like everything Oridé does.

At the start
Oridé would be naked
to end up fully dressed
at the end.

In that club on Moldy Green Street
cauldron of men
of males with towering frustrations
where hands don't hesitate
to grab dancers' thighs
where mouths leap
without warning to strippers' mouths
no fingertip had ever dared
do so much as brush Oridé's skin.
Ever.

"Only beauty
can tame such animals.
Not my beauty but
the beauty of the art I perform.

One can touch objects of art but not art.
To avoid being touched
there cannot be
any distance between the object and the art.
There cannot be."

"But most of all
if they don't touch me it's because
I don't desire it.
Especially because I don't desire it.
And they know.
Without understanding they know."

That's why
when the Inquisitor told her
that she was a woman asking to be raped
Jaz felt guilty.

In the name of what innocent look
in the name of what stray smile
in the name of what misunderstanding
did the man with Christ's eyes
feel invited to do that.

"And you have rape written
on every inch of your face
on the tips of your fingers
on the points of your breasts
on the ridges of your sex."

"I said get undressed and you got undressed
I said spread your legs and you parted your thighs
I said piss and you would have pissed if you could have
I said on all fours and you got down on all fours
like a dog
and when I sank my flesh
into the tremor of your flesh
you spread your ass of your own free will."

"Did you scream.
Did you call for help.
What kind of woman are you.

You're nothing but a slut.
Like all the others."

The woman takes the board and
holds it in front of her like
someone about to go to prison.
On the board is a number written
in an undecipherable alphabet.
Flash from a camera.
She presents her profile.
Another flash.
She puts the board down.
While talking, she loads the gun.
At the end, one chamber remains empty
for the bullet in her hand.

For life.
How long does a life sentence last.
How long does a life away from the rainbow last.

There.
Yes there.
That hole.
It's his grave.
It's where he's buried
from where the bullet roared earlier
to lodge itself in
the heart of all the virility in the world.

This morning.
He was waiting for me in front of the bathroom.
The man with Christ's eyes.
As he demanded
last Sunday.

His wife.
Why not.
What more could I hope for
now that he has frozen my life in
the only color that doesn't exist
in the rainbow.

"I'm your wife.
Oh yes I'm your delicate music.
I'm your archangel.
I'm your wife."

"Through you
I hoist myself up the mast of sensualities
through you
I'm penetrated by the exquisite turmoil
of self-surrender
when your shaft drills through me
through you
I'm filled with the entire universe's orgasm
until total exhaustion."

"You really are a knife
with a point as deadly
as a scorpion's tail."

No one.
At this time
on Sundays
China Blue Square is always empty.

Dressed like the last time.
Exactly like the first time.
Me too.
I don't know.
I felt I had to dress
like last Sunday that's all.

Yes.
Thursday I think.
On the stairs.
He was coming down I was going up.

No.
No.
No.

Same as usual.
He didn't look at me I didn't look at him.

Uncomfortable no.
More as if nothing had happened.
Because basically nothing had happened.
Nothing happened.

The idea didn't even cross my mind.
He passed me I passed him.
Like we've always done that's all.
The neighbors.
No more than with him.

He pretended he didn't see me coming.
There was no reason to be surprised.
I don't know him.
I put the coin in the slot
and the door opened.

Yes I knew he would push me inside
and we would be locked in together.

Not right away.
Exactly.
I waited for him to belch his
"Get undressed"
while waving his kitchen knife.

Obviously.
I took the gun from my underwear
it was the only place where
I could hide it I fired.
I fired.
At the exact place where supposedly beats
the heart of all the virility in the world.

Totally stunned.
He collapsed
looking at me in complete disbelief.
The Inquisitor with Christ's eyes died without understanding.

Proud.
Proud of what.

While he was thrusting
his swollen desire into Jaz.
No woman
can feel pleasure in such
circumstances.

I'm not here to talk about myself but to talk about Jaz.

No pleasure no pain.
Nothing.
Only the howl of the man
who was barking at her to repeat
that he is a knife
with a point as deadly as
a scorpion's tail.

Jaz repeated it.
"You are a knife
with a point as deadly as
a scorpion's tail."
Jaz repeated it.
Many times.
Jaz repeated it.
As many times as he demanded.
Jaz repeated it.
Until
in the throws of orgasm
a spurt
an epileptic howl
escapes from the throat of
the man with Christ's eyes.
Jaz repeated it.
Until the end.
Jaz repeated it.

Like that
it was the first time.
It was the first time for that too.
It was the first time for everything.
I know.

Jaz is my friend.
She is.

When
the man with Christ's eyes
realized that he was
the first male desire
to enter Jaz
he burst into tears.
Tears of joy.
Hallucinated joy.

He took Jaz in his arms
covered her face with kisses saying
"It's you it's really you."
After each kiss.
Detached.

No disgust no nothing.
Only detached.
Even from her own fear.

The man got dressed again.
Even more frantic *however*
the Hold Mail Service
can only be temporary.
His eyes were shining with insanity
the noncompliance of the
mailboxes will result in—
the zipper closed over
his desire now exhausted
like a plastic bag over a dead body.

A chatterbox.
Nothing that made any sense.
The same incongruous words.
He had finally found in Jaz
the Promised Land.
Their encounter and then their union.
There was no doubt.
Jaz was now his.

Their oath would cause the Tower of Babel
to crumble
one shit at a time.

Next Sunday
they'll meet again in the public bathroom.
And the Sunday after
and the Sunday after
and the Sunday after.
Every Sunday morning
that the Eternal grants them
they'll come to the public bathroom
in China Blue Square
so he can prove to her how much
he is all the virility in the world.

I'm not here to talk about myself but to talk about Jaz.

The man put his hand on the door.

"I'll leave first.
Count to a hundred before you leave."
"Make sure you count to a hundred."
So he could walk away.

"Count one two three to a hundred.
Slowly.
Or else.
Say that you'll come."

"Next Sunday
I'll meet you in front of this bathroom.
Like this morning."

"Good."

He kissed her on the forehead and disappeared.

They say that
within us is a music
that no one can hear but us
that cannot be played for anyone.
A music just for us.

They say that
it is made of one single note
a note that can be smelled
only by pinching our nose
a note that can be seen
only by closing our eyes
a note that can be heard
only by imposing silence to our ears.

They say that
after death
we continue to hear it.

They say that
our bones in the grave
continue to hear it.

They say that
our ashes
continue to hear it.

They say that
within us is a music
we may never hear.
Unless we create silence.

They say that
this music
is our Name.

Jaz didn't count.
Jaz didn't count one two three to a hundred.
No.

Sitting on the bowl
she pinched her nose
she closed her eyes
she silenced her ears.

And dove in.

First
a note
then another
note then again
another note
the same
one like a knock on the door a string of notes the same
one rubbing against each other as if trying to keep warm
a note made of every color including the one that
was banished
from the rainbow
a flood of notes the
same one made of every
sound mischievous
boisterous notes the same
one rushing to free the
secret from the silence
exploding as soon
as in flight to
give birth to
other notes the
same one even more
unpredictable
incandescent
volcanic and to
finally invoke the Name by
which she will never be called.

A note
then another
then again another
the same one
until
Jaz opens her eyes and realizes that
her dress in her left hand
her underwear in her right hand
she has just crossed
barefoot

China Blue Square
crossed
Golden Yellow Street
crossed
the watchful eyes of the awakening City
all the way to here.

She puts the last bullet in
the gun's last chamber.

Next Sunday
she'll meet him in front of
the public bathroom in China Blue Square
more radiant than a winter sun.

Remaining at your disposal
for any additional information
yours sincerely
what more can she hope for
now that she has been chased from the rainbow.

No disgust no pleasure
nothing.
Jaz doesn't see it as a duty.
Something to do that's all.
Like any other thing.

Next Sunday
in the morning
at the same time.
Go to the public bathroom in China Blue Square.
Pay no attention to the man's presence.
Put a coin in the slot.
Wait for the door to open.
For the man to push her in
and close the door behind them.
Not bat an eyelid
when he'll hold up his kitchen knife.
And then
take the gun from her underwear

it's the only place where
she'll be able to hide it
and lodge the bullet in Christ's eyes.

Jaz it's not me anymore.

Jaz.
Yes Jaz.
I have always been called Jaz.
Jaz.
I don't know anymore.
Simply Jaz.

END OF PLAY

Sébastien Ricard (Stan) and Daniel Parent (Sir) in *Big Shoot*, directed by Kristian Frédric at the Théâtre Denise-Pelletier in Montreal, Canada, 2005. Photo by Nicholas Descoteaux.

Big Shoot

2000

TRANSLATED BY CHANTAL BILODEAU

INTRODUCTION TO BIG SHOOT

A terrifying, disarticulated, and multileveled parable about the meaning of life, *Big Shoot* explores the fundamental question of the Old Testament: Am I my brother's keeper? This question that Cain, prompted by God, asks after he has killed his brother Abel resonates throughout the play. It is used ironically by the character Sir as he taunts his torture victim, Stan. Yet Sir, like Stan, is playing a role already scripted before their encounter. His role is to torture. Stan's role, on the contrary, consists in a self-conscious performance of rape and murder, crimes that would seem, in fact, to be only a figment of the collective imagination. This reconstructive performance of horror explains why death is the inevitable end of the line, a judgment that no one can or should escape. Looked at in this way, "big shoot" (which can mean at once a killing or death by firearm, a performance or film shoot, the ultimate high of intravenous drugs, and an orgasmic encounter with violence) not only hints at the inescapable confrontation with death but also at the fleeting possibility of love. If only one can recognize, truly look at, and really connect with an other—just as Sir once connected with a pig also named "Stan"—the divisions that spark dissent and dominance might disappear.

Downplaying this ethical (and perhaps grotesque) approach to the play—with its nod to Samuel Beckett's characters living by killing time while being killed by time, in a world more "in death" than "in life"—we can also see *Big Shoot* as an exploration of the mind of the torturer. Sir understands his work as an ever greater marshalling of power in a strangely complacent world. In his arena, the performance of menace and the extolling of disgusting imaginative constructs, including pornographic fantasies, are tools as useful as guns and electric shocks. Yet Sir, the tormentor, is insecure about all his performances, from telling bad jokes about Jean Cocteau to speaking French with an accent. And Stan, the victim, is not completely without arms to shake up his torturer: he too, for example, speaks French and speaks it better than Sir.

In this duel to the end, that is not an end (as is often the case in Kwahulé's plays), the audience is positioned, as in Jean Genet's *The Balcony,* as perverse mirror. Doubled by an imagined other audience that has come to enjoy the encaged gladiators as they try to best each other as actors and as linguists, the real theater public is prodded to consider its own sadomasochistic proclivities. Both Sir and Stan can thus be seen as part of a larger fragmented consciousness, a mind searching for a plot in order to narrate the ways in which each of us tortures ourselves. (Actor Denis Lavant's remarkable performance throughout Europe in 2009 as both Stan and Sir, in a production from Lausanne, Switzerland, reinforced this interpretation.) One might obsessively seek relief in young cultures (figured here as America) or regress to childhood in very old cultures (figured as Africa) or simply keep on keeping on in worn-out European cultures incapable of coming to terms with that which is apprehended as the "not-self." But relief is just as fleeting as love.

Notes for reading and performance:

1. Koffi Kwahulé's involvement with theater projects meant to help ease the effects of the Rwandan genocide on Rwandans (1994) led him to think about the complex dynamic between oppressed and oppressor. In the French text of *Big Shoot,* he does not differentiate, as has been done in the translation, between Stan's and Sir's lines. They answer each other as though musical instruments responding to cues, Sir in the typical rhythm of John Coltrane, Stan in the rhythm of Thelonious Monk.

2. In Kwahulé's French text, the Old Testament question "Am I my brother's keeper?" is always spoken in English. The question, a refrain throughout his play, has in the translation sometimes been kept in English and sometimes been moved to French—the latter indicating the linguistic play that Sir uses to demonstrate his superiority. In the translation, French phrases pop up from time to time as part of Sir's attempt at testing Stan. As the current dominant language of globalization, English has a different valence when used in a French text than French has when used in an English text. The translation into English cannot, unfortunately, capture the ironic coloration in the French text of having Sir use English as a torture weapon.

3. Jean Cocteau was a multitalented writer and artist, central to the devel-

opment of French arts from the 1930s to the 1960s. Cocteau was unabashedly gay and unerringly witty.

4. English version of French phrases used by Sir:

"Ta gueule! Enculé!"
(Shut up! Motherfucker!)

"Enculé. N'oublie jamais ce que je te dis: Vas-y doucement. Dou-ce-ment."
(Motherfucker! Never forget what I just said: Easy does it. Easy . . .)

"Vas-y. Tourne à gauche. Que vois-tu?
(Go on, Stan. Stop. Turn left. What do you see?)
"C'est bien, Stan. Une palissade?"
(Good, Stan. A fence?)
"Très bien, Stan, les fleurs?"
(Very good, Stan. Flowers?)
"Regarde mieux, Stan."
(Take a closer look, Stan.)
"Blanc . . . Roses . . . Rouges?"
(White . . . pink . . . red?)

"Pourquoi, Stan, pourquoi?"
(Why, Stan, why?)

"Mais elle ne peut pas avoir de chien."
(She can't have a dog!)

"visqueux"
(sleazy)

"Tu es malin, n'est-ce pas?"
(You're a smart ass, aren't you?)

"Seulement voilà, je suis prêt à te bourrer tout ce que tu veux mais ça non!"
(Only, I'd stuff you full of anything but not that.)

"Parce que je t'aime. Je t'aime parce que tu es différent."
(Because I love you. I love you because you are different.)

"Bien, Stan, très bien."
(Good, Stan, very good.)

"Pourquoi?"
(Why?)

"C'est très, très bien, Stan."
(Very, very good, Stan.)

"Alors, Stan n'a pas de hobby."
(So Stan doesn't have a hobby.)

"Ooh, la la!"
(Oh, my God!)
"Mon pauvre garçon!"
(Oh poor boy!)

"Dis-moi pourquoi?"
(Tell me why?)

"Ooh, la la! Mais tu parles français! Stan parle français."
(Oh my God! You speak English! Stan speaks English!)
"Merveilleux!"
(Oh wonderful!)

"Une ville magnifique."
(A gorgeous city.)

"Moi je l'ai souvent fait, Stan, prié et surtout pleuré pour l'Afrique . . . Mais New York . . . Ah, New York . . . Si le monde entier pouvait être New York! . . ."
(I did, I often prayed and mostly I cried for Africa . . . But New York! Ah, New York! . . . If the whole world could be New York! . . .)

"Et alors?"
(So what?)

"Continue, Stan, continue!"
(Go on, Stan, go on!)

"Morte!"
(Dead!)

"Très bien. Viens plus près . . . Allez viens . . . As-tu peur de moi? Il n'y a pas de danger, Stan . . ."
(Very good. Come closer . . . come on . . . Are you scared of me? It's all right, Stan . . .)

"Et Dieu dit à Caïn:
Où est ton frère Abel?
Je ne sais pas, répondit-il.

Suis-je le gardien de mon frère?
Et Dieu dit:
Qu'as-tu fait?
Ecoute!
Le sang de ton frère crie de la terre jusqu'à moi.
Maintenant, tu seras maudit
De la terre
Qui a ouvert sa bouche
Pour recevoir de ta main
Le sang de ton frère."
(Then the Lord said To Cain,
Where is your brother Abel?
I don't know, he replied.
Am I my brother's keeper?
The Lord said,
What have you done?
Listen!
Your brother's blood
Cries out to me
From the ground
Now you are under a curse
And driven from the ground
Which opened its mouth
To receive your brother's blood
From your hand.)

5. English version of the French spoken by Stan:

"Je ne sais pas."
(I don't know.)
"Le temps s'envole."
(Time flies.)

"Comment allez-vous?"
(How do you do?)
"Le mari de ma mère est mon père."
(My mother's husband is my father.)
"Je suis très heureux de vous rencontrer."
(I am glad to see you.)
"Mon voisin est pompier."
(My taylor is rich.) [not an exact translation]

"Nos cigarettes sont finies."
(Our cigarettes are finished.)
"Je ne suis pas un poisson."
(I am not a fish.)

"Je ne suis pas un chat."
(I am not a cat.)
"Je ne suis pas un poisson-chat."
(I am not a catfish.)
"Je suis un chien."
(I am a dog.)

"Je suis un pitbull."
(I am a pitbull.)
"Le vie ne commence que lorsqu'on est amoureux."
(Life begins when you're in love.)
"Je me considère comme un type chanceux."
(I am just a lucky so and so.)
"On ne se connaît pas assez."
(I don't know enough about you.)
"Parfois, je me sens comme un enfant sans mère."
(Sometimes I feel like a motherless child.)
"Vu les circonstances, M. et Mme Stan ont pu abandonner leur timidité et se laisser aller . . ."
(Under these circumstances, Mr. and Mrs. Stan could drop their usual shyness, and let themselves go . . .)

"Alors . . ."
(So . . .)

CHARACTERS

SIR: A man.
STAN: A man.

TRANSLATOR'S NOTE

The blanks in Stan's lines are an indication of how to handle the rhythm.

A glass cage. Perhaps a slaughterhouse. Without any smells or traces of blood. An excessively clean slaughterhouse washed with ammonia. Perhaps an arena. No wrestlers. Just an arena. In any case, not a boxing ring. Certainly not. In short, a glass cage. Preferably square. So in a square glass cage, two men.

SIR: *Ta gueule!*
Enculé!
Asshole . . . Pig . . .
Wimp . . . Jerk . . . Dickhead . . .
Prick . . . Moron . . . Idiot . . . Jackass . . .
Clown . . . Snake . . . Pimp . . . Hypocrite . . .
Dirt . . . Turd . . . Trash . . . Piece of shit . . .
Son of a bitch . . . Bastard . . .

(he sings)
Then the Lord said to Cain:
"Where is your brother Abel?"
"I don't know," he replied.
"Am I my brother's keeper?"

Cocksucker . . . Shithead . . .
Asshole jerk
Clown jackass bastard
Bastard trash cocksucker pig . . .
Slut . . . Son of a bitch
Son of a bitch bastard
Bastard son of a bitch
Dickhead . . . Wimp . . .
Asshole piece of shit
Pig bastard . . . Bastard pig
Moron . . . Idiot cocksucker . . .

(he sings)
Et Dieu dit à Caïn:
"Où est ton frère Abel?"
"Je ne sais pas," répondit-il.
"Suis-je le gardien de mon frère?"
Et Dieu dit:
"Qu'as-tu fait?"

Cocksucker . . . Son of a bitch
Fucking idiot fucking prick fucking jerk . . .
Piece of trash . . .
Fucking moron fucking asshole fucking pig fucking cocksucker . . .
Piece of shit . . .
Cocksucker . . . Moron . . . Son of a bitch . . . *Ta gueule!* You want me to smash your face? *Enculé!*

STAN: I was passing by.

SIR: Yes, I know, you were passing by . . . And then?

STAN: Nothing.

SIR: Nothing . . . Nothing . . . You were passing by . . . Nahnahnah nahnah, nahnahnah nahnah and then nothing . . . Shut up, you jerk! That's not a question! Piece of shit. You see how mad you make me with your fucking bullshit? Pathetic little turd . . . I can't tell you how much I feel like busting your ugly face. So stop being such a smart-ass. Relax. Take it easy. *Enculé. N'oublie jamais ce que je te dis: Vas-y doucement. Dou-ce-ment. . . .* Because that's all they're waiting for out there. For me to blow your brains out. Bang! Because these people came from far away, from very far, from the opposite end of the world, often on foot, you hear me, they came on foot from the opposite end of the world all the way to here! So stop your bullshit. Many of them, hidden in the dark out there, have saved all year from their meager salary to be able to afford this moment . . . So you can't fuck with them . . . Shut up! You open your mouth when I tell you to. Those people out there, you know why they made so many sacrifices in order to be here today? They're waiting for me to make them feel good, to indulge their sordid lust . . . So don't push me . . . Don't fuck with me . . . Because I could bend you over and give it to you deep, deep, deep. Easily. Just to see your flesh burn with pleasure and hear their screams of orgasm. That's what they're waiting for. That's what they paid for . . . But you're pissing me off with your stupid silence so now I feel a tickle, I feel an itch. God, do I feel an itch! Only, I'm not a cheap torturer. No, I'm an artist. All restraint, finesse, subtlety, grace . . . OK, let's go over this again. So? So?

STAN: I was passing by.

SIR: Good, you were passing by. And then?

STAN: Well I passed by.

SIR: Ah, we're moving forward at least. So you were passing by and then, pfff! You were passed? Like a deflating balloon?

STAN: In a way.
SIR: Like an overinflated beach ball.
STAN: If one wants yes.
SIR: Who's "one?" There's you, there's me, and nobody else. So who's "one?"
STAN: Like an overinflated beach ball.
SIR: There you go. So you passed by and you disappeared.
STAN: Yes.
SIR: But you're not going to disappear. Come back. Let's rewind the tape. Backwards. You come back backwards, soooooo! In fast motion. OK, you're now at your starting point. You haven't passed by. You're going to pass by. You understand? You haven't passed by, you're passing by. Is that clear?
STAN: It's clear.
SIR: Get up and walk. You're passing by. Go ahead, pass by! Tut, tut, tut . . . Hey, you're not leaving! Come back here! . . . You were walking like that?
STAN: I always walk like that.
SIR: No, I mean, at that pace?
STAN: I don't remember.
SIR: Never mind. Go on, walk . . . Didn't you stop at some point?
STAN: I think I did.
SIR: Then why didn't you stop now?
STAN: Because I'm not
completely sure that I stopped.
SIR: You're testing my patience, Stan . . .
STAN: Stan?
SIR: I know, I know . . . Your name is not Stan. But I want to call you Stan . . .
STAN: Stan.
SIR: What, you don't like it? Because I get a kick out of calling you Stan. So I don't care . . . I don't give a shit if you don't like it.
STAN: Stan.
SIR: Your name is Stan and you shut the fuck up, OK? Now let's start over, Stan, and this time, concentrate. No more acting like an idiot. *Vas-y.* Stop. *Tourne à gauche. Que vois-tu?*
STAN: A fence.
SIR: *C'est bien, Stan. Une palissade?*
STAN: Flowers.
SIR: *Très bien, Stan. Les fleurs?*
STAN: Amaryllis.

SIR: *Regarde mieux, Stan.*

STAN: Hibiscus now I

Stan sees hibiscus.

SIR: *Blancs . . . Roses . . . Rouges?*

STAN: Red!

SIR: *Oui*, congratulations, Stan. You see? We're getting somewhere! So why didn't you stop before?

STAN: Stan didn't think that

the fence blooming with hibiscus was so important.

SIR: It's cute how you say that. But everything is important in a reconstruction, Stan. Everything. OK, let's keep going. You see the fence and the red hibiscus? What else do you see?

STAN: Amaryllis.

SIR: Try again.

STAN: A mango tree.

SIR: Try again.

STAN: An apple tree.

SIR: Try again.

STAN: Hydrangeas.

SIR: Try again.

STAN: A sequoia.

SIR: Try again.

STAN: A dog barking.

SIR: No kidding!

STAN: Barking to death!

Stan still hears it barking to death.

SIR: Stan, what do I look like? I mean . . . Am I agitated? Angry? . . . Am I sweating? . . . Have I lost my self-control?

STAN: No none of that.

SIR: I'm calm, right, Stan?

STAN: Yes very calm.

He slaps Stan.

SIR: She's never had a dog! *So pourquoi, Stan, pourquoi?* Why do you want to push me to the limit? Why do you try to make me look like a cheap torturer in front of these people? I'm an artist, Stan, and never, in I don't know how many years of this vocation, have I ever stooped so low as to slap someone. I've always worked cleanly. Why did you make me slap you, Stan? I'll never forgive you. Never. I'm an artist, Stan, and like any artist, I need a good muse. But since the beginning, all you do is spoil my work. You don't throw the ball back, you short-circuit everything, you— . . . Viciously. She's never had a dog. You do sloppy work and I'm not happy with you, Stan, not happy at all. She's never had a dog. And I'm not the only one who's not happy with you! Those people sitting in the dark, did you think about them? Selfish pig. She's never had a dog. Since the beginning, you've been fucking with them and fucking with me. In a way, you're mocking them, you're making fun of their sacrifices. You keep them on tenterhooks and that's not professional, Stan, that's not right. So I'm not happy with you. She's never had a dog. I warned you, right from the start I could have forced you on all fours and spilled myself inside you, flooded you. Easily. But I didn't because this time, I want to create a true masterpiece. Not some dirty, perverted, tasteless thing . . . No . . . No more bloody stew for intellectuals in garter belts! . . . No . . . Something grand, clean, correct . . . So, Stan?

STAN: Stan sees it now.
Behind the fence
there was a house.

Silence.

Now Stan sees it.
It looked like a picture
a painting.
SIR: Describe it.
STAN: Stan can't.
Stan says.
I mean
I didn't look at it with the idea
that I would have to describe it later.
In fact
I didn't look at it.
Stan saw it but didn't look at it.
SIR: Don't start again, Stan.
STAN: A dog barked
maybe she doesn't have a dog.
SIR: *Mais elle ne peut pas avoir de chien!*
STAN: She doesn't have a dog
but a dog barked.

SIR: Are you bullshitting me again with this dog business?
STAN: No I'm not
SIR: Don't freak out, it's cool, Stan, it's cool. So you're saying there's a dog left in this city?
STAN: Stan even thought
that's strange where does this dog come from?
SIR: Why didn't you come to tell me?
STAN: Because Stan says.
I thought about it
it went straight out of my head.
A dog barked
while she was looking at the street
from her window.
A dog barked to death.
SIR: Hmm . . . Let's forget, for now, this whole dog story and tell me what happened instead. So you pass by, you see the fence . . . By the way, did you stop for the blooming fence or for the woman in the window? . . . I mean, the hibiscus first or the woman?
STAN: The thing is Stan is not sure that he stopped.
SIR: But you said . . .
STAN: Things had to move forward
the story had to progress.
SIR: Even at the cost of a lie?
STAN: Stan said.
I'm not completely sure.
Completely.
Which means it isn't certain
that I didn't stop.
Maybe I stopped
maybe Stan stopped
but I could have forgotten.
Stan said.
I'm not completely sure.
But he could also have said the opposite.
Completely.
That's what Stan said
and you can't say the opposite.

SIR: Oh, Stan, Stan, Stan! Am I angry? Am I foaming at the mouth?

STAN: No you're calm.

SIR: Only calm?

STAN: Very calm.

SIR: I'm starting to like you, Stan. So I'm going to talk to you like someone who likes you. Can I do that?

STAN: Yes of course.

SIR: Thank you, Stan. You're the kind of guy in front of whom one comes to measure the extent of his own stupidity. You're dirty, Stan. You're very dirty. *(pointing to his own head)* It's slimy inside. There's something *visqueux*, something rotten in you. You're repulsive, Stan. You have a vicious and twisted mind. *Tu es malin, n'est-ce pas?* Aren't you just a smart-ass, Stan?

STAN: Stan's never thought about it.

SIR: Oh yes, you're very clever. I'm telling you, you're one hell of a smart-ass, my little Stan.

STAN: Thank you.

SIR: Not at all. You complicate everything: one step forward, three steps back. You're strong, very strong . . . Do you know this story, Stan? I know you know it. You're too wise not to know it. Do you know the story of Cocteau and the Angel? It knocks your socks off that I know Cocteau, huh? You see, I don't look it but I do know a thing or two . . . Anyway, it happens during a meal. People are talking of this and that. Between glasses of cognac, they reinvent literature and the world. They talk behind people's backs. Then suddenly, silence. Dry spell. Not a word. Since it's the custom, someone shouts: "An angel is passing by." Right away, Cocteau replies: "Let's catch him and fuck him in the ass!" They all laugh, they start reinventing the world again, they gossip, and so on. Fifteen minutes later, another silence. The phrase comes out right away: "An angel is passing by." And Cocteau: "Let's catch him and fuck him in the ass!" They all laugh again and so on and so forth and all the rest of it. Then another silence and despite Cocteau's threat, the angel passes by a third time. So someone says: "This angel, he wouldn't be a little queer?" That doesn't make you laugh, Stan? Because it's a funny story, or at least it should be, so you should be laughing, Stan.

STAN: I know. But Stan was waiting for the punch line.

SIR: That's my Stan in a nutshell. All finesse and subtlety with irony on the tip of his tongue. I tell it wrong, Stan? Come on say it, I tell it wrong?

Shut up! *Ta gueule!* That's not a question! *Enculé*. You're a smart one, Stan, but you're only as smart as a book. Since I threatened to stick it to you, you've been bugging me, annoying me, pissing me off. But April Fool, Stan! April Fool! That's my job! Usually from the very first threat, they shake like leaves, they sweat like pigs, they cry their eyes out, they choke, they belch, they fart, they vomit, they piss, they shit, they faint, and they confess everything and its exact opposite which is nothing at all. But they confess. I don't know why but this trick always works—the prospect of getting an assful really terrorizes a guy. But you, no . . . Clearly, it doesn't . . . You'd like that, huh, piece of trash? *Seulement voilà, je suis prêt à te bourrer tout ce que tu veux mais ça non.* It's not my thing, Stan. Sorry. I'm not like that. So stop bugging me. From the moment we met, I've made real efforts . . . I've been open . . . I've been tolerant . . . You can't say I haven't been tolerant. Admit it!

STAN: You've been tolerant.

SIR: I try to be considerate . . . Am I not considerate, Stan?

STAN: You're considerate.

SIR: I open my heart to you . . . I lay my cards on the table . . . Don't I always lay my cards on the table, Stan?

STAN: All the time you lay your cards on the table.

SIR: Nothing in my pockets, nothing in my hands, nothing up my sleeves . . . All in plain view. Clean, I'm clean. But you, what do you do? You create confusion, chaos. You stab me in the back. You make me wear the dunce's cap in front of all these people! *Enculé*. But go ahead! Keep at it! Keep making fun of me and you'll see what I do to fucking asslickers like you. I, alone, push the rock all the way to the top and as soon as I get there, with an irony, a flick, a pirouette, you throw it right back down. But I'll keep pushing it, again and again, until the rock is perched at the very top of the mountain. And why so much abnegation, Stan? *(in an intimate tone, almost whispered) Parce que je t'aime. Je t'aime parce que tu es différent.* You're not like the others, Stan. In fact, I don't remember the others and I don't care. You're the one, Stan. You. And I want you to make it. I don't want to have to put a bullet in your head like . . . puh . . . all those dogs killed recently . . . That'd be like putting a bullet in my own head . . . That's all they're waiting for. It's their right. It's why they've saved all year, why they've come here on foot, from the opposite end of the world, why they've made me a hero. So you have to help me, Stan. We need to stick together and let no doubt, even as thin as cigarette paper, come between us. No hiding. You have to tell me everything. You promise to tell me everything, Stan?

STAN: From now on I will tell you everything.

SIR: *Bien, Stan, très bien.* Now let's start over. Up until now, I've gone at it the wrong way. I've proceeded as usual, as with the others. I take the blame and we wipe the slate clean. You're not like the others so I must raise myself to your level . . . You forgive me?

STAN: Yes of course.

SIR: Thank you, Stan, from the bottom of my heart.

STAN: But if you want—

SIR: No, no, Stan. It's up to me to make an effort . . . Up to me. So first . . .

While singing "Et Dieu dit à Caïn . . ." in a syrupy manner, Sir removes his uniform, button by button, and lays his gun on top of it.

Here you go, no more uniform, no more gun. Only a man, a new man in front of you. See? I'm calm again. Don't you agree that I'm calm?

STAN: Yes you're very calm.

SIR: Go back to your place, Stan.

Sir takes out a pack of cigarettes.

Cigarette?

STAN: Don't smoke.

SIR: That's good, Stan. Smoking attacks the lungs and you die in terrible pain. *(a beat)* Not at all? Not even one from time to time?

STAN: From time to time
one
like that
like everybody
I suppose.

SIR: Then let's have one! . . . Just one. Between the two of us. The peace pipe . . . It'd make me happy.

Stan accepts the cigarette. They smoke.

Any kids?

STAN: No.

SIR: That's very good, Stan. Kids are a pain in the ass. They scream, they wail, they cry, they piss, they shit everywhere and they do all kinds of stupid things. And the cruelty! Just like prison, it eats years out of your life.

And when those years are gone, they're gone . . . A real pain, I'm telling you. I know what I'm talking about, I have some . . . Well, I used to have some . . . Married?

STAN: No.

SIR: Never?

STAN: Never.

SIR: That's good, Stan . . . Everything starts with a woman and everything ends with a woman. Now that it's just the two of us, I can tell you: Everything started with the breast of a woman . . . The left breast.

STAN: Everyone knew.

SIR: The whole city?

STAN: This is the origin of the night.
Low-ranking official.
A woman your office.
A small office oozing boredom
like a local newspaper.
Without much hope you try a request
"Would you be so good, *Madame*,
as to indulge my eyes with the sight of your left breast?"
Then delicately
like a prayer unfolding
the woman opens her blouse.
Her breast.
Her naked breast.
Her breast like a wafer
resting on the tongue of your eyes.

SIR: Do you realize, Stan? Do you realize! . . . I'd asked just like that, without even— . . . and suddenly, she shows me her left breast!

STAN: One day two days.
And the third day
a woman another one
in the small office
boring like a local newspaper.
You ask her
just like that
again without much hope
if she would agree to show you her breasts.

SIR: And bingo, she shows me her breasts! I say to myself: Wait, this is not a joke, you have this power, this power lives inside you. I was petrified, Stan. But little by little, I gained confidence. It turned into a game. Every woman who entered my office would end up indulging my eyes with her breasts. Some even came back. To unbutton their blouse a second time. But careful, Stan, I never touched or did so much as brush a single nipple . . . I only looked.

STAN: Everyone knew.

SIR: And the more I saw, the more I wanted to see. Of every color, every shape, every kind . . . Do you know, Stan, that Arabs have seven different words to describe women's breasts? And they're right . . .

STAN: And then one morning   fate
chuckles in your brain.
It whispers
What if you pushed a little further
and asked   for example
that they surrender their lives
so you can make
a spectacle of their deaths?

SIR: Of course, Stan, since without a promise of life or threat of death I'd gotten them to show me their breasts! . . . So it became madness . . . Women brought me their lovers, their husbands, their brothers, their fathers . . . The city fell into darkness—everyone wanted to be part of the show . . .

STAN: Everyone
men women
the governor the mayor
dogs cats
one after the other
they came and
offered their necks
so you would put a bullet in them
and save the others from boredom.

SIR: *Pourquoi?*

STAN: Stan doesn't know.
Maybe because of the fascination
you exert on women.
And when one fascinates women
the rest . . .

SIR: I wasn't in control anymore . . . But I took responsibility . . . Until the very end, I will take responsibility . . . Is it true? You find me fascinating, Stan?

STAN: Yes something.

SIR: Yet, at the last moment some of them wanted to back out, wanted to jump ship. But it was too late . . . A shoot! The first time, it was like a shoot. The second time, the third time . . . Every time it was the same shoot. I flew way up high, as high as one can go. But every time, I still hoped for something more. Oh, not a lot, a hair, just a tiny hair to . . . you know, Stan, get over the edge . . . To get over the edge and fall on the other side of infinity . . . Too late. It was always too late. Even before the first shoot, the audience was already involved. They were coming from everywhere, every time in greater number, every time from further away, from the opposite end of the world, more and more on foot, paying every time more money, at the cost of huge sacrifices . . . And when the audience gets involved, Stan, the ifs, the buts, the whys, the maybes . . . No, no . . . No more time to get over the edge . . . The show must go on! So everyone had to take responsibility . . . I took responsibility . . . And when every soul will be eliminated, I, alone, will continue to take responsibility for everyone . . . Everyone until you. *(a beat) Pourquoi, Stan, pourquoi?*

STAN: Stan doesn't know.

SIR: You don't know . . . You don't know . . . Ah, my poor Stan . . . *(a beat)* A fiancée?

STAN: No.

SIR: Crushes?

STAN: Not even.

SIR: Very very good . . . *C'est très très bien, Stan.* Who dares look at a breast loses a kingdom . . . But mind you, women are nice. They keep you company . . . No they're nice . . . Especially in the beginning they're— . . . But after . . . always asking you to tell them that you love them . . . always quibbling, splitting hairs . . . They can be a real pain in the ass! But hey, they keep you company . . . In any case, they're better than kids . . . And they can be very strong . . . You wouldn't know just to look at them but women are tough . . . Very tough . . . And they keep you company. *(a beat)* A job?

STAN: So-so.

SIR: You mean sometimes yes, sometimes no.

STAN: Exactly.

SIR: So you come, you go, you breathe, and that's it.

STAN: More or less.

Stan passes by.

SIR: By the hibiscus, like the last time.

STAN: That's it.

SIR: A hobby?

STAN: No   it was the first time
that Stan was passing by the hibiscus.

SIR: No, I mean in general . . . A hobby in general.

STAN: Oh. That? No.

SIR: Not even a stamp collection? Tin soldiers? Old coins? No? I know . . . Panties! That's the big thing right now, the collection of schoolgirl panties . . . Not even that?

STAN: Not even.

SIR: Jockstraps?

STAN: No   no collections.

SIR: You're being a little difficult, Stan. *Alors, Stan n'a pas de hobby.*

STAN: I'm sorry
Stan apologizes.

SIR: Please don't . . .

STAN: Oh yes   knitting.

SIR: Knitting . . . Knitting?

STAN: Yes   Stan knits.

SIR: With?

STAN: Yes.

SIR: And a?

STAN: Yes.

SIR: Of wool, I imagine.

STAN: Oh yes   for what I do
wool is more than adequate.

SIR: You do know that knitting is a girl thing.

STAN: Stan knows but hey.

SIR: *Ooh, la la!* So Stan likes to knit! You knit with two long needles and a ball of wool . . . Like an old woman?

STAN: Stan says
I don't know if
it's like an old woman
but the fact is that I knit.

SIR: And that's the only hobby you have?

STAN: Yes.

SIR: *Mon pauvre garçon!* But at least it's useful. Baby clothes . . . Sweaters . . . Scarves . . .

STAN: No
nothing like that.
Stan knits   that's all.
Without a goal.
Like others do painting   or poetry . . .

SIR: Oh no, Stan, no! Don't be vulgar! Vulgarities are my department, they're part of my job. And I don't know if you've noticed but it's been a while . . . I haven't said any . . . So don't you start now! Cocteau doesn't knit! Picasso doesn't knit! Césaire doesn't knit! Shakespeare didn't knit! This habit, today, of wanting to put everything on the same level in the name of open-mindedness! You knit, it's your right. But even so. People have been burned for less. You know that, Stan?

STAN: Yes.

SIR: Then don't gild the lily! You knit, OK, you knit, fine . . . But don't go mixing poetry with that. When I think of all the hobbies you could have . . . But no, two big needles and a ball of wool . . . *Pourquoi, Stan, pourquoi? Dis-moi pourquoi?*

STAN: *Je ne sais pas.*
It relaxes Stan
helps him meditate
find himself
le temps s'envole.

SIR: *Ooh, la la! Mais tu parles français! Stan parle français!*

STAN: Yes   Stan says—

SIR: Stop acting like an idiot . . . Stan says, Stan says, Stan says . . . Stan doesn't know, Stan thinks that . . . Stan, Stan, Stan . . . Stop acting like an idiot!

STAN: I will stop acting like an idiot.

SIR: So you speak French?

STAN: Yes   I can get by.

SIR: *Merveilleux!* Stan speaks French!

STAN: *Oui.*

SIR: Say something . . . Something longer . . .

STAN: Well if it makes you happy

yes why not.
But first I have to think.
I have to
for example
Comment allez-vous?
Le mari de ma mère est mon père.
Je suis très heureux de vous rencontrer.
Mon voisin est pompier.
Nos cigarettes sont finies.
Je ne suis pas un poisson.
Je ne suis pas un chat.
Je ne suis pas un poisson-chat.
Je suis un chien.

He acts like a dog. He barks.

Je suis un pitbull.

He shows his teeth.

SIR: Lie down, Stan, lie down . . . I said lie down!

Stan lies down.

That's it?
STAN: No not at all.
I can say much more
complicated sentences
like
La vie ne commence que lorsqu'on est amoureux.
Je me considère comme un type chanceux.
On ne se connaît pas assez.
Parfois, je me sens comme un enfant sans mère.
Vu les circonstances, M. et Mme Stan ont pu abandonner leur timidité et se laisser aller . . .
But I've lost a lot.
Lack of practice.
You know how it is.
You forget to talk
you get rusty
and then it's over.

Because there was a time
when I had almost no accent.

SIR: What are you talking about? Your French is excellent! So you do have another hobby, and a real one at that. You speak French! You know, it's a hobby to speak French. It's not like other languages . . . You know what I mean? Sort of— . . . with no balls . . . Languages in love with themselves . . . No, with French it's like being on top of the world! It gives you a hard-on . . . You must have noticed that from time to time, out of the blue, I allow myself a line of French . . .

(theatrical)
Et Dieu dit à Caïn:
"Où est ton frère Abel?"
"Je ne sais pas," répondit-il.
"Suis-je le gardien de mon frère?"
Et Dieu dit:
"Qu'as-tu fait?"
"Écoute!"
"Le sang de ton frère
crie de la terre
jusqu'à moi."

And bingo! I'm on again, I'm recharged! Speaking French gives me such a high. It's worse than coke. But careful, you do what you do but you have to keep your head straight, know what you want. I'd rather get high on French than on coke.

STAN: You say that
but one often leads to the other.

SIR: Yes, sometimes. There have been cases, yes. But we can't generalize.

STAN: Certainly not.

SIR: *(declamatory)*
Et Dieu dit à Caïn:
"Où est ton frère Abel?"
"Je ne sais pas," répondit-il.
"Suis-je le gardien de mon frère?"

STAN: You have a bit of an accent . . .

SIR: That's because I don't speak French, I speak Parisian. It's more chic, you see, and most of all, I get more of a high . . . But the ultimate is to speak Haitian. That's— . . . that's true nirvana, it's— . . . it's a completely different planet, it's— . . . The height of snobbery is to speak Haitian with a Moroccan accent. But that's not easy, you have to work at it, you have to deserve it. Especially with the Moroccan accent. But for me right now, it's Parisian and that's already plenty. Because you don't just speak Parisian. Oh, no. You have to earn it first.

STAN: Yes but you have an accent anyway.

SIR: Just a touch?

STAN: No no a real accent very thick.

SIR: Really? When I say:

(more and more theatrical, stretching words like a bad Shakespearian actor)

Et Dieu dit:

"Qu'as-tu fait?"

"Écoute!"

"Le sang de ton frère

crie de la terre

jusqu'à moi."

You think I have an accent?

STAN: Absolutely.

But mind you

it has a certain charm.

SIR: Ah, at least . . . In New York, I'm always a hit with the ladies.

STAN: Even without the accent you would be a hit.

SIR: Thank you, Stan. Ever been to New York?

STAN: New York?

Never.

SIR: You should go, Stan, you should. A gorgeous city. *Une ville magnifique.* For sure the most beautiful city in the world. Because New York is a girl. From Long Island. A lascivious girl lying on her back, with long and perverse legs spread wide with expectation. Many times I've imagined having a rough tongue and slipping it into this gaping hole, this unfathomable abyss open to the sky between the Big Apple's moist and transparent thighs. Many times I've dreamt of breasts full and round, topped with juicy nipples that rise with insolence to taunt the tip of God's tongue . . . The first time with New York—it's the only city for which there's always a first time, like for a woman . . . The first time, it was abrupt and violent. Hardcore. Divine. A city to take from all sides. Evil. Like youth. Like all of America. America will stay eternally young, Stan. It's doomed to stay young. Youth is its fatal flaw, but it's also its religion and its strength. Not like Europe. Europe is stopped. Frozen. Content to be old. From time to time, they fix a road, a bridge, a law. They fix but they don't change. They tinker. Europe is happy to sit in her rocking chair and be an Old Continent . . . She's not a promise anymore, she's a string of memories. And Africa . . . Africa got old before the world did. Like a scrawny kid . . . Because she was born too early, before term, before everything. Africa was never young. She was born, she got old. Like a fruit rotting on the tree before it has time to ripen . . . Africa is so old that she's regressed into a second childhood . . . I bet you've never prayed for her, Stan . . . *Moi je l'ai souvent fait, Stan, prié et surtout pleuré pour l'Afrique . . . Mais New York . . . Ah, New York . . . Si le monde entier pouvait être New York!* . . . Now honestly, Stan, you think I have an accent?

STAN: Yes.
But not unpleasant.
I've heard worse.

SIR: An accent . . . Stan, from now on you say "Sir" when you address me.

STAN: Fine.

SIR: Stan.

STAN: Fine Sir.

SIR: This woman in the window, behind the hibiscus . . . There was a woman, right, Stan?

STAN: Uh   yes   yes
there was a woman
a naked woman   Sir.

SIR: Yes?

STAN: She   she smiled while looking at me.

SIR: She looked at you or you looked at her?

STAN: She didn't look at me.
She was looking at the street and
since I was passing by
there on the street
inevitably   unless
she'd been blind or shortsighted
she had to have seen me
without necessarily having looked at me
looked distinctly at Stan in particular at Stan   but
me as part of the street
me as an element

a mere component of the whole
no more important than another
no more important for example than
I don't know
the lamppost
the yellow lamppost
the green and yellow lamppost
the red, green and yellow lamppost   or
the bus stop   or
the trash can   or
but maybe we should
I hope you're following me?
SIR: You bet!
STAN: But no less
because this also has to be said
since I should tell the truth
since I promised to tell the plain truth
since Stan swore not to hide anything anymore
no less important than another
another element   or
one could think for example
that the lamppost
the red, green and yellow lamppost
because it's bright   colorful   would
one way or another
draw more attention
but it's the whole
that has to be taken into consideration
because   this also has to be said
without Stan
not because it's Stan in particular
but it's like that
without Stan this whole could not have existed
nor the look.

Long silence.

SIR: So?
STAN: In any case

and this I absolutely have to say
because between us there can't be
a doubt even as thin as cigarette paper
I have to say this
to avoid any misunderstanding
not as it was when she looked at the street
while I was passing by
without thinking
that someone
much less a woman
naked on top of it
would look at the street from a window
hidden behind a blooming fence
but it's a random element
at least I think it is
a fence blooming with red hibiscus.
SIR: And not amaryllis.
STAN: Exactly!
SIR: *Et alors?*
STAN: *Alors . . .*

Long silence.

But they could have been amaryllis or tulips.
SIR: Why not since we're at it?
STAN: This said it doesn't mean that—
No.
SIR: Obviously. Tell me, sweetheart, you wouldn't have suicidal tendencies by any chance?
STAN: No.
Why do you say that Sir?
SIR: No questions! Don't you ever ask me any questions! And don't add anything! You know, Stan, I'm not here to save souls but to eliminate them . . . So let this be the last time you ask me a question . . . So?
STAN: What I want to say
is that she saw me before I saw her
but I looked at her before she looked at me.
SIR: Huh?

STAN: Looking at her
while passing by.
SIR: You pass by without noticing anything?
STAN: I don't understand.
SIR: Around the woman's neck?
STAN: Around her neck.
SIR: She wears . . . She wears . . .
STAN: She wears . . .
SIR: A necklace?
STAN: A necklace a . . .
SIR: A?
STAN: A pearl necklace!
She wears a pearl necklace!
The woman in the window
wears a pearl necklace!

SIR: I really have to give you all the answers, Stan. You're hopeless. And to think that when I saw you, I got all excited: "Smart as he is, it's going to be a ball." Faced with what is perhaps your last life, I expected you to have some guts. To become a king, you have to work, Stan, work on yourself like a slave. Do you value your life?

STAN: Enormously Sir.

SIR: Then fight for it! Get moving, Stan, time is running out . . . You won't say afterwards that I didn't do everything to get you out of this.

STAN: I won't say Sir.

SIR: I've seen people at this time of life, guys who weren't much to look at, with little going on upstairs, rip their guts out to try to save their skins. I've seen guys stand on their heads or dance on their big toes or suddenly break into tears while begging, in an extraordinary language, a language never heard before, for their lives to be spared. I've heard here ridiculous pleas where language was constantly twisted, manipulated, and pierced by streaks of poetry, a language so rich in innovation that it had become secret again. But nothing moved me. In the end, I put a bullet in all of their necks. But you, you don't even do half of one-tenth of what didn't save the others. You just keep saying: "There was a fence and I passed by." Only that. Do you really think you're helping me with that? You live in slow motion. You align words one at a time, without rushing, as if they were notes from a stammering piano. You don't move, don't stir, life in you never cries out. Instead, you insist on knocking down all the obstacles I put up between you and your destiny, as if you were in a hurry to meet your own destruction. Which is something that, in I don't know how many years of this vocation, I've never seen before. So what new trick are you plotting in your head, Stan?

STAN: Looking at her
while Stan passes by.
As he gets ready
to round the corner
and let the woman looking at the street
vanish behind him
I stop.
She called out for Stan.
I think she called out for me.
Or at least Stan saw
or thinks he saw
the woman's lips move.

SIR: From where you were you could see her lips move?

STAN: From where I was   yes.
As if the frame
had suddenly tightened around her lips.

SIR: OK.

STAN: A close-up
shot
of two lips moving.

SIR: OK.

STAN: For a brief moment
I saw nothing but that.

SIR: OK.

STAN: Those lips.

SIR: OK.

STAN: And now I can say it

SIR: OK.

STAN: I don't think   I know
I know her lips moved
to smile and say:
Come.

SIR: *Continue, Stan, continue!* Now you have it! Don't let it go!

Sir sings softly "Then the Lord said to Cain . . ." to encourage Stan. At the same time, he acts out Stan's "deposition."

STAN: The frame widened to include the window.
Like when Stan saw her
for the first time.
Then she appeared.
I don't know.
Stan opened the door
without taking his eyes from her and
suddenly I thought
This woman must have created
a lot of confusion
in men's hearts.

Stan stops, short of inspiration.

SIR: OK . . . Stan? You're in the house . . . Stan! . . . Are you listening to me?
STAN: Stan is listening Sir.
SIR: OK. You've just entered the house . . . Now you're in the house of the woman with the pearl necklace . . .
STAN: She's in bed.
She's waiting for me.
I don't know why but.
Maybe because of her smile
which seems to mumble a prayer
maybe because of the impatience
of her pointed breasts
maybe because of her fleshy lips
open like an invitation
like a supplication
maybe because of the intoxicating smells
escaping from the depth of her thighs
to embrace the walls
embrace the floor
embrace the furniture
embrace the curtains
the light the light the light
SIR: The chimney, Stan . . . The chimney . . .

STAN: The chimney
everything
the entire room.
The chimney.
Yet it was why Stan went up.
But all of a sudden
I wanted her to
stop smiling
I wanted her to
fold her arms over her breasts
I wanted her to
bring her thighs together
I wanted something else
suddenly
I don't know why.

SIR: *Continue, Stan, continue!* We're almost there . . . Almost . . . Just relax and throw yourself into it. There was a metal rod in the fire . . .

STAN: A metal rod
a poker yes   a   poker
forgotten
forgotten in the chimney and
turned red-hot
by the fever of the flames.

SIR: You took the poker out of the fire . . .

STAN: Yes Sir.

SIR: To silence the supplication of her flesh . . .

STAN: Yes Sir.

SIR: You plunged it between the open thighs . . .

STAN: Yes Sir.

SIR: Plunged it.

STAN: Yes Sir.

SIR: Plunged it.

STAN: Yes Sir.

SIR: Plunged it.

STAN: Yes Sir.

Sir screams as if in pain.

No   she didn't scream

SIR: Yes, she must have screamed!
STAN: She didn't scream   no.
Believe me   she didn't
she didn't even moan.
Even with a red-hot poker
nothing.
She simply stopped smiling
her eyelids lowered
and her nipples dissolved
into her melting breasts.
She was calm
peaceful.
Like the last silence.
And beautiful.
SIR: She was most of all *morte*, Stan. *Morte!*
STAN: God   she was beautiful . . .
SIR: Dead! You took the rod out and stuck your flesh into her dead flesh because that's how you like them, right, Stan, cold limp lifeless open totally open? Dead flesh turns you on, doesn't it? Doesn't it?
STAN: I admit it yes.
Everything.
I confess.
Everything.
But I beg you
don't talk about this anymore.
SIR: How many times did you force yourself inside her?
STAN: I don't know.
SIR: How many?
STAN: Hours
the whole day
the whole night
I don't remember
until the next day
maybe.
SIR: How many burials have you desecrated like this, Stan? How many?
STAN: I don't know
dozens
probably hundreds
thousands.

SIR: Look at me, Stan.

Stan looks up and discovers that Sir has removed all of his clothes.

No, no look! . . . What do you see? Huh? What do you see?

STAN: Nothing.

SIR: Oh, Stan, Stan, Stan! That's very low. It's not nice to upset your friends like that.

STAN: You are naked Sir.

SIR: There, what do you see there?

STAN: Hair.

SIR: Look more closely.

STAN: Your—

SIR: I beg your pardon, Stan?

STAN: Your—

SIR: Cock. But look even more closely.

STAN: Testicles.

SIR: Stan!

STAN: Balls.

SIR: *Oui*, very good, Stan. *Très bien. Viens plus près . . . Allez viens . . . As-tu peur de moi? Il n'y a pas de danger, Stan . . .*

STAN: You scare me   Sir.

SIR: I scare you, Stan? *Ooh la la!* But look at me, I'm calm . . . I know I got a little excited earlier but now I'm in control. And even when I'm not in control, I don't say anything vulgar, right, Stan?

STAN: You haven't said
anything vulgar in a long time.
You're in control.
You're in control of the situation.
You're in control of everything   Sir.

SIR: Come on, take them.

STAN: I can't Sir.

SIR: Yes, you can. They're not going to bite you . . . There . . . The other one too . . . Both of them, Stan . . . With both hands . . . One in each hand . . . That's good, Stan, you're a good sport. Feel them . . . I said feel them! . . . How are they? Shy, huh? . . . Now squeeze them . . . Go ahead, squeeze them! Relax and squeeze! . . . That's it! . . . Now squeeze harder . . . Again . . . Again . . . Harder . . . Harder . . . With all the strength of your fingers . . . Harder . . . Harder . . . Harder . . .

STAN: I can't squeeze any harder Sir.
SIR: I'm happy to hear it. Did I scream?
STAN: No Sir.
SIR: Do you see any tears?
STAN: No Sir.
SIR: How do you find them, Stan?
STAN: Hard.
SIR: Only hard?
STAN: Very hard.
Like stones.
SIR: You're flattering me, Stan.
STAN: No no I'm not flattering you Sir.
And if I may
I would say that
you have balls of steel Sir.
SIR: That's nice, Stan. Very nice. So now that you know I have balls of steel, what do you think is going to happen if you keep fucking with me?
STAN: I guess
I will regret it Sir.
SIR: You're guessing right, Stan.

Sir gets his gun and aims it at Stan.

Because I'm very angry with you, very very angry. I've had it up to here. You want to die, is that it? You want to die? Well, you're going to die! I'm tired of you taking me for a fag! I'm tired of you making shit up! You keep being vulgar, sordid, tasteless. Even though you know how much I want to create something proper, decent, and clean. And you lie! You've been lying all along. Your metal rod never existed. And what's with the chimney? There's never been a chimney! No more than a pearl necklace. There's never been anything! This woman, it's bullshit, she doesn't exist. At all. There's not the tiniest bit of woman. Admit it!
STAN: No yes
she doesn't exist
but I thought that you—
SIR: You thought what? You thought that I what?
STAN: I'm totally confused.
SIR: Oh, because you think I'm not confused? You think I understand why, even though I'm neither the mayor nor the governor of this city, you all came here one after the other, without being forced? Why you offered

me your necks so I could put a bullet in them and serve your deaths as fodder to these animals? Did I seek you out, Stan? Did I drag you here by the hair?

STAN: None of that   Sir.

SIR: You came of your own free will, like all the others?

STAN: Like all the others   Sir.

SIR: You could have run away, right, Stan? Or left the city?

STAN: Nothing stopped me from running away   Sir.

SIR: Then what?

STAN: I don't know   Sir.

SIR: Because on a boring day I looked at a woman's breast? No, Stan, no . . . Nobody understands. But we try to do our best, to put one foot in front of the other, 1-2, 1-2 . . . Blindly . . . One foot in front of the other, 1-2, 1-2 . . . Like soldiers . . . Heads up, stand straight . . . Like good little GIs, one foot in front of the other . . . Left-right, left-right, left-right . . . Until one day, everything goes back to dust. We don't pretend to be smarter than we are. We play along. As best we can. That's all. Nobody's ever been able to understand, Stan. Nobody! . . . But maybe you can perform a miracle? You, who are so smart and have ideas about everything . . . Right, Stan, maybe you can enlighten me?

STAN: Stan says
I don't know.
Vanity.
Perhaps loneliness.
Vanity and loneliness and boredom   perhaps.
Perhaps also
because   ultimately
life is no more than a sketch of death
that's what Stan believes.
Perhaps
simply vanity
Stan says.
I don't know.
Perhaps because
we're only human.
Perhaps
basically I don't know
Stan says.

SIR: I don't know . . . I don't know . . . That's all you can say. I don't know . . . You never know anything, Stan! . . . Now, what do you suggest to fix this mess? *(a beat)* A poem? A song? A tap dance? What? . . .

STAN: Stan doesn't know any poem.
Stan is tone-deaf.
Stan has two left feet.
I'm sorry I cannot be
of any help Sir.

SIR: And to think that I'm busting my ass to save—to spare a life! So, Stan?

STAN: Nothing absolutely nothing.
You saw
when Stan tried to lie
you saw?
Believe me Sir
I have no talent.

SIR: Yes, you do. You know how to knit and you speak French rather well . . . *(silence)* Well, since you keep asking for it by draping yourself in silence and spoiling everything I do with your vulgarities, I have no choice but to pull the trigger. Show me your neck, Stan.

STAN: You won't betray
the thread of Stan's existence Sir.

SIR: I kind of like you, Stan, but I'm really sorry . . .

STAN: Because first your gun
would have to be loaded.

Silence.

SIR: You're a fucking pro, Stan, you're very very strong. A real fucking pro. *Alors?*

Sir acts out what Stan says.

STAN: You're going to point the gun
at my neck
then cock the hammer
before recounting . . .

SIR: When I was a kid, I wanted a dog. Dad hated animals in general and dogs in particular. So Mom offered me a pig—a piglet—as a pet. I called him— . . . Obviously you know what I called him.

STAN: Stan.

SIR: Everywhere I went, Stan followed. You wouldn't know just to look at them but pigs are very smart, smarter than dogs, and infinitely more endearing. And contrary to popular belief, they don't stink. They smell like pigs but that's a good smell—it's like bacon. Stan was so poetic that even Dad fell for him. Little by little, my father made him his companion. With no regard for me. He took him everywhere: To work, to his friends', to parties . . . Stan ate at the table and at night he slept in my parents' bed between my father and my mother. So one day I came up with the idea of killing Stan. Since his affection had been stolen from me, I had to kill him so nobody else would enjoy his company. After all, he was my pig. I dragged him very far, outside the city, and into the forest. I tied him to a tree. But when I raised the hammer to smash his head, Stan looked at me and his eyes smiled. For the first time, I saw him smile. And everything fell apart. Suddenly, he wasn't "my pig" anymore. But he wasn't a human being either. He was himself. Stan. Simply Stan. Stan died much later, very old, of a natural death, in his bed between my father and my mother.

STAN: And now you're going to pretend that
your finger is hesitating on the trigger
because
you made the mistake
of getting attached to Stan.
And that
we get attached to everything
so long as we give it a face.
And that
Stan has become your
Promethean rock.
And that's a tragedy.
And that.
And that.
And that.
But it's not true.

Stan turns around.

Shoot.

He opens his mouth and, in an obscene gesture, wraps his lips around the gun's barrel.

Because
it was never your intention
to shoot Stan.
From the very beginning
you knew that
you would spare Stan.
Didn't you make sure
to unload your gun
for fear that
with all the stress and excitement
an unfortunate bullet
and bang!
Not because
you've become attached to me no but
because
you have no choice
because
you're the only one left
because
I'm the only one left.

SIR: Also because I finally understand . . . And you're the one who taught me, Stan, you're the one who taught me . . . I finally understand that real power, absolute power, lies not in our capacity to inflict death but in the choice we make not to kill when everything is forcing us to. I finally understand that, thanks to you, Stan.

STAN: Because
you want things
to be different than usual
because
they came from the opposite end of the world
often on foot
because
they paid a lot of money
with the secret hope that
this time
something else will happen
because
they too

hope that
you'll spare me.
Because above all
fear says
What if Stan weren't
The Big Shoot.

SIR: Because in the end, Stan, the show must go on.

STAN: Now
you're going to whisper in Stan's ear

SIR: You learn fast, Stan, and I'm happy that it's you. Finally. But you have to keep your end of the deal, respect the contract, go all the way . . . We're pros, right, Stan? So I'm going to put one bullet in the cylinder. Russian roulette. One chance out of a hundred million to hit the right hole. One out of a hundred million. And tomorrow, they'll come from even further away, and they'll pay even more money, not for an execution anymore but for a leap into the void. The ultimate thrill. And they'll come back, and come back, and come back until one day, without expecting it, they'll hear the bang! The Big Shoot! Because you know it, right, Stan? Smart as you are, you know that you're the Big Shoot? Are you ready?

STAN: I'm ready.

Sir takes a bullet from one of his pockets. Drum roll. He shows the bullet to the audience, like in a circus act, then loads it into the gun.

SIR: We've finally reached the placenta of life, this place with no before or after. As we've all noticed, Stan here is an exceptional character. An extraordinary character. A true one of a kind. And it'd be a shame to lose such a unique individual in—how should I say—such a crude way. So for the first time, I'm going to leave it up to chance. Russian roulette. This bullet will be the ultimate judge . . . And now, Ladies and Gentlemen, the pathetic encounter of dust and its collapse.

He hands the gun to Stan.

Stan?

Stan takes the gun and points it at his temple.

Stan . . . before you— . . . Because we never know . . . Out of a hundred million, there's still a chance . . . We never know . . . So a question, which I know won't be the last . . . A question. When I say:

(with no theatrical affect and a genuine lack of affectation)
Et Dieu dit à Caïn:
"Où est ton frère Abel?"
"Je ne sais pas," répondit-il.
"Suis-je le gardien de mon frère?"
Et Dieu dit:
"Qu'as-tu fait?"
"Écoute!"
"Le sang de ton frère
crie de la terre
jusqu'à moi.
Maintenant, tu seras maudit
de la terre
qui a ouvert sa bouche
pour recevoir de ta main
le sang de ton frère."
When I say that, Stan, honestly . . . You think I have an accent? Honestly?
STAN: You have an accent Sir.
A thick and terrifying accent.
SIR: There's no two ways about it, you're a fucking pro, Stan . . . Whenever you want.

Drum roll. Stan pulls the trigger. Gun shot and blackout. When the lights come up again, Sir is laughing hysterically.

April Fool, Stan! April Fool!

Stan is sitting on the chair, his arms hanging and his body pitched forward. Sir takes the gun from his hands and pushes him with his foot. Stan collapses on the floor. While crooning "Et Dieu dit à Caïn . . . ," Sir removes the used bullet and shows it to the audience. Applause. Then, as in an illusionist's number, he removes, one by one, several unused bullets—way more than the gun could normally hold.

April Fool! . . . Death is a lot more vicious than you, Stan. Oh yes, a hell of a lot more vicious. *(a beat)* To insist that I have an accent!

(mimicking Stan)
"You have a bit of an accent"
"A real accent very thick"

"A thick and terrifying accent . . ."
Fuck you and your fucking accent! *Enculé!* What do I care about the Why? Dickhead, idiot, pig, jackass, bastard . . . Cocksucking son of a bitch . . . Me? An accent? *(he closes his eyes in an ecstatic pose)* Silence. The silence of the Big Shoot is finally born. Real. Absolute . . . Young at last. Young forever. Like America!

A dog howls to death. Sir opens his eyes and listens. The dog howls again.

The dog! . . . And the woman in the window . . . Tough, they're tough . . . Because . . . it's inevitable . . . the beast is always the sign of the woman . . .

Third howl.

Oh, Stan, Stan, Stan!

Blackout.

END OF PLAY

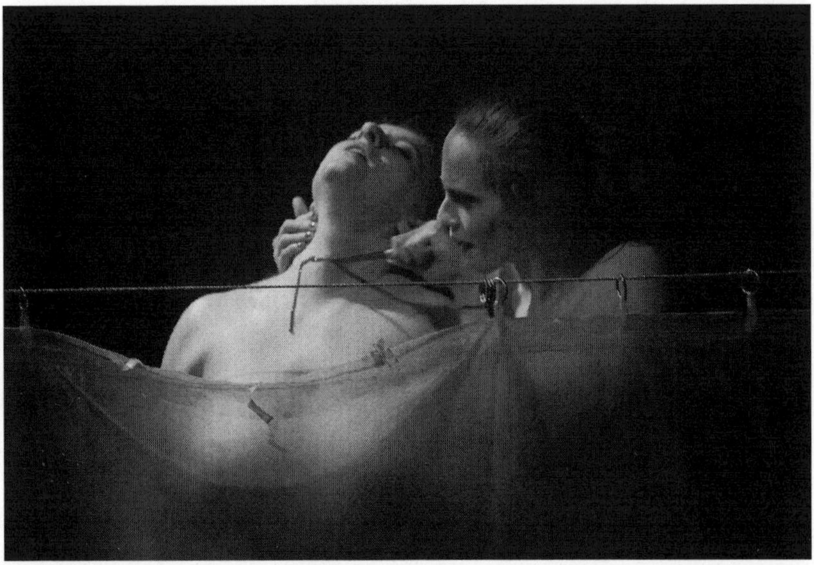

Tiffany-Jane Madden and Camille Giacobino in *Misterioso-911*, directed by Cédric Dorier, at the Théâtre Vidy-Lausanne, Switzerland, 2014. Photo by Mario del Curto.

Misterioso-911

2005

TRANSLATED BY CHANTAL BILODEAU

INTRODUCTION TO MISTERIOSO-911

Never ask the way from someone who knows it
because then you cannot get lost
—Rabbi Nahman of Bratslav

One of Kwahulé's darker and more abstract dramatic works, more like an oratorio than a play, *Misterioso* equates the insanity of the world responsible for 9/11 with the traumatized and maddened inmates of a women's prison. Through a series of dramatic movements and musical riffs on themes of abandonment and frustration, we gradually understand the fantastic ritual taking place—but also having already taken place, as we are again in the realm of temporal circularity that characterizes much of Kwahulé's later work. To the background music of Thelonius Monk's *Misterioso*, a haunting and explosive jazz piece that slides from fugue-like progressions to piercing sax solos (in this case played on a cello by one of the inmates), passive-aggressive prisoner Linda kills the prison drama teacher. The teacher has indeed requested this, suffering as much outside the prison's walls as the inmates do inside. She had come to the prison to offer some creative outlet and artistic discipline to these forsaken women, plagued by horrendous pasts: victims of psychological battering, incest, and marginalization, perpetrators of infanticide and murder. The drama teacher, like the inmates, will never leave again. As in the blackest of masses, that should be read metaphorically, the inmates' ultimate "cannibalization" of the teacher, a sacrificial victim to the collective psychological trauma, is figured as an act of love. It is, however, also a sign that their pain cannot be transcended, for part of the great suffering of this group is their invisibility. With the death of their teacher, the drama they have been rehearsing will never be performed and thus never acknowledged.

In individual monologues that punctuate the choral movements of the undifferentiated voices (whom we might identify as the nostalgic woman, the woman with big breasts, the woman who loves children, the woman with the hammer, the immigrant), inmates recount haltingly and in syncopated phrasing how the absence of a meaningful existence and the lack of counting for something led them to kill. Each murderous act should also be understood as a form of suicide. Always, even as children, they have been bombs ready to explode. Each time they "go off," they wreak havoc outside as well as inside themselves. Incarcerated, the meanness, wounding, and battles they experience in prison are little different from what they had known before entering. An archeological history of the prison space, with its convent-like *voussoirs*—a history intoned by one of the inmates—indicates that the prison, like the women, has indeed harbored years of massacres and repression.

We might characterize this play as a musical drive toward inevitable death, with any chance of resurrection suspended. In this light, the women's stories can be thought of as a mosaic of circulating violence and pain that constitutes a meditation. The embedded dramatic text rehearsed by the inmates hints at a parallel with Holocaustal horrors. As historical "intertext," the Holocaust, a central instance of cultural madness, is also invoked in the repeated references to a crematorium. *Misterioso-911* would have us ask questions about violence begetting violence, about the connection between sexual longing and destruction, about masochism as both responsible for and resulting from existential emptiness, and about the perverse need to absorb the other in order to be full of oneself. If there is an opportunity for beauty here, it is in the musical form of the play, in the intercutting lines, the rhythmic drive, the constant return to the musical question posed at the beginning of Monk's *Misterioso*: Where will this repetitive, hallucinatory theme take us? To a volcanic implosion? To a launch into emotional freedom? To the stasis of defeat?

Notes for reading and performance:

1. Koffi Kwahulé works often with various groups of people, including troubled adolescents and battered women, who use drama therapy and drama workshops to deal with trauma. He wrote *Misterioso-911* after the terrorist attack on the Twin Towers of the World Trade Center as a way to think about violence. In it, he continues to explore the impact of jazz structure by imagining the voices of the characters as individual instruments whose recurring phrases help identify them.

2. Thelonious Monk was one of the giants of jazz piano. A composer known for dissonant harmonies and angular melodic twists, his haunting composition "Misterioso," featured in the 1958 album of the same name, builds slowly into a swinging melodic blues and ends in a series of chordal progressions, with space for virtuosic sax, trumpet, bass, drum, and piano solos.

3. Elena Hebrayova is the fictional author of the play within the play. Her name suggests Russian Jewish origins.

4. *Voussoirs* is the term for the wedge-shaped stones used in building arches or vaulted ceilings.

TIME

Sometime after September 11, 2001.

SETTING

A women's prison.

CHARACTERS

At least six women. Ideally, eight or ten. Possibly more.
A cellist.

TRANSLATOR'S NOTE

This play should be approached like a piece of jazz. The goal of the author is to create a blueprint, or theme, around which artists are free to improvise. Since there are no stage directions and lines haven't been assigned to specific characters, actors and directors are encouraged to use the text to create their own narrative. No language may be added but lines and scenes may be reordered and/or deleted to serve each artist's vision.

* indicates a rhythmic line break. In the original French version, these breaks occur after the word "que." In the English version, since "que" translates into different words, I have added an asterisk to make the pattern clear.

I. A HAPPY CHILDHOOD

Does anyone know the girl who keeps playing this heart-wrenching music

Why do I have to prove myself every time

I had a nice childhood. A happy childhood. Affection. Love. I received a lot of love. From my father. From my mother. Good parents

Look, I managed to sneak a hammer in

This country, I was born here more than twenty years ago yet—how do I put this—I just don't feel I belong to this country

So tell me

It's private

To feel lonely is to crave someone to love

All this blood

Can't that girl play anything other than a chant luring death to our door

This blood everywhere

I love caresses because the rest is boring

It's only blood
It's only blood
It's only blood

To caress is to tease the flesh

He thinks they're too big

A man to love

Oh, come on

After

He used to say that they frightened him

After what

A man who lets me love him

My father always says To kill is to turn off the light inside us

Big breasts frightened him

Give me the hose

Can I see them

After. After in a while

After the blood. And turn on the faucet

I love his caresses

Maybe I knew but didn't want to accept

All this blood, it reminds me of the first time, when my man laid me on his butcher's block—he's a butcher, my man—and he split me and split me and split me like a watermelon

Six months I've been here and I've already gained ten kilos

I love kids. I used to work in a kindergarten. I've always loved kids

For someone with big breasts, you have very delicate nipples

Come on, tell me

You say that just to be nice

Not now, I said

The night before, he'd told me for the zillionth time You need to get an operation

Hurry up! Let's clean up! Let's clean up before Mother Superior gets involved

In America, after a year, I'd feel like an American. But here

I like that he teases my flesh

If anyone tells that I have a hammer, I'll crush her forehead with it

I had good parents. A happy childhood. Love.

II. A LIFE WITH NO WINDOWS

Look at me, I'm not from here, from inside, I'm from outside. I live a life with no windows. I have no dog, I have no cat, I have no goldfish, I have no friends, I have no husband, I have no children. A life with no windows. Perhaps that's why I like being here, inside. Look at me, I'm not from here, from inside, I'm from outside. Look at me, I'm an actress, a drama teacher, I'm inside as a replacement, at the last minute. A few weeks that I've been coming here, inside. Every Thursday. The previous teacher fell from the seventh floor. They say A suicide. They also say She didn't fall on her own. They even say She was pushed. But an accident, they concluded. Before her, two others disappeared. Leaving no body. Look at me, in a few Thursdays my contract will be over and the doors of the inside will close behind me, for good. And that day, that Thursday, I pray to God it never comes. Because my only window is here, inside. Look at me, in a few days I'll be dead. That girl says it to everyone, says it everywhere, without shame, screams it at the top of her lungs to make sure it reaches my ears. Look at me, do I look like a cow? Do I look like a pig? Am I fat? Because it's me. I'm the fat cow. I'm the fat pig. I'm the fat one. Look at me, in a few days that girl will have killed me.

III. A FLEETING GLANCE

On the first day I almost . . .
Someone was playing, room 911, a cello, *Misterioso* . . .
I was walking in the cloister, she'd just arrived. I didn't see her, I didn't look at her. I simply felt her arrive, a foreign vibration in this place, a foreign presence, a female presence of course. No man ever comes here. I didn't look at her, I don't like to look. I don't like to be looked at. I never look. Almost never. Sometimes. Just to make sure that*
nobody is looking at me, just for that. They all know it here. We passed each other. I said good morning, I heard good morning. And I knew that*
she'd turn around and that*
she'd look at me. I turned around. She looked away. Quickly. She had looked at me. And I saw in that*
fleeting glance, and I saw in the trail of her look this thing . . .
about me that*
I'd never seen . . .
that*
I'd never wanted to see . . .
I didn't know that*
it'd be her . . .
I didn't know yet that*

it was her . . .
But I almost . . .
right then, in the cloister . . .
while a cello, somewhere, was playing *Misterioso*.

IV. POM-POM GIRLS

So tell me

That*
fat cow, I think I'm going to kill her

Tell me

What did I hear

Nothing

Tell me

Who's the fat cow

Nobody

Come on, tell me

Who is it

Are you deaf? I said Nobody

Do you hear how she talks to her

It's private

My breasts are too big

And she doesn't even respond

I don't intend to do this all my life
I don't intend to do this all my life
I don't intend to do this all my life

Shhh

Do you have your hammer with you

A long time

The blessed fruit of thy womb

More than twenty years that I was born here

OK, back to your places. Focus. And don't forget: Energy and smile. Everybody smile . . . Smile! One, two, look at the audience . . . Look at the audience, I said . . . The audience is over here . . . Good. Three, four, sway your hips and flirt with the audience, like this . . . Five, six, seven, eight

Look, they're too big

Will you tell me

I don't think so

One, two, shake your pom-poms . . . three, four, five, and turn . . . six, seven, sway your hips . . . eight, nine, ten

He thought they were too big

The flesh of my flesh

I've started a diet

Well, he's a fag

Or I should say, I'm careful about what I eat

Shhh

Real men like big breasts

But not cow udders

Oh, the nasty bitch

Shhh

Shut up

What

Nothing

That's not true

She said Shut up
She said Shut up

She said Shut up

You want Mother Superior to find out

I don't give a shit

A fag

Breasts like cow udders, he said

You know, gay

One, two, three, four, and move back

I don't see how he could be

. . . five, six, stretch your arms! Seven, eight, and hold it

He doesn't like it when I play the pom-pom girl

Stretched arms

He comes to see me less and less

In America, everything would be—how do I put this—simpler

And turn, and down, and up, and stay, and sway your hips

Other men looking at me, he doesn't like that, it hurts him too much

Good. Now, music

I'm like everybody, I need a little love, that's all, it's no more complicated than that

And one, and two . . . Girls, get ready, with the music and the chorus . . . And one, and two, and three . . . Chorus, take it away

The market square is empty. . . . It's raining. A light rain. A man tries to start his motorcycle parked by the fountain. A child—she looks like Little Red Riding Hood, how we imagine her—and a woman cross the market square. The woman holds the child by the hand. . . . The man kicks the tires of his motorcycle. The woman and the child reach the door of the community center. The T36 bus. The woman knocks on the door. No one is waiting at the bus stop. T36 stops. No one gets off. The man puts his hands on his hips. He walks around his motorcycle. T36 leaves. . . . The woman and the child look through the window of the community center. I need to call my bank. The woman and the child dressed in red come back to the door of the community center. The woman knocks on the door. The door opens. A man appears. He's smiling. He seems to be. He's happy to see the woman and the child. Maybe. The woman and the child go inside the community center. The man has managed to start his motorcycle. I didn't see him leave. T36 arrives. From the opposite direction. A man gets off. Angry. He seems to be. He screams at T36. At the driver probably. . . . I'm sure I have a huge overdraft. T36 leaves. I'm listening. A coffee. The market square is empty. The woman comes out of the community center. Without Little Red Riding Hood. The woman runs. The woman crosses the market square. The woman crosses the street. The woman passes the café. Mrs. Keller. Worry on Mrs. Keller's face. Maybe not. Mrs. Keller disappears. It's a shame that the market is only on Sundays. A car went by. Red. Yellow. Orange maybe. 4:23 p.m. Mrs. Keller reappears. She's followed by Mr. Coulanges. In his pharmacist's lab coat. And by a policeman. Mrs. Keller, the pharmacist, and the policeman cross the street. A man goes by on a bike. The thieves! They're going to slap me with a fine. Bank employees are rats. If they give me a fine, I'll fill their heads with lead. Calm down. You'll do nothing at all. . . . Mrs. Keller, Mr. Coulanges and the policeman cross the market square. The market square is empty. The market twice a week, that wouldn't be bad. T36 stops. No one is waiting for T36. A glass of water and the bill. T36 leaves. Tap water. No one got off T36. It's strange after all this coffee I still don't feel awake. I must have an overdraft. T36. From the opposite direction. Bank employees are swindlers. Mr. Coulanges comes out of the community center. Alone. Mr. Coulanges crosses the market square. T36 leaves. Mr. Coulanges runs. Crosses the street. Passes the café. Worry on his face. Disappears. Another coffee, please. Tomorrow will be a great day for picking mushrooms. The market square is empty. . . . It's raining. A light rain.

Break

It's clear, I'm going to kill that*
fat cow. What*
she did . . . What*
she did to me . . . What*
she makes me do . . . What*
she makes me say . . . Anybody would kill her.

V. AND THAT'S WHY YOU'RE KILLING ME?

Excuse me . . .

It's going well, isn't it?

Why do you want to kill me? You're telling everyone, everywhere. It's finally reached me.

I won't take you by surprise. Right before, I'll kiss you in front of the others. I'll kiss you on the mouth, with my tongue. And if you're nice, on that*
day, I'll come to you, in a rush of commiseration, I'll come to you naked, in bright daylight, in the middle of rehearsal, in front of the others. Isn't that*
what your look was begging for?

I looked at you?

The day that*
girl was playing *Misterioso* all day.

I may have looked at you? And that's why you're killing me?

Did you notice that*
for as long as I've been standing in front of you, I haven't lifted my eyes? Did you notice? I almost never look, I hate to be looked at, to be looked at the way you looked at me that day.

Was this look insolent? Was it arrogant? Did it seem to be prying?

Let me touch your eyes, I'll tell you . . .

You're hurting me . . . Please, stop . . .

Don't beg. Demand. You're in charge, you're the teacher, you're the authority, don't beg, demand . . .
You like what*
you're doing with us?

What?

Pom-pom girls, fancy music and theater?

If I didn't I wouldn't be here.

Are you ever on TV?

No, never.

What about movies? Are you in movies?

No.

Do you sign autographs?

No.

You're not famous then?

No, I'm not famous.

Otherwise, they wouldn't have sent you here. You're here for the money, right? No, you're only doing this for the art. Obviously. They said Young girls impossible to rehabilitate. They said Make them do theater, girls like theater, it improves character and it doesn't cost a dime, a few pieces of string and *voilà*, it's theater. They also said Be careful, they're all insane . . . Isn't that*
what they said? . . . You know, your colleague, not an accident, not a suicide either . . . Before her, two others disappeared. No body, not even a piece of clothing. Nothing. The one who fell from the seventh floor, yes. But the other two, no. They came in and never went out. No trace. No trail. No clue. No evidence. As the police say. Did you know? . . . You can't not have known. Ah, the desperate need to feel useful! You knew and you threw yourself to the wolves. Performed your civic duty, as they say. And also for the money. Not primarily, of course . . . How much do they pay you for this? . . . Come on, tell me, what*
price did they put on your life?

Look at me when you talk to me!

If I look at you, I kill you.

Then look at me.

In the end . . . in the end . . . What*
price? . . . It's one of your creations, huh?

Don't touch me! . . . What?

What*
you make us do. Theater, fancy music and pom-pom girls. It's one of your

creations? A new concept, as they say? That's what*
they chose you for, isn't it? It's one of your ideas?

No . . . not at all. It's very common . . . Everybody does it . . .

I've always dreamt of being a pom-pom girl.

Well, I'm pleased.

But you came here, you pointed at me and you said You'll be the chorus. Everyone else, You'll be the pom-pom girls, the Golden Girls. I, alone, make up the chorus. Why do you make me do this? I hate that*
Elena Hebrayova and what*
she says and what*
she writes and what*
you make me recite while the others wiggle around, show off their breasts and shake their asses. Why did you choose me?

I didn't choose you . . . I had to pick someone . . . And it fell on you . . . That's all . . . Maybe because you were isolated from the others . . . Slightly to the side . . . Not part of the group . . . I don't know . . .

. . . *The market square is empty. The market twice a week, that wouldn't be bad. T36 stops. No one is waiting for T36. A glass of water and the bill. T36 leaves. Tap water. No one got off T36. It's strange after all this coffee I still don't feel awake. I must have an overdraft* . . . Maybe it works for you, maybe it amuses you, makes you feel smart, gives you the sensation of floating on a bed of subtle emotions but I find it old and stupid and a pain in the ass.

I didn't think it would offend you . . . offend you this much . . . If you want— . . .

I want nothing. I want nothing anymore. Nothing, you hear me? Nothing. You humiliated me. By choosing me for this, you humiliated me, as if everything in me was unworthy of being a pom-pom girl, you humiliated me. After looking at me the way you did, in the cloister, while the cello was struggling with *Misterioso*. I've dreamt about this. When the other one, your colleague, fell from the seventh floor, I got really excited because in her concept, I never had a place . . . And when I discovered that*
you wanted to use pom-pom girls, I got even more excited. I'd waited for

you for so long. Like for a last chance. I told my parents, my friends . . . all my friends . . . everybody . . . I told everybody: I'm going to be a pom-pom girl. But here I am sitting on a stool, isolated from the others—the real beauty queens—like a leper, constantly repeating the platitudes of that*

idiot—

An idiot? . . . Elena Hebrayova, an idiot?

Yes, an idiot! I've always despised what*

that woman writes. And I'm sick of the crap you're making me repeat. How do you expect us to develop an interest in theater with this pretentious bullshit? I've always hated her posturing but now I'm stuck with it.

It's not fair!

It's not fair!

It's not fair!

. . . *The woman and the child reach the door of the community center. The T36 bus. The woman knocks on the door. No one is waiting at the bus stop. T36 stops. No one gets off. The man puts his hands on his hips. He walks around his motorcycle. T36 leaves. . . . The woman and the child look through the window of the community center. I need to call my bank . . .* Everything she does sounds affected, false, and dumb! Majorly dumb! It's enough to put you off theater forever!

I've heard enough, get out of my way . . . Please, Miss . . .

Demand! I'm not your friend, I'm not your girlfriend, you're in charge, you're the teacher, you're the authority, demand!

Get out of my way! Immediately!

There you go. Right before, I'll kiss you.

You're just a troubled young girl . . . trying to draw attention to herself . . . You don't kill people for something like that . . .

Who says that*

I'll kill you only for that?

Don't touch me!

We'll talk about it later.

We won't talk about it again . . . Don't touch me, I said!

I'm sure that*
your lips are deliciously salty.

VI. THOSE DIRTY THINGS

The worst is to have no sense of humor

Was he good

He spends his time trying to guess what other men imagine doing to me that he hasn't done yet

I love caresses

Will you tell me

I could have hated her, detested her, if only because she invaded my body

I love his caresses

Sometimes I think that being a stripper wouldn't be so bad

Not after being a pom-pom girl

I love when he caresses me

She boarded me like a secret passenger

Of course it hurts him

This country, I was born here more than twenty years ago. Yet

What I miss most, it's not freedom, it's my childhood

I'm not telling you

Can you show me your hammer

I didn't think he'd do it because he always said big breasts frightened him

All those dirty things

For me, it's hairy men

For me, it's as smooth as a shark

Me, I only love caresses. Because the rest is boring

That's not true, it's obvious that you're dying to

Those things I wish he would do to me

Would have done to me

Would do to me

Would have done to me

Would do to me

Would have done to me

Don't confuse her

Holding it in my hand makes me feel all . . . It's better than a man's dick

Finding a bra my size is always a big ordeal

The blessed fruit of thy womb

Would do to me and would enjoy doing but he doesn't dare because he thinks it's dirty

You don't look like you've gained weight

The flesh of my flesh

It's here, here and here that I've gained the most

Yours, they're exactly the way men like

Yeah but I wish they were a little bigger

To caress is to tease the flesh

Mine, my man, he's as smooth as a shark

Distance. She should have kept her distance

In America, I'd already feel like an American

The first time he caressed me, I realized I was a desire that had never been awakened . . .

VII. THE WORST

I'm like everybody, I need a little affection, that's all, it's no more complicated than that. First, he said We need to talk. About us. But he was saying that while thinking about my breasts. The night before, he'd told me for the zillionth time You need to get an operation . . . It's strange what that girl is playing. No. Not what she's playing but the fact that she only plays this, all the time. At night, during the day. At wake-up time, shower time, exercise time, arts activity time, visiting time, breakfast time, lunchtime, dinnertime, lockup time, bedtime. All the time. The same piece, all the time. Without sleeping, without waking up, without eating, without drinking, without exercising, without receiving visits, without sleeping. All the time. Like a penance. Like a vow. That's what's so strange, to only play this, all the time . . . Show me. My breasts? Your breasts. Here? Here. In front of all these people? It's none of their business. The train is coming. Well, we'll miss the train. I can't. Not here. Show them your breasts. They'll tell you that your breasts are the most . . . like that in the world. Because they've never seen breasts like these. I can't. You can. Not here. Here. Here? Here. I didn't think he'd do it because he always said big breasts frightened him. So on a subway platform . . . But already his hands had slipped inside my blouse. Had opened it. I was paralyzed with shame. Obviously, people were looking at us. He wasn't caressing them. Anyway, he's never caressed them. But for the first time, he was holding them without fear. He was simply touching them. Feeling them. Weighing them with both hands as if they were on a scale. He was gauging them. He was gauging me. They felt enormous, even more enormous than usual. And misshapen. People are looking at us. Nobody's looking at us. Maybe he was right because I couldn't lift my eyes. I could only watch, in my mind's eye, his two hands weigh my breasts. And you know what, fuck them! It's none of their business. This is between you and me. Between us. You worry too much about other people. You worry too much about your breasts and you miss out on a lot of things. You miss out on us. You keep saying that you feel lonely but to feel lonely is to crave someone who loves you . . . No . . . I think it's to crave someone to love. A man to love. A man who lets me love him. A man whose return I'd wait for impatiently. A man I could kill from love . . . Well, I'm here. I'm right here. While he's gauging me on a subway platform, his hands inside my blouse. Look, they can't believe their eyes. They're all looking at you. They're looking at them. Because they're beautiful. In their own way, they're beautiful. That's what they're looking at . . . It's this stunning beauty, here, in my hands, that they're looking at. He suddenly withdrew his hands and shook them. But you still need to get an operation. As if he'd just taken them out of something liquid. Like this, he shook his hands. Like this. Your breasts are warm and sweaty like cow udders. Maybe he didn't say it to hurt me but I immediately saw myself as a cow, standing in the middle of those people on my four cow legs, with my heavy cow teats dragging on the concrete floor. I must have screamed because he started to laugh. Loudly. Cow udders, you have cow udders! He was laughing. Don't make this face, cow udders, it's a compliment. He was laughing. But you don't get it. He was laughing. Because you have no sense of humor. He was laughing. The worst is to have no sense of humor. He was laughing. It's even worse than to have cow breasts. He was laughing. The train was coming. He was laughing. I didn't have time to feel humiliated, he was laughing, I just thought You're right, but I'm not just missing out on a lot of things, and on us, I'm most of all missing out on myself. And I pushed him. The rails screeched as if horrified by the blood and scattered flesh that steel was pressing against steel. The attorney pleaded sudden insanity. I told the judge I wasn't crazy, that it was the only moment since I met him when I'd had all my head. I'm like everybody, I need a little affection, that's all, it's no more complicated than that . . . Does anyone know that girl, the girl who's playing this music?

VIII. I THOUGHT ABOUT YOU

Here, this is for you . . . I'm offering it to you.

But I— . . . Good morning.

Oh yes, I'm sorry, good morning . . .

A Bible? . . . You can't give someone a Bible . . .

Then receive from me this heresy.

But I— . . . Keep it, it'll give you something to read . . .

I've already read it and reread it.

Yes, but I— . . . I don't need it . . .

You'll need it. You'll see, we always need it. To ask forgiveness. Please, take it and forgive me for what*
I did last week . . . For what*
I said, what*
I said about Elena Hebrayova . . . I don't like Elena Hebrayova but what*
I said about her, I didn't really mean . . . Usually, I control myself, I keep myself in check. But with you, I'm not in control. I think I'm in control then suddenly, it takes me, like an attack of epilepsy. I don't know what*
I want from you . . . Please, accept my apologies.

Well, thank you.

And this too.

No, that's too much . . .

It's just a knife . . . I wish I could offer you a real one but here, even needles are considered weapons. The rules. So I drew it. Almost a painting. Don't you think?

It's very well done.

All week, I more or less sharpened it. For you.

Thank you.

I did it while thinking about you.

Thank you.

Every day . . .

Thank you very much.

Did you think about me?

You're forgiven.

Every day I thought about you.

You're forgiven.

Every night.

You're forgiven.

Every hour.

You're forgiven.

Every minute.

You're forgiven.

All the time I thought about you.

You're forgiven.

Did you think about me?

You're forgiven.

Did you think about me?

You're forgiven.

You're here but already, I miss you.

I thought about you.

Then take me in your arms . . . Please.

I can't . . . I'm not allowed . . . The rules . . .

Please . . . Nobody will know . . . Thank you . . . thank you . . . thank you . . .

Don't cry . . . Or rather yes, cry . . . cry.

You really forgive me for everything that*
I did to you? You didn't even complain to Mother Superior. The first time that*
someone's taken me in their arms . . . It's very soft here, your skin, behind your ear . . . I love your smell. I want to tell you about myself. Ask me some questions. I want to tell you about myself but first ask me some questions. Where I'm from. My age. My parents. My friends . . . How I ended up here . . . Please . . . I'd like to tell you about myself, to open up to you. But maybe you don't feel like it? . . . Don't want to? . . . Hear about me?

Of course, I do . . . Your life . . .

Call me Linda. My mother used to call me Linda . . .

No, that's not possible. The rules . . .

Nobody will know that*
you've called me by my first name.

I never call the participants by their first name. It's a principle.

Me. Call me by my first name. Please. Me.

Well . . . Linda . . . Your father?

Did you think about me?

I thought about you.

Often?

Often.

Often and often and often?

As often as possible. I think about you very often. Your father?

Don't talk about him.

Then your mother?

I like your perfume . . . Who do you wear it for?

Please!

I'm sorry . . . I shouldn't stick my nose in other people's business . . . Do you hear? The cello . . . do you hear it? In room 911? . . . It's her again, that*
girl, the girl who, on the day you arrived, when you secretly looked at me—

I don't remember secretly looking at you.

—was desperately trying to play *Misterioso*. She's practicing scales. I recognize her bow. Hesitant. Disjointed even. Falsely troubled.

Have you ever felt like killing one of the other participants because of—

Killing? . . . Killing them? Never. I hate them . . . I despise them. They have nothing but Diet Coke in their heads. Spend their time talking about boys . . . And he took me like this . . . And he took me like that . . . And me, we were on the train and we did it during the whole trip, in the bathroom . . . And me, on his butcher's block—he's a butcher, my man—in a pool of blood, he split me and split me and split me like a watermelon . . . And me, mine, as smooth as a shark . . . Words, wind, nothing real. It's all in the Diet Coke that*

serves as their brains . . . They're showing off as if they were somewhere other than here . . . As if they were watching their lives on the screen of a movie theater . . . As if the rainbow hadn't shut them out . . . They're showing off. Pretending that*

they're somebody . . . I despise them all. And we can only kill what*

we love. Even if they stared at me or showered me with the most vicious insults, I wouldn't kill them. I despise them too much . . . What*

did they do to deserve being here? I'm not inside because I was caught selling a few grams of hash! To end up here I didn't just steal a lipstick, or solicit men for a guy who would have promised all the love in the world, or commit I don't know what*

girly crime . . .

I've killed!

I've killed!

I've killed! . . .

I'll end up liking what*

that girl is playing in room 911 . . . Your skin here really is soft and smooth . . . Right behind your ear . . . Soft and smooth . . . I like your perfume . . . and I love your smell . . .

You're hurting me . . . I said You're hurting me! . . . Are you out of your mind? You bit me . . .

I forgot myself . . . I'm sorry . . . I let myself go . . . But we can only kill what*

we love . . . I forgot myself . . . You hate me, don't you? Because . . . because of my nerves. I don't control them. I don't keep them in check. Because of what*

I said . . . last Thursday . . . about Elena Hebrayova . . . You hate me otherwise you would have bit me back . . . I saw a man in the middle of a pack of wolves the other day. He was dancing with the wolves. Real wolves. Not a movie. On TV. A documentary. The man was calling them by name and rolling around in the grass with them. Then at one point, one of the wolves forgot himself, let himself go and he bit the man. The man immediately bit him back, not to remind him who the master is, who the man is, who rules over the world, but to raise himself to the level of the beast's love. Because that's* all it was, love . . . But you, you don't understand, you can't see it . . . you— . . . There's a language, I don't remember, maybe it's Yoruba, maybe Baoulé, maybe Xhosa . . . I don't remember. The verb to eat is exactly the same as to make love. I eat. I eat you. You eat. You eat me. You eat me. You eat me. We eat. We eat each other. I eat you. You eat me. We eat each other. To make love. To eat. Eat me. Eat me. Eat me. We eat the person that*

we love . . . But you, you can't see it . . . One day, the cameras won't be there anymore and the wolves will eat the man. The man knows it. He expects it. But you, you don't see it . . . you don't see anything . . . Next week, don't come back. Don't ever come back.

Go back to your place, the other girls are coming.

IX. THE DIRTIER THE BETTER

I used to work in a kindergarten. I love kids. I've always loved kids

Do you think she has her hammer with her

So tell me

It's private

To feel lonely is to crave someone to love

And you let him do that to you

A man to love

Receptionist

I still think they're too big

A man who lets me love him

I like socializing, talking to people

Hair on a man's chest, I find that

Do you have your hammer with you

My mother took care of her

Breasts like cow udders

This country, I tell myself—how do I put this—I tell myself it's too late, more than twenty years it's too late, you'll always live outside of this country

Do you have your hammer with you

In any case, when it comes to love
the dirtier the better
the dirtier the better
the dirtier the better

I like that he teases my flesh

Oh, come on

Do you have your hammer with you

A time when diseases appear out of nowhere, diseases with no rhyme or reason

Was it at your place or his

Why do I have to prove myself every time

Or gas station attendant

Mine, my man, he's as smooth as a shark

Will you tell me

Can I touch your hammer again

I keep telling you it's private

Just to caress it

I wonder who planted that thing in me

I love his caresses

I don't even weigh myself anymore

In New York, the buildings' hair floats among the stars

At least, gas station attendant, it's original

Distance. She should have kept her distance

The first time I saw him, I got goose bumps

Again. Linda, once again

She's calling her by her first name

The market square is empty. . . . It's raining. A light rain. A man tries to start his motorcycle parked by the fountain. A child—she looks like Little Red Riding Hood, how we imagine her—and a woman cross the market square. The woman holds the child by the hand. . . . The man kicks the tires of his motorcycle. The woman and the child stand in front of the door of the community center. The T36 bus—

Ms.— . . .

Linda, do you hear

She called her Linda

. . .—if she keeps saying the text the way she does, I don't see what we're doing here

She called her Linda

I'm dreaming, she's calling her by her first name

If Mother Superior finds out

Ms., it's true! If she doesn't want to say it

She called her Linda

Because I care about this show

Linda, do you hear? Once again

I can't believe it, she's calling her by her first name

The market square is empty. . . . It's raining. A light rain. A man tries to start his motorcycle parked by the fountain. A child—she looks like Little Red Riding Hood, how we imagine her—and a woman cross the market square. The woman holds the child by the hand—

It's too fast. Don't rush. Do it again but this time, keep the rhythm

The market square is empty. . . . It's raining. A light rain. A man tries to start his motorcycle parked by the fountain. A child—she looks like Little Red Riding Hood, how we imagine her—

Linda, don't comment. Just give the information, don't try to comment on it

Stop calling me by my first name! Who gave you the right to be so familiar? Who gave you permission to say my name? I've opened my Bible to you, I've given you a drawing, I've let you hold me in your arms, I've caressed you with my index and middle finger, caressed that*

spot so soft right behind your ear! So what? I'm not your girlfriend and I have no intention of becoming your girlfriend! So stop calling me Linda!

X. VISIT

Here, inside. Before Jesus Christ. Or right after, with the Romans. But what's certain is that there was an arena here, on the Plateau de Beaumont, which wasn't called Plateau de Beaumont yet but Pré des Loubatous. *Loubatous*, name given, at the time, to the inhabitants of the region, that means: Those who hunt wolves. Those who beat up wolves. *Loubatous*. Wolf beaters. Gladiators killed each other here. Executions too. Until 1870. Already? What about the abbey built at the end of the 12th century over the ruins of the arena, where, among others, Isabelle d'Angoulême and Jean Sans Terre, brother of Richard Coeur de Lion of the Plantagenets dynasty, stayed? Until 1870. What about the Château de la Vilaine, built over what was left of the abbey in the 17th century by James Scott, Duke of Monmouth, head of the Protestants and illegitimate son of Charles Stuart II? . . . Isn't there anyone here who can silence that cello? . . . We'll have to talk to Mother Superior . . . Silence it, at least for a while . . . Anyway it's from here, from this castle, on the Plateau de Beaumont, formerly Pré des Loubatous, name given, at the time, to the inhabitants of the region, that means— . . . that James Scott drew the plans for his failed rebellion against James II, failure which, predictably, caused his execution in 1685. Until 1870. Not yet. At the beginning of the 18th century, the castle was taken over by the Church and used to perform exorcism ceremonies. In reality, they were performing abortions on . . .

Young nuns who'd fallen prey to the temptations of evil.

Young nuns who'd fallen prey to the temptations of evil.

Young nuns who'd fallen prey to the temptations of evil.

In 1792, during the first Reign of Terror, the Church was evicted from the castle of James Scott, Duke of Monmouth. Torture and executions were performed in the castle until the fall of Robespierre. It was razed to the ground in 1794, a few days after Robespierre's execution. When do we get to 1870? Now.

Ah!

Ah!

Ah!

Yes, it's in 1870, over the ruins of the Château de la Vilaine, more precisely on the Plateau de Beaumont, formerly Pré des Loubatous, name given, at the time, to— . . . that the Parisian architect Alfred Normand built this complex. The building, located between the railroad and the street Pont de l'Alma, street that the city—if we can believe people in the know—is about to rebaptize, in the next few weeks, boulevard Général de Gaulle because the recent discovery of the alleged homosexuality of Marshal Pierre Jean Bosquet who, as everyone knows, contributed, on September 20th, 1854, on the shores of the Alma, to the victory of the Anglo-French troupes over those of the Russian Alexander Sergheïevitch Menchikov, has tarnished the name Alma forever, and because furthermore— . . . Argh, that girl is really pissing me off with her cello! . . . If at least she could play it well! . . . Mother Superior cannot not hear this! . . . The building, of hexagonal shape and neoclassic style, with walls made of white Charente stone—also called shell stone—adorned with oculus windows and carved *voussoirs*, eventually became a convent for young girls of good families.

A few dates:

1968: The complex burns down during the events of May '68.

1969-1977: Renovation and restoration of the building.

Beginning of 1978: Nomination to the National Register of Historic Places.

End of 1978: The Marine Corps moves in.

1999: The Marine Corps moves out. The building becomes what it is today.

And I am,

And I am,

And I am,

Inside.

XI. LET HER DIE

Let her die if you've decided she must die.

Let her die.

Let her die.

Let her die.

But hurry up! And spare us your prissy manners! Your moods! Your qualms! Does it burn your tongue to recite Elena Hebrayova? Who do you think you are to refuse to recite Elena Hebrayova? Who do you think you are to be above being called by your first name? Does it prick your eyes to be called Linda? Does it rip your flesh to be called Linda? Does it turn you into a leper to be called Linda? . . . If only I was the one with a hammer . . . Because in the end, it's irritating. Annoying. Stressful. At first, it was kind of—how do I put this . . . You think It's weird what that girl is playing. But you get used to it. After a while, you get used to it. But now, it's just garbage. At first, you think It's cool. She wants to be cool. She's trying to be cool. Except, it's not even music anymore. The way she makes her cello squeal. I'd say meow. Me, her cello, I think she makes it squeal. Maybe, but for me, it meows. Me, I'd say—how do I put this. Indecent. I'd say Indecent. That's it, that's what it is, that's what I'd say too: Indecent . . . You keep harassing this poor woman. You call her names. You turn all her efforts to ashes. You tell everyone that you're going to kill her . . . You say she's a cow. You say she's a pig. You say she's fat. But have you looked at yourself? You act like you're so smart, so clever, so tough but have you looked at yourself? Don't you wonder why you're not a part of the Golden Girls? Look at you, look at me, look at us. You're disgusting. You're repulsive. You're ugly. That's why you're not a part of the Golden Girls. Look at us, look at me, look at you. So stop sabotaging our show. Because I've invested a lot in it, and I continue to invest, day after day. Because I want to know, I want to finally know if we're capable of anything other than to make a body disappear . . . Because even if I don't understand, even if we don't understand, we feel she's trying to say something, to tell a story. So we follow her. Without knowing where exactly. But we follow her. We trust her. Up to a certain point, we trust her. And we follow her because we think She's searching. And it'll happen. Sooner or later, we'll recognize a passage. Hook up to a melody. Identify a few notes. But no, nothing. It's not the kind of . . . thing you can listen to in the background. And absorb. Or forget. You have to pay attention to it. You must pay attention to it. That's how it is . . . My father, my mother, my brothers, my sisters, my girlfriends, my boyfriend, everybody knows, and everybody is coming to see me . . . I want to impress my boyfriend, I want to blow him away. Because in case you didn't know, I have a boyfriend. In case you didn't know, I have a boyfriend. Me, I have a boyfriend. And I feel like getting out of my head. So everything here is worth grabbing. Everything is worth grabbing here if only to remind ourselves that we're alive, or better, that we're free. Here, everything is worth a dream. A dream where a boy waits for you, alone, in the cold, on the platform of a train station. A dream where a boy lowers his eyes and trips over words because he's about to tell you I love you. A dream where a boy undresses you in a deserted church, and splits you open in order to spill the incandescence of his desire inside you while whispering I love you in all the languages in the world. A dream where, in the blood of a butcher's block, a butcher splits you like a watermelon. A dream so good it hurts where a boy cries because you're so beautiful . . . The more she plays, the more she erases her steps like she's trying to prevent us from remembering where she was. It's not music anymore. It's bullshit. It's noise . . . She's fucking with our heads. She's trying to be cool. For weeks, she's made this cello squeal. Meow. Squeal. Meow. Squeal. Whatever but in the end it's irritating. Annoying. Stressful. If only I was the one with a hammer . . . And Mother Superior doesn't say anything! . . . Obviously, these are not things you can understand. You think To think that way they must be really dumb. Grass-chomping asses, you think. Well, fuck you! And watch out. I'm not like that woman. She's from good stock. Well bred. Well mannered. So civilized she'd offer the other cheek. Let you spit in her face. But me, I'm a bitch, a real fucking bitch. So stop pissing on my pride. Stop farting in my joy. Stop spreading your shit on the wings of my dream. Stop! Or else, I'll pop your teeth . . . You understand? . . . I'll pop your teeth, one by one, with a hammer. Or else, I'll destroy you body and soul and you'll come out of this shower feet first. Or else, I'll rip out your stinking pussy with my own teeth. So get rid of her once and for all and stop playing cat and mouse with our dreams. Let her die if— . . . Who's the whore who keeps playing this music that's like quicksand?

XII. 911

I know I can't ask you to forgive me again, that*
would be too much . . .

Good morning.

Oh yes, good morning . . .

Here, this is for you. Please don't think that I feel obligated because of the Bible and the knife—well the drawing . . . everything you gave me. It's a gift, that's all.

Is it gold?

Plated. Only plated. I wish I could offer you a paper cutter, not a drawing, a real one . . . Because . . . Well, in the end, I chose a nail file. It's discreet. You can go in and out, back and forth, without arousing suspicions . . . When I came in earlier, the metal detectors went off. I was searched, I was body-searched, my bag was searched but nobody said anything, maybe they didn't even see it . . . A nail file is not very noticeable. Especially in a woman's purse. Yet it's a weapon, in a way it's a weapon. I first thought of a paper cutter, or even a small knife, because of what happened in New York but the rules . . . I thought you might need it . . . I know you'll need it . . .

I'm confused . . . I don't know what to say . . .

Then don't say anything. I had the idea after what happened in New York, on TV. My God.

The planes? God . . . I know . . . I saw them. At first, for a long time, I thought that*
it was just another one of those stupid movies that*
they show on TV. I flipped the channel but it was the same image. I flipped again but again the same image.
I flipped,
I flipped,
I flipped . . .
but everywhere the same image. A silent, mesmerizing image. A plane dives into a building like into a gigantic house of cards. Then the second plane appears and sets the other building on fire. I think There's something wrong. Why are all the channels showing the same stupidity? Because I can't imagine that*
it's really happened . . . Those two planes penetrating the two towers . . . . then coming back, always the same two planes, again and again, penetrating the two twins . . . Again and again
and coming back and penetrating . . .
and penetrating and coming back . . .

and coming back and penetrating . . .
and penetrating and coming back . . .
and coming back and penetrating . . .
and penetrating and coming back . . .
and coming back and penetrating . . .
and penetrating,
and penetrating,
and penetrating,
until . . .
I feel it rise from the depths of my flesh and spread through me like an explosion, from the roots of my hair to the tip of my toes, an incredible orgasm, while before my eyes that*
still can't believe it, the twins' bodies, exhausted by so much pleasure, melt in the sacrificial blood, among the trumpets' piercing cries and the requiem of our wailing. And
I thought,
I thought,
I thought
What*
has America done to deserve so much love? What*
has America done to deserve to be the Host through which humanity will exorcize the new millennium . . . Because that's*
what it is, love . . . Always love. A love so powerful that*
it even drowned the sacrificers . . . Dust drank their blood. Dust reverted back to dust. The holocaust was accepted. The millennium, exorcised. So may God bless America . . .

America wants to bite back . . . wants to love back . . .

How could America bite back the world when she's herself made of the world's flesh?

Who did you kill?

To protect the daughter from the mother. He used to tell me— . . . In those moments, he used to tell me . . . To protect you. I'm doing this to protect you. From your mother. That's*
what fathers are for, to protect daughters from their mothers. That's*
what he used to tell me in those moments . . . You know, your colleague, it wasn't me. She's one of the Golden Girls but I won't tell you which

one . . . She'd served her sentence and didn't want to go outside. All of us here, we're afraid of one day, having to go outside. So she came up with that, to push that*

woman from the seventh floor in order to prolong her sentence . . . My mother. I couldn't stand how she let my father treat her. Her docility. Her genuflections. I couldn't stand what*

she let my father do to me . . . She should have left him.

I would have killed my father.

I couldn't kill him because I didn't love him . . . He didn't protect me enough from my mother . . . In a way, he didn't protect me enough from her . . . Because he was right, that's*

what fathers are for, what*

fathers should be for: To protect daughters from their mothers. Unfortunately, I've expiated my crime. I'll soon have to face the outside. And I don't like it. I feel better here. I don't want to go out. I don't like their freedom. I don't like this straitjacket that*

they put on life. That*

they put on everything. I can't imagine being among them without having a terrifying desire to throw a bomb at the whole thing. Yet I don't love them. Nothing about them really offends me. Nothing about them really moves me. Nothing about them stirs a dream in me. But the idea of throwing a bomb in there to once again feed from the very roots of the dream . . . A bomb to flatten everything and re-create the dream . . . Don't you want to know what happened to the other two, the ones whose bodies were never found? . . .

XIII. SHE'S BAD

Maybe I knew but didn't want to accept

Go ahead, tell me

To exit me! Not to be born, to exit

My mother wants me to go back to school

She's bad

In America, dreams are bigger than anywhere else

Come on, tell me

He wanted me to get an operation

Do you have your hammer with you

I had a childhood to die for. Parents to die for

Caresses and I

I can't stand that girl, I really can't stand her

Will you tell me

Can I touch it too? I'm the only one who hasn't touched it yet

It's private

Because in a way she invaded my body. I could have hated her, detested her

Going to school is a waste of time

Maybe I didn't do everything I could have done to feel like one of them

She boarded me like a secret passenger

With small breasts, you can create the illusion that they're normal, but with breasts that are too big, you're automatically a trucker's whore

Maybe I didn't take the necessary steps to—how do I put this—reduce the gap between them and me

A man to love. A man who lets me love him

Now they also take girls in the army

They're mean

Will you tell me

It's private

You've slept together at least

Your mother is right: You should go back to school

I love kids. I used to work in a kindergarten. I've always loved kids

God, it was about time

God, what took you so long

God, I was starting to wonder

At first, I didn't want to be a pom-pom girl

Going to school takes too long and it makes you stupid

He said Your breasts are warm and sweaty like cow udders

Hair on a man's chest, I must admit that for me

He's the one who said You have no energy and you don't smile enough, you should learn to be a pom-pom girl

Where

At your place or his

When

This morning. On the train

During the trip

I like socializing, talking to people

As smooth as a shark

Diseases with no rhyme or reason

Yesterday, my mother brought me this bra. With lace. Special

I wonder who planted that thing in me

It makes me feel like the first time I touched a man's dick

Plus with that, you can crush a life in less time than it takes to say it

That's what she said, a man's dick

That girl, I can't stand her, she's bad
That girl, I can't stand her, she's bad
That girl, I can't stand her, she's bad

The first time his lips touched my nipples, I fainted

It's almost impossible to get lost in New York

That's what I'm saying, to caress is to tease the flesh

Avenues are straight and wide in New York. And streets too

Come on, tell me

Like cow udders

Back to your places. Once again

. . . Bank employees are rats. If they give me a fine, I'll fill their heads with lead. Calm down. You'll do nothing at all. . . . Mrs. Keller, Mr. Coulanges and the policeman cross the market square. The market square is empty. The market twice a week, that wouldn't be bad. T36 stops. No one is waiting for T36. A glass of water and the bill. T36 leaves. Tap water. No one got off T36. It's strange after all this coffee I still don't feel awake. I must have an overdraft. T36. From the opposite direction. Bank employees are swindlers. Mr. Coulanges comes out of the community center. Alone. Mr. Coulanges crosses the market square. T36 leaves. Mr. Coulanges runs. Crosses the street. Passes the café. Worry on his face. Disappears. Another coffee, please. Tomorrow will be a great day for picking mushrooms. The market square is empty. . . . It's raining. A light rain.

XIV. MOM

Distance. She should have kept her distance. As long as she kept her distance . . . My mother took care of her . . . I didn't hate her. I didn't detest her. Or anything. I just never expected her. I wasn't expecting her. Didn't expect her. I never felt her inside me. From the beginning until she came out— . . . showed up, I never felt her. I didn't realize. Never knew. So when you've never expected someone. When you've never imagined someone. When you've never learned, in your mind, to love someone. Because that too has to be learned, it doesn't just fall from the sky . . . To love has to be learned too . . . Can't that girl play anything other than this piece? It's like a chant luring death to our door. Like she doesn't know anything else. But it's beautiful. You could say it's beautiful. I think it's beautiful . . . Yet from what they say, it takes up a lot of room. Day after day, it grows and stretches in all directions, like mangroves, like weeds, and it dances inside your belly. I saw it, not on me but I saw my little brother dance inside my mother—mean little steps against the drum of her belly . . . I wonder who planted that thing in me. At the hospital, it didn't surprise them. It's more and more common, the doctor said . . . She had such eyes, that woman! Sunny blue eyes framed by short, black hair. Like the hair of an Indian. She smiled at me convinced that what was happening was the most beautiful thing in the world . . . But at home, all around me, everybody was surprised. Not that it had happened but that no one had noticed during all those months. Maybe I knew but didn't want to accept. Maybe everyone knew without knowing. So they wouldn't have to ask awkward questions: Since when? How? Where? With whom? Especially With whom? So they wouldn't make me uncomfortable. Wouldn't upset me. My mother took care of her. I couldn't convince myself that it was a part of me, that— . . . How does he say it, the man who comes from time to time to rummage through my brain like a tramp through garbage? . . . The flesh of your flesh . . . That's it, the flesh of my flesh. In fact, what was happening was much simpler than what the man rummaging through my brain was looking for . . . How do I put this? . . . I love kids. I used to work in a kindergarten. I've always loved kids. But in this case—that's what I said to the judge—there was no kid, there was more or less nothing. Nothing. I never gave birth to this kid. One day, I felt something in my belly. I got scared. I thought it was a cancer or a strange disease . . . Aren't we at a time when diseases appear out of nowhere, diseases with no rhyme or reason? I told no one, I went to the hospital. Alone. Because—that's what I was saying—I knew without knowing. And I didn't want any witness the moment I wouldn't be able to pretend not to know anymore. The woman with the sunny blue eyes and the hair of an Indian told me the one thing I knew she'd tell me. So I said Then get it out! They tried everything but it didn't want to exit . . . or I didn't want it to be born from me. To exit! Not to be born, to exit. In the end, they had to cut my stomach, from here to here, to extricate it. The woman with the hair of an Indian who was smiling with her blue eyes convinced that what was happening was the most beautiful thing in the world said It's a girl! I immediately closed my eyes. She was screaming and I hoped—that's the first time what the prosecutor, the jurors and the journalists called The Atrocity danced in my heart. She was screaming and I hoped it was because the nurses were strangling her. Not out of hatred or anything. I just never expected her. I never felt her dance inside me. Never expected her. Never suspected she was there. Never imagined her. Never expected her. Never learned to love her. Because that too has to be learned. To love has to be learned too . . . I could have hated her, detested her because in a way, she invaded my body. In a way, she boarded me like a secret passenger. In a way, she raped me. So I should have hated her, but no. My mother didn't make a fuss, she took care of her. Until the first babbling, until The Atrocity . . . That's it, a chant luring death to our door . . . She's getting better. I feel she's getting better. Her bow is rounder, silkier, richer. I like it. I like it more and more . . . I never hated her or detested her. But when she blurted out her first word, Mom, her arms extended, open like the world's first smile, with a kind of meek gratitude in her eyes . . . After I had done everything to— . . . It was to her, to my mother she should have said that, Mom, not to me! I'd never taken part in their sentimental number! I'd never had anything to do with her! So like that, all of a sudden, Mom. NO! Distance. She should have kept her distance. As long as she kept her distance . . . MOM. No. No. No . . . When my mother came back from the bathroom, she looked for her, in silence. First in the baby carriage. Then around the baby carriage. Then under the baby carriage. Then in the entire room. With her eyes. In silence. Then she turned towards me, her eyes suddenly inquisitive, but still without a word. Also without a word, I turned my head and, with my eyes, indicated the microwave . . . She tried to scream but her throat tightened up at the sight of what the prosecutor, the jurors and the journalists called The Atrocity. Then she vomited her scream, she vomited. She vomited. She vomited her horror at the microwave. Then she fainted and collapsed in her own vomit . . . I didn't hate her but. As long as she kept her distance . . . She's getting better. Or at least, her cello handles Thelonious Monk better and better. Beautiful . . . A beauty that resonates more in the ears than in the guts. But it's beautiful. In its own way, it's beautiful . . . Otherwise, Mother Superior would have said something . . . "You're nothing but"—that's the prosecutor all choked up with outrage— "You're nothing but a cold-blooded monster and a perverse liar! . . . How do you expect a newborn of less than a month to stand up in her carriage, climb out, walk towards you and call you Mom?" . . . Less than a month. Yet I saw her climb out of the carriage and walk towards me. I heard her say Mom with a smile, her arms extended towards me . . . Climb out of the carriage. Walk. Extend her arms. Say Mom. This fucking word, Goddamn, nobody will ever erase it from my eyes, I saw it fly out of her mouth. Nobody can erase that from my head . . . "But it's her right—" . . . that's the prosecutor again screaming at the top of his lungs. "Even if by some strange miracle, she'd stood up in her carriage, walked towards you with her arms open with love and called you Mom . . . it's her most absolute right to call you Mom since she is the blessed fruit of thy womb!" . . . The blessed fruit of my womb. But who planted it there, that blessed fruit? During the entire trial, I felt as if it wasn't about me . . . As if they were addressing someone else. The attorney they had assigned me was in despair. She kept repeating:

My God, a child of less than a month in a microwave . . .

My God, a child of less than a month in a microwave . . .

My God, a child of less than a month in a microwave . . .

She kept repeating that instead of telling the judge and the prosecutor and the jurors the truth: I was innocent. I hadn't done anything . . .

I'm innocent . . .

I'm innocent . . .

I'm innocent . . .

Who is that girl who keeps using her bow like a matador defying death? . . . Distance. I never wished for her. I never wanted her. I never desired her. Nothing. Except this nothing raped me. So she should have kept her distance. As long as she kept her distance . . .

XV. JUST LIKE THAT, ON THE TRAIN

So are you killing her or not

Will you tell me

Pom-pom girls have a lot of energy and they smile all the time, he used to tell me

Just like that, on the train

She boarded me like a secret passenger

When did you meet

The blessed fruit of thy womb

This morning. In the train station

Hair on a man's chest, with only the tip of the nipples showing, I find that

The worst is to have no sense of humor

I like talking to people, exchanging ideas

He thinks they're too big

And once on the train

The way he teases my flesh

Real men like big breasts
Real men like big breasts
Real men like big breasts

In America, girls are twenty-five, they're blonde and they have blue eyes

I love my breasts licked to death by his skin as smooth as a shark

My mother took care of her

Because he loves watching pom-pom girls

Yes and right away, on the train

Gas station attendant, that's not bad

Receptionist

Have you made your decision

Is she ever going to use her hammer

In a way, she invaded my body

Even without the hammer, this girl scares me

But I can't be a pom-pom girl all my life

But not a stripper

He was right, I'm going to get an operation. I feel like a cow

He's fast

I'm fast

Feel them, they're enormous and flabby

Except with me

In New York, I'd already feel like an American

But he wants me to keep being a pom-pom girl

Like cow udders

No . . . I don't think so

The first time he collapsed inside me, I finally believed in death

So are you killing her or what?

XVI. FORGIVE ME

I'm here to give you back the look you didn't dare to give me. The day we passed each other.

We passed each other?

We passed each other in the hall that leads from the refectory to room 911.

And I looked at you?

One day.

I don't remember.

The day you arrived.

I don't remember.

The day you arrived.

I don't remember.

The day you arrived.

I don't remember.

You remember.

I don't remember.

That*
day was filled with what*
that girl kept playing. *Misterioso*. Constantly playing.

I can't remember. What happened on that day, the day I arrived, when you say we passed each other in the hall that stretches like a hyphen between the refectory and room 911, it was only that, the cello, that I remember, that only, the cello, hesitant but determined and fierce, trying to make *Misterioso* fly. I remember only that.

You looked at me as if I were a woman.

I looked at you, me, as if I were a man?

No, as if I were a woman.

How long have you been standing there?

One two three minutes that*
I've been here. One two three minutes that*
I've been standing here, motionless, like eyes in the dark watching the obscenity that is theater. One two three minutes that*
I've been looking at you. From head to toe while your breath— . . . While your eyes were hiding behind a veil of soap, I looked at you. I took the time to examine every inch of this flesh for which you looked at me as if I were a woman.

Today I'm going back outside, for good. I don't want to talk about that look anymore. I'm exhausted. I won't come back and I want to be done with this. That's why I waited for you . . . I always come here after the other girls. I prefer it. I feel calmer. I know no one will come. After the frenzy of the rehearsals, I need this moment. To relax. Breathe. Relax. And also, it's nice to be the one whose responsibility it is to leave the ship last. But today I lingered, a little, under the water, a little on purpose. For you. To give you time to decide. Time to make a decision. Since you're after me. Since you're spreading the word to make sure your love reaches my ears. Since earlier, you kissed me in front of the others. I waited for you in the shower to see just how far your love will go . . . Do you have the nail file?

I have the nail file.

Take the soap. Take the sponge . . . Today I rubbed and rubbed and rubbed. Lazily. I'm not washing myself. Only dead bodies can be washed. Today I'm not washing myself . . . I'm making myself clean. Because I guess for that too, we must be clean . . . Don't wash me, don't tease my flesh, don't make my flesh moan, don't caress me, make me clean . . .

Your throat, from here to here, is as intoxicating as the scent of rain over red earth.

It's the soap . . . only the soap . . . No, don't let your tongue run along my flesh . . . Don't tease my flesh . . . Please, remove your teeth from my breast . . . Remove your fingers, I beg you . . .

The tips of your breasts are fragrant like jasmine that's*
been trampled
and trampled
and trampled
and trampled . . .

It's the soap . . . only the soap . . . Have you always known?

It's in your eyes that*
I saw it . . . That*
I saw myself.

And that's why you're killing me . . .

For that too. Because I'm afraid of going outside. And you, you're afraid that*
today might be your last day inside. Because you want me to. You asked me. You gave me a nail file. A nail file. Because I must convince myself that*
what I saw in your eyes, the day you arrived, the day the girl was trying to trap Thelonious Monk in a cello, that*
this flame that*
I saw burning in your eyes was for me. For all that. Also because of Elena Hebrayova. But mostly because we only kill what*
we love . . .

Remove your teeth from my breast . . . Here, on my neck, this spot that you find so soft, look, there's a vein . . . You're hesitating. Your hand is shaking. You see, it's not easy to love with this kind of love. If I loved you with the kind of love you claim to love me with, I would have already planted the nail file in the supplication of this vein, here on my neck, here, on this spot that you find so soft . . . Pick up the nail file and try again. Here, where my blood is calling, on this spot that you find so soft . . .

Forgive me . . .
Forgive me . . .

Forgive me . . .

In my locker, it's not locked, you'll find your Bible. Take it back. It's my turn to offer it to you. Because you'll need it.

Forgive me . . .
Forgive me . . .
Forgive me . . .

At least, look me in the eye. For the first and last time. Let me see how dark your love is. Let me at least see your eyes.

XVII. EUCHARIST

Here. The heart

Hurry up

In New York, avenues are wide, straight and endless

Now is not the time, let's clean up

Streets too

Let's clean up before Mother Superior gets involved

Will you tell me now

To feel lonely is to crave someone to love

Let's divide it up

It compresses the sides and lifts the breasts

A man to love

Private. It's private

The heart should be yours

So

I said It's private

A man who lets me love him

I love his caresses

I didn't think she'd do it

Are you going to see each other again

I didn't think she'd do it

They'll never be like yours but it shows them nicely

I didn't think she'd do it

You have to admit, that text by Elena Hebrayova was desperately boring

I like socializing, talking to people, exchanging ideas

To exit! Not to be born, to exit

I left him yesterday. He'd shaved his head, his beard, his chest, his whole body down to his crotch

Enough to put you off everything, that Elena Hebrayova

In front of the other passengers

I didn't think he'd be willing

Who didn't get her share

In the bathroom

She's just showing off

Maybe I knew but didn't want to accept

Was he good

Oh no, that's way too private

Who didn't get her share

Your bra, I'd be very surprised if my breasts fit in it

Who didn't get her share

I've always loved kids

Because there's still the head

More than twenty years that I was born in this country

In the crematorium

Like the others

Distance. She should have kept her distance

Come on, tell us, was he good

It's not a crematorium

I even screamed

She's just showing off

You're jealous

Who didn't get her share

Your breasts are warm and sweaty like cow udders

The head

I'm totally hooked

She's just showing off

She's the worst of all of us

Where is he in the audience

Sometimes, I think a bit of hair here and there would add a zest of wildness to his body as smooth as a shark

Girls, let's clean up

I love caresses because the rest is boring

There's a kind of bra that makes breasts look smaller

To kill is to turn off the light inside us

Breasts just like that
Breasts just like that
Breasts just like that

Over there

That's what my father likes to say

I tried it once, it didn't work

He's not much to look at

I could have hated her, detested her because

All it did was give me bruises all over my breasts

The head

But the dirtier the better
But the dirtier the better
But the dirtier the better

The head

Yes, the head

With the guts

People often tell me For someone with big breasts, you have very delicate nipples. Look

Let's throw it away with the guts in the same place as the others

Come to think of it, leave me the head, I have a hammer

It's true that you have incredibly delicate nipples

In America, girls are twenty-five and they're blonde with sin sparkling behind the blue innocence of their eyes

But that doesn't make me feel better

In the crematorium

The head, the chin, the chest . . . without any hair, he looked terminally ill

It's not a crematorium

A time when diseases appear out of nowhere, diseases with no rhyme or reason

Here, the heart is yours

I'll eat everything except the heart

Then in the crematorium with the guts

No. In my room. I want to keep it alive in my room

Are you out of your mind

She's out of her mind

You're completely insane

In three days, I'm supposed to be outside

Oh, yes, it's true

Oh, I see

Oh, I understand

You don't understand. None of you understands. You can't understand . . . The first time that*
she laid eyes on me, I peed my pants

Elsewhere, in America, after more than twenty years, I—how do I put this—I'd feel at home. American. Fully American. But here

So

Private, it's private

I'm like everybody, I need a little love, that's all, it's no more complicated than that

I've always loved kids. I used to work in a kindergarten. I love kids

Why do I have to prove myself every time

Does anyone know the girl who keeps playing this heart-wrenching music
Does anyone know the girl who keeps playing this heart-wrenching music
Does anyone know the girl who keeps playing this heart-wrenching music?

END OF PLAY

Jean-Pierre Olinger (The Man) and Romaine Cochet (The Woman) in *Blue-S-Cat*, directed by Jean-Pierre Olinger at the Théâtre Astrée of Villeurbanne, France, 2011. Photo by Julie Romeuf.

Blue-S-Cat

2005

TRANSLATED BY CHANTAL BILODEAU

INTRODUCTION TO BLUE-S-CAT

He who sits in the heavens laughs,
the Lord scoffs at them.
—Psalm 2:4

An uncomfortably comic pendant to *Misterioso-911*, *Blue-S-Cat* is as much about bodies as about voices. The voices rattle around, but the bodies communicate the anguish of nonmovement. A Man and a Woman, stuck in an elevator, each in his or her own bubble, misprize, misinterpret, and misbehave. (Is that a knife in his pocket or maybe something worse? What is it that she seems to be craving?) Thoughts collide and stumble, blend and separate. Language lies and sets up false expectations. The audience, too, gets caught up in this game of mistaken assumptions. The Woman is, it turns out, hysterical and craving a cigarette. The Man is distracted and replaying in his head the scene with the tax collector, remembering his wife Mélidésha's injunction to be tough. The Woman projects her mad desire for a cigarette as the Man's desire for her. He wonders finally if she is trying to communicate. He is inhabited by the banal and the bureaucratic and she by a fixed notion of man as savage hunter. Neither can see beyond their personal boundaries.

Louis Armstrong's "What a Wonderful World," which begins the play, floating the elevator upward until it freezes in place, commences again halfway through. With this musical reintroduction blossoms their joint hope of escape from the claustrophobic tension that keeps the Man and the Woman in their spaces, tension being the only thing they share in the elevator. They participate, at least in fantasy, in a blissful dance number, conjuring Fred Astaire and Ginger Rogers and the electricity of a fully engaged presence. We see how solidarity might be possible. But during a second wordless conversation, one gaffe sends their momentary harmony into chaos. Nothing moves further, except the Woman's increasing paranoia. The Man at last decides to try to speak with her. The feared but expected final misunderstanding finds her annihilating him with her high-heeled shoes, as he offers her surrealistically, and too late, a rose. What kind of wonderful world is this?

Notes for reading and production:

1. Louis Armstrong was a pioneering cornet and trumpet player and a foundational influence in American jazz. He was famously skilled in scat singing, a type of vocalizing using sounds and syllables instead of lyrics. "What a Wonderful World" (by Bob Thiele and George Weiss), first recorded by Armstrong in 1968, optimistically extols a future of ever more intelligent babies and blue skies. The song has frequently been used ironically.

SETTING

An elevator.

CHARACTERS

A MAN
A WOMAN

Ascent.

She's elegant.

He's elegant.

Ascent of the woman and the man to "What a Wonderful World" by Louis Armstrong (the sweetest version).

They both seem happy. Or at least untroubled.

They sway to the music, imperceptibly.

Each in their own little world.

Ascent.

They seem, although their bodies are relatively close, not to notice/not to care about the other's presence.

Each one is in his/her own bubble, happy. With their eyes half-closed, they perform, in unison but without being aware of it, the same tiny dance moves.

Subtle ballet of weightless bodies. Imperceptibly in sync with one another. Happy.

Ascent.

But soon the music coughs, cracks, becomes slurred, whiny, tearful—as if all its springs had lost their zing—and dies prematurely.

The man stops dancing and opens his eyes.

Her eyes half-closed, the woman doesn't seem to notice anything and keeps "floating" . . .

Until the elevator stops.

At last, the woman opens her eyes and stops dancing.

* * *

The woman, barely breathing, listens for a sound, a voice, a sign. Nothing.

WOMAN: Is someone there?

Silence.

She runs around in circles like a trapped mouse.

It's not happening again?
It's not happening again?
It's not happening again?

Suddenly, perhaps out of rage, perhaps out of frustration, she bangs her head against the wall of the elevator . . .

* * *

The man doesn't react, doesn't move in the slightest, as if the scene of the woman banging her head against the wall of the elevator wasn't happening.

* * *

WOMAN: Brute. He's a brute. Someone else would have said Stop you might hurt yourself. You're going to hurt yourself. You're hurting yourself. For Heaven's sake stop. The kind of words you say in a situation like this. They may not seem like much these little words these tiny gestures these little nothings but they soothe. Someone else would have worried would have pulled out his handkerchief. Are you hurt? Let me see? Let me help you, Miss. But this man here remains unflappable hands in his pockets both hands deep in his pockets. I won't fall for it others might but I won't.

She feverishly opens her purse.

She starts to take something out then hesitates.

She looks at the man, observes him.

The man looks at her, neutral.

A beat.

She quietly withdraws her hand without taking anything out of the purse.

She closes it slowly, her eyes intent on the man.

Brute.

* * *

MAN: It was right there.
We refused to see it.
Refused to feel it.
Refused to hear it.
We looked away,
we stuck our heads in the sand,
we shut our eyes,
we pinched our noses,
we covered our ears,
we looked away from it.
We acted as if.
But,
when it keeps aligning itself
with your line of vision,
with the direction of the wind,
when it keeps howling in your ears,
you realize that.

You become aware that.
You accept.
It hits you just like that,
like a tile.
From the roof.
From the sky.
From.
And you finally understand that
your life is as insignificant as
most lives.
As all lives.
A simple recognition.
One day you accept.
Without surrendering.
You flex your muscles,
you clench your teeth and,
with a Buddha's smile in your heart,
you throw yourself into the fray
for 37% instead of 20%.
Mélidésha says
It's worth it.
Mélidésha says
No way we're going to let people walk all over us.
Mélidésha says
We need to have conviction.
Mélidésha says
It's essential.
Mélidésha says
Out of the question to give up anything.
We can't let others
take us for.
No.
We can't crawl at people's.
No.
Under the pretext that.
No.
We can't lay down and die because.
No.
We can't.

We can't.
We can't.
We must refuse to be lambs,
Mélidésha says.
Clench our teeth,
clench our eyes shut,
clench our butts.
Not give up anything.
We'll never be forgiven for creating dissension in the ranks.
So act as if.
So clench.
It's amazing how good it feels!
To clench everything.
Body and soul.
Clench.
At peace.
At peace because we know,
—a calm, serene knowing—
the ridiculousness of it all.
To realize that,
without parentheses,
without quotes,
without ellipses,
without margins,
without before or after,
to realize that,
like that,
makes one serene.
At peace because
from now on we know that.
That much we know.
Only, as
Mélidésha says,
we can't let people walk all over.
Because 37% is not 20%.

* * *

WOMAN: And this craving that won't leave me alone! Resist. Hold back. Until everything gets back to normal. Resign myself. I have no other choice.

A beat.

He's going to whip it out. Short and thick. No. Long and slender. Curved. Slightly. Like a crescent moon. He's going to whip it out. Answer his smile?

A beat.

She smiles.

He's playing shy. He's lowering his eyes. My breasts. On my breasts. His eyes on my breasts. He's lowering his eyes on my breasts. It's always the same thing the sensation that I'm nothing but these breasts when people look at them that they take on the weight of my whole body. That they swell. The more he looks at them the more they swell with this slimy God knows what that's oozing from his eyes. He's looking at them. Go ahead don't be shy let your eyes roam free rummage in my cleavage. Go ahead what's stopping you? Grab them with your eyes grab them with your eyes feel them with your eyes squeeze them. Are they to your taste? Are they as big as tender as juicy as you like? Or would you rather feel small buds tits as firm as a rock under your anxious tongue?

A beat.

She checks that her clothes are not too this or that.

She presses a button.

She crosses her arms on her chest.

Nervous. He's averting his eyes. He's averting his eyes from my breasts. A little nervous huh?

* * *

He smiles again.

She doesn't return his smile.

His smile disappears.

A beat.

MAN: It's appalling
the dishonesty sometimes!
The blow to one's pride when
forced to recognize that
one has made a mistake.
It would mean that
he doesn't do his job well.
Not well enough.
Not sufficiently well enough at least.
No matter what proofs we shove under their noses.

She presses the button.

He smiles.

She doesn't.

He doesn't smile anymore.

He examines his fingernails.

Almost.
A smidgen.
And I was there.
I could have.
All I had to do.
Extend a finger.
Just like that.
And.
Because
my first time
seeing one.
From up close, I mean.

A beat.

Actually I had never seen any.
From up close or from afar.
As far as I can.
My first time seeing one.
I've always thought
They don't exist.
I've always thought

Only in movies.
I've always thought
A big machine.
Sort of like a nuclear plant.
A big computer.
A small computer.
They make very small ones these days
that can hold tons and tons.
Anyway, a computer.
That swallows all the forms.
When it spits them back out,
after multiplying, adding, subtracting and dividing
all possible and inconceivable numbers,
you know, to the decimal, the exact amount that
you owe the State.
And that's magical.
At least I find it magical.

A beat.

Obviously someone has to cram them in.
They don't arrive there by themselves.
A hand has to do it.
Has to put in the forms.
Even if it's the computer in the end.
Otherwise it wouldn't be magical.
It wouldn't be magical otherwise.
Someone necessarily has to decide.
I mean according to what.

A beat.

Until this morning.

A beat.

Mélidésha was right.
I had to go.
I had to get myself there.
I had to find out who was breathing behind the machine.
Because

behind the machines there were indeed men.
Again Mélidésha was right.
There were machines.
Yes there were plenty of computers.
But there were most of all men.
They're always the ones who decide.
In the end always they're the ones who decide.
What
you owe the State.
To the decimal.
Always the ones who decide.

A beat.

I won't answer her smile.
73% of people who continue to smile
without a reason, without a response,
are fundamentally stupid.
Statistics don't mince words.
Twice she's rejected my smile.
Well then on her own.

* * *

WOMAN: There he goes again acting like his pigheaded self like he hasn't seen anything doesn't see anything doesn't even notice that I'm here close to him pore to pore my chest almost bare. Because you couldn't stop rummaging in my bra with your eyes because I crossed my arms over my breasts so swollen with sins they were ready to burst?

She uncrosses her arms.

He smiles.

She smiles again.

Ah you're smiling again. I prefer when you don't smile when you act like a grumpy kid. Look at him! There he is leaning against the wall both hands in his pockets smiling. At peace. He's telling me I'm at peace. I have nothing to feel guilty about. I have both hands in my pockets I'm leaning against the wall at peace. And I'm smiling. I'm at peace so be at peace too. He's trying to numb me. He's letting me stew in the juices of my anxiety. He's waiting for me to first wet myself and then . . . It makes the flesh more tender. That's what they say. I saw it on TV a documentary the guy took the fish by the head a carp still alive I saw it dipped it in boiling oil and laid it on the plate among sculpted carrots and zucchinis I saw it. The head was still alive. The eye was bright and clear and the gills red with life but the rest of the carp was cooked fried apparently crispy. A man pulled the plate to him. He methodically skinned the fish with the bright and clear eye and the gills that were still breathing. Stress that's what they say makes the flesh more tender. So like everyone else you let me fry in my fear first.

* * *

MAN: People are so perverse!
Wait until I tell Mélidésha.
If I hadn't insisted.
With them you always have to insist.
The only way they understand
is when you get all up in their faces.
But even then, even with insistence.
No matter how much I shoved the forms under his nose,
practically crammed the numbers into his eye sockets,
he remained unfazed.
No, no and no.
He was right and
I didn't know a hawk from a handsaw.

A beat.

A handsaw from a hawk.
A hawk from a handsaw.
A handsaw from a hawk.
Hawks from handsaws.
Handsaws from hawks.

A beat.

Why do we say that?
Why wouldn't we know a handsaw from a hawk?
Unless vice versa.
It means absolutely nothing.

A hawk from a handsaw.
Amazing what people come up with!
Why wouldn't we know handsaws from hawks?
It's stupid.
But people say that like it's true.
I should discuss it with Mélidésha.

A beat.

She's pretty.
She might have been beautiful.
OK, she is beautiful.
Women are more beautiful.
It's undeniable, these days
women are more beautiful.
The numbers.
All the studies agree.
Women are more beautiful.
Cosmetics have a lot to do with it.
More refined, more sophisticated.
Any woman today can be beautiful.
Can appear to be beautiful.
It's been proven beyond doubt.
The numbers are stubborn.

A beat.

Why did I think
She's not beautiful?
Her smile.
She doesn't have a nice smile.
Forced.
It's obvious that
she's forcing herself to smile.
To break the ice.
Because
she's scared.
It's only natural that
she be scared.
To be here, in this situation, with a man.

Because
if I were.
I could.
I don't know how Mélidésha would take it if.
As jealous as she is.

* * *

WOMAN: Ask him to grant me that. No hold back instead. Resist the tyranny of the craving. I have no other choice. He'll say no.

A beat.

He's going to whip it out. He keeps it hidden at the bottom of his pocket. Maybe he doesn't have a pocket. A false pocket.

She presses the button.

She opens her purse.

She rummages through her purse.

She checks the content of her purse.

She takes a pack of cigarettes out of her purse.

She hesitates then puts the cigarettes back in her purse.

She closes her purse.

I'm fine. I'm fine. I'll be fine. I prefer natural elevators with a wire-mesh gate that opens like a folding fan natural because mechanical because manual. The old ones. The ancient models. The antiques. The ones you see in black and white movies. The ones they display in museums to hopefully stop the passage of time. Because in those you can see hear feel what's happening outside. When they break down it's less stressful you can see what's happening outside and the air never runs out. You're almost outside. It's just a matter of being patient. Of waiting for the emergency team. You can even scream. They hear you. But with these modern electronic elevators that open at the sound of your voice drop you in front of your place based on your scent go up and down at the mere formulation of the thought you can scream bawl as much as you want. Nothing. They do exactly as they please. If on top of all that you're with unsavory characters.

A beat.

So I prefer antique models well prefer in a way. Because really when you live on the 73rd floor you have no choice it's like flying you just have to.

A beat.

He's holding it against his thigh. A false pocket for sure. Pressed all along his thigh. Long with a flat head like the ones sugar cane cutters have in Cuba. Or the West Indies.

A beat.

Since he insists let's smile at least when we smile.

* * *

Silence.

"What a Wonderful World" rises, the voice of Louis Armstrong, sweet.

At first, the intrusion of the music seems to worry them.

They no longer smile.

A beat.

They smile again, knowingly.

* * *

WOMAN: It's about time. The craving was becoming unbearable.
MAN: Finally the end of the tunnel.
WOMAN: It's a sign.
MAN: It's a strong sign.
I'm sure that
Mélidésha is waiting.
Worried sick.
WOMAN: A way of telling us
MAN: We didn't forget about you.
WOMAN: We're doing all we can
MAN: to get you out of there.
WOMAN: Hang on!
MAN: Hold on!
WOMAN: Hold on tight!
MAN: It's only a question of.
WOMAN: Even seconds.
MAN: Everything goes so fast these days.

WOMAN: These days everything goes so fast.
MAN: There is so much progress these days.
WOMAN: These days all the progress there is.
MAN: Our firemen are among the best.
WOMAN: Our firemen are the best in the world.
MAN: Or at least
WOMAN: their rescue techniques
MAN: are.
WOMAN: The entire world recognizes it.
MAN: The numbers. All the reports prove it.
WOMAN: The entire world envies us.
MAN: They've saved people
from situations far more perilous than
being stuck in an elevator.
WOMAN: Thousands of lives have been rescued from impossible flames
MAN: as journalists of all persuasions
WOMAN: say
MAN: report
WOMAN: write
MAN: it's a real sight
WOMAN: our firemen in action.
MAN: We would like to see them more often in action.
WOMAN: A lot more often.
MAN: But hey.
WOMAN: You don't always get what you want.
MAN: Secretly want.
WOMAN: Maybe the entire building is here.
MAN: The entire building might be here.
WOMAN: All the tenants.
MAN: Even tenants from adjacent buildings.
WOMAN: The entire neighborhood maybe.
MAN: All the nearby neighborhoods.
WOMAN: The city.
MAN: To be part of a news item.
WOMAN: Of current developments.
MAN: Of the show.
WOMAN: Even if it's not as beautiful as a fire.
MAN: It's true that a fire is something else.
WOMAN: It's far more gratifying.

MAN: They would have talked about it on the news.
WOMAN: No doubt the journalists would have talked about it.
MAN: They certainly would have interviewed us.
WOMAN: Our pictures.
MAN: Our stories.
WOMAN: Everywhere
MAN: in the papers.
WOMAN: Maybe even in a film.
MAN: Who knows?
WOMAN: Everything gets turned into films these days.
MAN: These days everything ends up in films.
WOMAN: It's true
MAN: that a fire
WOMAN: is far more
MAN: gratifying.
WOMAN: What about a tsunami?
MAN: A tsunami? Well!
WOMAN: Variety shows.
MAN: Talk shows.
WOMAN: The radio.
MAN: Newspaper columns.
WOMAN: A bestseller.
MAN: In a word—fame.
WOMAN: I didn't dare say it.
MAN: Because
it's not something you say out loud.
WOMAN: Exactly.
MAN: Out of.
WOMAN: That's the word.
MAN: But hey.

* * *

They suddenly go quiet while "What a Wonderful World" swells . . .

Their bodies, seized by the music, start to move.

The elevator, apparently under the music's pressure, explodes. The walls fly up or disappear into the wings.

The light becomes magical, as in a Hollywood musical.

Their bodies are not just moving, they're dancing over the entire length of the stage.

It's a light and fluid dance. A sweet dance.

Separate at first, in their own worlds as they have been since the beginning, their bodies, carried by the music, move closer, merge, become one . . .

Hands crawl, lips search for other lips.

They grab one another, embrace, break apart, catch one another again.

We're transported into the world of Hollywood musicals. With all its clichés.

But the choreography must avoid falling into caricature. There should be no judgment or comment on the musical. Even if the actors are not dancers, they should perform a minimal choreography that never looks clumsy. We must believe it.

After the music has died out and the dance come to an end, the woman and the man go back to their initial places in the elevator—now in one piece again—as if the "musical" had never happened.

MAN: A 37% tax abatement that's something.
The dishonesty sometimes!
To try to make me swallow that,
in my situation,
a 20% tax abatement would be preferable while
he knows perfectly well, yes perfectly well,
the thief, that
with 37%, or
even 30%, or even
25%, we're not talking about the same thing anymore.
Ooooooooooooh no,
we're not talking about the same thing at all.
I'm in a different bracket, I don't owe any.
Or so little. Insignificant. A trifle.
And if I don't owe any.
That really irritates him. That
I not owe any in the end.

Or so little.
But it's not like the money is going into his pocket.
The scum!
That money is not his, it's the State's.
And what belongs to the State belongs to everyone,
starting with me.
He's neither the father nor the mother of the State,
he's just an obscure tax collector.

A beat.

Unless they're paid on commission?
No other explanation.
I would understand.
The wife and kids to feed. It makes sense.
But it's not my pocket he's going to pick.
Wait until I tell Mélidésha!
I had to
shove the form under his nose, to
explain everything to him in painstaking detail, to
basically do his work for him,
the work for which we fatten him.
With our money.
Yet he remained obtuse and as stiff as a board.
The nerve sometimes!
It was clear as day that
he had lied.
Hidden the truth, lied.
But he was determined
to pull a fast one on me,
to double-cross me,
to shaft me.
Out of principle.
Out of professional habit.
Out of perversion.
Because
these people are naturally perverse.
That's basically how
you recognize them.

But when it comes to money
I too am capable
of spontaneous violence.
That 37%,
I'm not stealing it,
I have a right to it,
it's the law,
period.

* * *

WOMAN: Craving. It had to hit me now I'm craving it. For once not listen to myself. For once get a grip. I have no other choice.

A beat.

I have no idea who he is I've never seen him. In the elevator or the hall. Or the parking lot. Anywhere. And I never take the stairs. No one ever takes those stairs. In fact why are there stairs if no one ever takes them? It's not like they make the place look nice. Stairs are always ugly. Since no one takes them. Then why have stairs at all? We saw it in New York. Because even in the event of a fire or something like what happened in New York we saw it it's always faster to go down in the elevator and if by chance the elevator is broken because it does happen sometimes the elevator sulks people would rather jump out the windows than take the stairs. We saw it in New York. People chose to jump out the windows. At least you can gather up the body. The ripped scattered strewn apart pieces of flesh you put them side by side and it makes a body. You recover a body. Even a head even an arm even a toe that makes a body. Mourning can take place. Because those who stayed in the buildings in New York those who had no other choice but to stay well they were vaporized. Vaporized. Vaporized. No body to honor. And then it's impossible to mourn. You pretend to save face but it's not mourning. And it's then in the absence of the body that the real tragedy begins.

A beat.

Make a move as light as a butterfly's wing. As nothing as a blink. Just try to take your hands out of your pockets. Try. And I'll rip your throat. And it's not an image and it's not literature. Literally I'll rip your throat. With my bare teeth I'll rip your throat. I'll hit you right there with my knee and sink my teeth into your throat. And it's not an image and it's not literature. I'll clamp my teeth around your throat until your blood howls your allegiance in my mouth and then I'll break your skull with my stilettos. So a piece of advice keep smiling keep being a gentleman a well-bred man a civilized man hands deep in your pockets. Don't let your little urges dominate you. Don't let them set your groin on fire.

A beat.

I'm craving it like crazy. But he won't agree. He'll say no with a smile. He'll hide behind You can't do that in a public space. It's not the place. The time certainly but not the place. That's what he'll smile to me. And it's his right. Anyway I refuse to ask you for anything. Don't expect me to crawl at your feet and beg like a dog. No. Oooooooooooh no I won't give you the pleasure of saying No to me.

* * *

MAN: It's strange.
I've never seen her here.
In the elevator,
or the halls.

A beat.

I could be wrong.
I may be wrong.
Maybe I'm.
Probably.
I'm.
I'm way off track.
I'm.
I'm missing the mark.
I'm.
I'm barking up the wrong tree, the wrong forest,
and even, let's not be stingy,
the wrong ecosystem.
Altogether.
Mélidésha always tells me
You're a lamb and
lambs don't know a thing about women.

But something tells me that.
She's teasing me.
Something tells me that.
She's enticing me.
Something tells me that.
She's tempting me.
Finds me to her liking.
Finds me something.
A sort of.
Finds me a sort of something to her liking and is tempting me.
But I could be wrong.
I could be way off track.
Be missing the mark.
Not know a handsaw from.
Unless it's a hawk.
It's possible.

* * *

WOMAN: Not kid myself the thing is to not kid myself especially not.

* * *

The woman turns to the man. She tells him a story with gestures.

What it is not: pantomime or sign language. She's simply talking without words, with awkward gestures, like a Cassavetes film.

The man becomes animated too, answers with more gestures just as awkward. That's it, he recognizes the story. He's heard it before. On TV or on the radio. Unless he read it in a newspaper somewhere. Or simply heard someone tell it. But it's clear that it's the same story. He even points out a detail, apparently significant, of the story.

The woman, without questioning that detail, rectifies it. It may be about the shape. Slender, not thin. Or the size. 5'5, not 5'4.

The man remains convinced that it is in fact 5'4. He positions his hand at a certain height so the woman can visualize what he's saying.

The woman doesn't budge. She indicates with her hand a height slightly higher than the man's.

Etcetera.

Finally, without being convinced, the man accepts the woman's view.

They each, in turn, tell a part of the story. There's no doubt, they're talking about the same thing.

What are they talking about? It doesn't matter whether the audience knows or not. The main thing is that they're "talking," that they've found something to "say" to each other.

Suddenly, the man bursts out laughing. A frank and resounding laugh . . . that breaks the thread of the woman's silent story. Maybe because of what the woman is saying. Or because of her excessive gesturing, her somewhat exaggerated way of telling the story. Maybe.

The man falls silent as suddenly as he started laughing.

The woman looks at him, on the verge of apoplexy.

The man is visibly appalled by his own laughter. He stares at his shoes, contrite—one cannot do that, cannot laugh about that. One can laugh about anything but not that.

They "break apart" and return to their own respective bubbles.

* * *

MAN: It's true that
these things happen.
We don't think about it but
they do happen.

* * *

WOMAN: Because . . . because if he throws himself at me a knife at my throat and demands it . . . I can scream yell . . . But in the end . . . In the end. So plan prevent prevention.

* * *

MAN: Because if I were.
One of those.
One of the ones we.
One of the ones who.

They talk about it more and more
on the news,
all over the papers.
The radio.
People on the street.
In pubs.
Hair salons.
Public transports.
Theaters.
Movie theaters.
Markets.
Supermarkets.
Bakeries.
Flower shops.
At home.
Everywhere in fact.
The news.
TV films.
Documentaries.
Variety shows.
Reality shows.
On Sports Weekend.
Everywhere on TV in fact.
The news . . .
But it's not fiction.
The fact that it's on TV
doesn't mean that.
It's a lot more frequent than
we would like to admit.

* * *

WOMAN: So watch for the moment when he takes his hand out of his pocket . . . Because afterward it'll be too late.

* * *

MAN: And we don't even have all the numbers.
Because numbers.
81.23% of women have been.

Statistics are relentless.

A beat.

Who wouldn't be scared?
Because
she's scared.
It's obvious that
she's scared.
In her position I would be scared.
Who wouldn't be scared in her position?
Nothing is written on my forehead.
It's healthy that
she be scared.
It reassures me that
she's scared. It makes me feel better.
Because
in a way it normalizes the situation.
That she be scared.
In a way.
We hear so many things these days.
And we see so many.

A beat.

So it's up to me
to take the first step.
To do something to.
To try something.
To take fate in my own hands.

* * *

He smiles.

She smiles.

He takes his left hand out of his pocket.

Open palm. His hand is empty.

He starts to move, this time to take his right hand out of his pocket.

She immediately kicks him in the groin

and bites his throat.

Blood.

While he's groveling in pain

she removes one of her stilettos

and hits him in the head with a sudden rage.

Blood.

He falls to his knees.

Blood.

Silence.

Stillness.

The woman frantically opens her purse.

She takes out a cigarette.

She lights it.

She fills her lungs with smoke.

Soothed.

Silence.

The man is on his knees,

a dazed smile on his face,

his hand still in his pocket.

* * *

MAN: A 37% tax abatement!
When I tell Mélidésha she won't believe me.
When I tell Mélidésha she won't believe me.
When I tell Mélidésha she won't believe me.
When I tell Mélidésha she won't believe me.
That
I didn't let anyone walk all over me.

That
I fought every inch of the way.
That
I wasn't a lamb.
I wasn't a lamb.
I wasn't a lamb.
I wasn't a lamb.
Clear that
When I tell Mélidésha she won't believe me.
When I tell Mélidésha she won't believe me.
When I tell Mélidésha she won't believe me.
When I tell Mélidésha she won't believe me.
But luckily, numbers are what they are.
But luckily, numbers are stubborn.
But luckily, numbers don't have mood swings.
But luckily, numbers don't have moods.
37%, it's definitely something!

At last, the man takes his hand out of his pocket.

He opens his hand, for the audience, like one would take the oath.

His hand is empty.

The woman is devastated.

Suddenly, a rose sprouts in the man's open right hand.

The woman is devastated.

She takes the flower from the man's hand.

The woman is devastated.

She smells the flower.

The woman is devastated.

She paces in circles like a caged animal.

The man collapses.

Lifeless.

The woman freezes.

Devastated.

* * *

WOMAN: Someone?

She waits for an answer.

Someone's there?

She waits for an answer.

Is there someone there?

She waits for an answer.

There's someone there?

She waits for an answer.

Is there someone?

She waits for an answer.

Is someone there?

She waits for an answer.

Is someone there?

She waits for an answer.

Is someone there?

Silence.

Then, as the only answer, the voice of Louis Armstrong, "What a Wonderful World," rises while the woman, curled up in a corner of the elevator, finally breaks into sobs. Sobs soon drowned by the music.

Blackout.

END OF PLAY

Roch Amedet Banzouzi (Schmeckel) and Kader Lassina Touré (Corporal Bonkers) in *Brewery*, directed by Christophe Merle at the Théâtre de Cahors in Cahors, France, 2012. Photo by Patrick Béhin.

Brewery

2006

TRANSLATED BY JUDITH G. MILLER

INTRODUCTION TO BREWERY

Humor asks for yet one more thing from man: that he make fun of himself, so that once one idol has been overturned, unmasked, and exorcised, it won't be immediately replaced by another.
–Vladimir Jankélévitch

Where is your brother?
I don't know. Am I my brother's keeper?
–Genesis 4:9

Brewery skewers military greed, neocolonialism, and economic collusion between the wealthy North (Europe and America) and the hungry South (Africa, in this case). It also targets fantasies of living in a continuous performance mode with no real roots and no commitments. Kwahulé's satire means to make its audiences (African and non-African) laugh in order not to cry, guffaw in order not to kill, and chortle in order to live with themselves. A subversive response to marginalization and chaos, *Brewery*'s humor is adolescent, noisy, and jubilant. It is what makes the equally omnipresent violence (sometimes substituting for plot) bearable.

Kwahulé's farcical four-hander takes place in an unnamed African country at the end of a bloody civil war. The remaining and victorious militia, a clown duo, "Corporal Bonkers" and "Commandant Fuck Death," assault the last-standing institution, the Brewery, once a veritable fount of wealth for the government. Having conquered the factory workers, all of whom are represented by a single man, "Schmeckel" or "Little Prick," Corporal Bonkers and Commandant Fuck Death set about negotiating with the distillery's supervisor, the German cabaret performer "White Magic." The four partners plan to take over the government, make a fortune on beer, and eventually escape to Las Vegas.

Brewery offers a roller-coaster of parodic exchanges and portraits, with different rhetorical styles highlighting the hypocrisy and often pure idiocy of the universe created on stage. Commandant Fuck Death provides a sardonic pastiche of Martin Luther King's celebrated "I Have a Dream" speech. Bonkers talks "dirty" with the stamina of a fifteen year old. Schmeckel, whose name suggests the anxiety attendant upon a male figure who might not have the goods, meditates on the vagaries of sex in a raunchy catalogue of prick sizes. White Magic, an unapologetic figure of "white guilt," takes the offensive from her first entrance on stage and her tirade in German. Her only real passion is her cell phone, "MySweetie," which connects her to Europe's most famous cabaret, the Moulin Rouge. A globalized power field, both boss and star, White Magic binges on sex with Schmeckel as she might on cookies. Through his pitiless targeting of egomania, Kwahulé foregrounds neocolonial absurdity.

A German cantata, sung by children and introduced at the beginning of the play, comes into full force at its end. We could interpret this singing as an army of neocolonialists in the making. But these voices might also signal the possibility of renewal, a fermentation that will explode the Brewery and create other sites of desire and hope. Depending on production choices, the voices might weave a safety net around the characters' grotesque shenanigans or they might reveal a terrible sense of emptiness. It is possible, however, that Kwahulé wishes to keep both potential meanings alive in a kind of ebullient jazziness, buoying the audience as well as recalling the threat of continual corruption.

Notes for reading and for performance:

1. Known also as the Bavarian Josephine Baker, White Magic evokes a form of heightened minstrelsy. Baker, herself, a famous African American cabaret performer, seduced European audiences, particularly at the Moulin Rouge, in the first half of the twentieth century by giving them back the exotic image they projected on her.

2. Babylon in this play, as elsewhere in Kwahulé's work, represents a consumerist hell, a form of modern enslavement; he thus interprets negatively the meaning of the famous ancient city that can now be physically located in what is modern Iraq.

3. White Magic's song references most pointedly the Four Horsemen of the Apocalypse from the book of Revelation in the Bible and equates erotic love with destruction.

4. The English translations of the passages White Magic speaks or sings in German (passages signaled in the texts with superscript letters as below) are as follows:

a. It's always the same story. Incapable of doing anything on their own. What has White Magic done this time?

b. Hello Gianfranco? It's me . . . Josephine Baker . . . Yes, yes, Josephine Baker . . . Where am I? . . . You're not going to believe this, but I'm with Captain Fuck Death . . . No, no, the real Captain Fuck Death . . . That's the one. They also call him El Comandante. You know, the buddy of Corporal Bonkers. What? . . . Yes, but he's so stupid, it's depressing . . . On the other hand, Captain Fuck Death is a perfect gentleman . . . I don't know. *(To Captain Fuck Death.)* My agent, Gianfranco, would like to know if you already have somebody to represent you? . . . He says not . . . Why not? It's time! . . . What? Hello Gianfranco . . . I don't understand a word of his German. He has one of those accents! My impresario is Italian, Neapolitan, to be precise. No, I'm still here . . . Exactly, soon all the impresarios will try to grab him . . . Yes . . . yes . . . yes . . . What do you say to Gianfranco taking care of your business?

c. Hello Gianfranco. Captain Fuck Death is asking for time to think about it . . . No, no, not now . . . Because I don't have time . . . Listen I'm calling you for something else . . . Tell the Director of the Moulin Rouge that I won't be able to perform tomorrow . . . That's right, I can't be in the show tomorrow . . . No, no, I'm not being held against my will . . . Don't do that . . . Not that . . . No police . . . No press . . . Can I count on you? . . . I'm counting on you . . . Thanks for this . . . No, no, no ransom . . . I'm telling you I've not been kidnapped . . . This whole thing will be over by tomorrow . . . Exactly. I'll be back in Paris by tomorrow . . . OK here's a hug . . . Me too, I kiss you everywhere . . . Yes, everywhere, everywhere, everywhere . . . Till tomorrow . . .

d. Where are you, my dear Father?

e. The world will talk about it!

f. You big lazy prick!

g. No . . . no . . . no . . .
Where are you, dear Father?
Yes . . . yes . . . yes . . . no . . . no . . . no . . .
Where are you, dear Father!
Come save me, dear Father . . .

h. . . . For here I am again

Impaled on the delightful bite
Of his night sword . . .
Here I am again
A host
Posed on the peak of his furious sex . . .

i. Search
Search my sex
Search my body
Search beyond my body
Search beyond my sex
And kill me with your secret pleasures . . .

j. Where are you, my dear Father?
Come save me, my dear Father
For he's opening me
Opening me with his night sword
From head to toe
From right to left . . .

k. My body exhausted with sweet suffering
Is quartered on the altar of our devilry
Around me run
Four horses
Their nostrils streaming
All the fires of hell

Where are you, dear Father?
Come save me, dear Father
His night sword
Is still raised
Four horses carry me away, plunge and fill up my multiplied body
Racing in the winds
Of the East's pummeled pleasures
Of the South's forbidden charms
Of the West's abolished satisfactions
Of the North's impossible love.

Where are you, dear Father?
Come save me, dear Father.
For now from the altar
Where the horses with flaming nostrils
Have left

He laughs
His night sword pointed at the heavens
He laughs
He laughs
Drunk with the transgressions
He will make me taste again.
And he laughs
He laughs
He laughs . . .

SETTING

We are in an unnamed African country at the end of a Civil War.

CHARACTERS

CORPORAL BONKERS
CAPTAIN FUCK DEATH
WHITE MAGIC
SCHMECKEL

TIME

The time is now.

I. CANTATA

Dusk: Noise of clashing knives, machetes, pistols, machine guns, missiles, canons . . .

A battlefield . . .

Silence . . .

Captain Fuck Death, also known as "El Comandante," and Corporal Bonkers appear. They are covered in blood as though just emerging from a slaughterhouse.

Corporal Bonkers, seemingly gone crazy, waves his machete in the air and fires his machine gun, shooting wildly at nothing and everything.

CORPORAL BONKERS: This time we have to finish it . . . finish it . . . finish it . . . finish it off . . . end it all!

CAPTAIN FUCK DEATH *(managing to grab hold of Bonkers):* Take it easy! Take it easy! It's over . . . It's over . . . *(He strokes his head as a mother would a child who was having a nightmare.)* It's OK . . . It's OK . . .

CORPORAL BONKERS: It's over?

CAPTAIN FUCK DEATH: It's over. Easy now . . . Easy . . .

CORPORAL BONKERS: The war is over?

CAPTAIN FUCK DEATH: The war is over. We won the war. The war is finished. Nobody's left. Nobody.

CORPORAL BONKERS: Nobody's left?

CAPTAIN FUCK DEATH: Only silence, emptiness, and the night.

CORPORAL BONKERS: But just a minute ago . . .

CAPTAIN FUCK DEATH: Nobody.

CORPORAL BONKERS: But over there . . .

CAPTAIN FUCK DEATH: Nobody.

CORPORAL BONKERS: But I thought I saw, over there . . .

CAPTAIN FUCK DEATH: Nobody. Not there, not anywhere.

Captain Fuck Death shoots off a round with his repeating rifle, as though he were asking a series of rapid-fire questions . . . No answer.

You see? Nobody. We wiped them all out. We created silence and emptiness.

CORPORAL BONKERS: But there? . . . Even there?

Captain Fuck Death turns on his powerful searchlight and slowly surveys all of the space, finally turning the light on the audience.

You see, Comandante, they're still there . . . Don't you see? . . .

Bonkers lunges towards the audience, his machete raised.

CAPTAIN FUCK DEATH: That's enough, you big idiot! Can't you see there's nothing there? They're just shadows!

CORPORAL BONKERS: Shadows!

CAPTAIN FUCK DEATH: Just take a look!

Corporal Bonkers stares at the audience. He bends his head to the right and looks. He bends his head to the left and looks. He bends over and looks at them between his legs.

CORPORAL BONKERS: Yeah. It's just shadows . . . Always under our feet. Wherever we go, whatever we do, always under our feet.

CAPTAIN FUCK DEATH: That's what shadows are . . . So you might as well get used to it.

CORPORAL BONKERS: Whatever. But those fuckers really scared me . . .

CAPTAIN FUCK DEATH: Don't call them that. And pack up that machete!

CORPORAL BONKERS: You know I almost chopped them to bits, crushed their bones . . .

CAPTAIN FUCK DEATH: Pack that up, you big idiot! . . . I hope your brain hasn't cancelled the reason we're here?

CORPORAL BONKERS: Of course not, boss . . .

CAPTAIN FUCK DEATH: So prove it to me; I want to hear you recite your speech to the shadows.

CORPORAL BONKERS: We came here to take the brewery.

CAPTAIN FUCK DEATH: And so?

CORPORAL BONKERS: So we took the brewery . . . We've been fighting all the other militia groups for months in order to take that brewery. We fought the Fire-Breathing Rambos of the Great Northern Insurrection. We fought the Warrior-Gravediggers of the New Troupes of the Great Center. We fought the Revolutionary Red Ninjas from the Great South. We fought Marshal Sabotage's Crazy G.I.s from the Great Western Rebellion . . . We fought everybody in the jungle, because those gangs of syphilitic rats wanted to stop us from getting to the brewery. And we won. We cut off their ears with our machetes; we cut off their noses with our machetes; we cut out their tongues with our machetes. With the butts of our guns, we squashed their eyeballs in their sockets; we cut off their pricks and stuck them in their mouths . . . And each time, they threw themselves at our feet and begged us on their knees to finish them off. "We're not men anymore, we're not soldiers anymore, defeat has defiled us and turned us into bugs. For the love of your mothers, kill us!" And so we killed them. A real slaughter. The bravest of the lot blew themselves up with grenades . . . Look at those trees covered in scarlet . . . Look at those puddles of blood . . . Look at those pieces of flesh strewn around, hanging on branches . . . A real slaughter. And the stink of the rotting corpses . . . But that's war. That's always been war, war was never anything else but that. . . .

How did I do, boss?

CAPTAIN FUCK DEATH: Not bad, even if you seem to enjoy boasting about the violence and perversity . . . But I've heard worse. All the same, you forgot to tell them why we had to take the brewery, regardless of the cost.

CORPORAL BONKERS: Oh yeah . . . So here goes: it's not enough to win the war. You also have to win the peace. The State's coffers are empty. Even the banks' coffers are empty. The ex-President devoured all the money. Not a penny left in any coffer. So we have to fill them back up, because from now on we're the new masters of this country, because we kicked the hell out of all the others, cleaned out the lot. It's our turn now. And the only way to get fresh money, fresh and fast, is to sell beer. So we're going to reopen the factory to fill up the coffers, and once the coffers are filled up again, we're going to disappear to America with all the money, because it's our turn now . . .

CAPTAIN FUCK DEATH: You big idiot! . . . You never miss a chance to screw up . . . Don't listen to him! Corporal Bonkers is out of his mind, as usual. Everything we're doing, we're doing for the good of the children, all the little children of this country. And for democracy . . . You big idiot! . . . In any case, you managed to get the most important stuff across: empty coffers, need for new revenue to relaunch the economy, necessity of taking the brewery by force . . . Hey, there's a miracle! . . . Do you see what I see?

CORPORAL BONKERS: Boss!

CAPTAIN FUCK DEATH: What now?

CORPORAL BONKERS: Can't you hear it?

CAPTAIN FUCK DEATH: Hear what?

CORPORAL BONKERS: The Music! . . . la la la la la la la la . . . It sounds like children . . . It is children . . . In German . . . They're singing in German.

CAPTAIN FUCK DEATH: Shush . . .

He listens. And indeed we hear coming from far away, softly as if from a transistor radio in the middle of the night, children singing a cantata.

CORPORAL BONKERS: Children singing in German! . . .

CAPTAIN FUCK DEATH: I don't hear anything!

CORPORAL BONKERS: Listen more carefully, Comandante, children singing in the middle of the night! . . .

CAPTAIN FUCK DEATH: Nothing. Absolutely nothing. I hear nothing because there is nothing.

CORPORAL BONKERS: Come on, Comandante . . . children's voices . . .

The cantata grows louder. The sound takes over the space, forcing the men to speak louder and louder.

Do you hear it now?
CAPTAIN FUCK DEATH: No.
CORPORAL BONKERS: Listen better.
CAPTAIN FUCK DEATH: I don't hear anything.
CORPORAL BONKERS: What?
CAPTAIN FUCK DEATH: Nothing . . .
CORPORAL BONKERS: What?
CAPTAIN FUCK DEATH: What?
CORPORAL BONKERS: What?
CAPTAIN FUCK DEATH: What?

The cantata abruptly stops. Nevertheless . . .

CORPORAL BONKERS: What?
CAPTAIN FUCK DEATH: What?
CORPORAL BONKERS: What?
CAPTAIN FUCK DEATH: What?
CORPORAL BONKERS: What?
CAPTAIN FUCK DEATH: That's enough, Corporal Bonkers, there is nothing there! . . . Do you hear me? Nothing. No German child in the neighborhood. You're hallucinating, you're hearing things, and nothing else . . . Try to look for a change . . . Do you see what I see?
CORPORAL BONKERS: You'd have to be deaf not to see what you see, Comandante.
CAPTAIN FUCK DEATH: Not deaf, blind.
CORPORAL BONKERS: What?
CAPTAIN FUCK DEATH: You'd have to be blind . . . You said, "You'd have to be deaf . . ."
CORPORAL BONKERS: Did I say that?
CAPTAIN FUCK DEATH: I'm telling you, you did, you big baloney.
CORPORAL BONKERS: Well then: you'd have to be blind not to see what you see, boss.
CAPTAIN FUCK DEATH: And what am I seeing?
CORPORAL BONKERS: I don't know, boss.
CAPTAIN FUCK DEATH: What do you mean, you don't know?
CORPORAL BONKERS: When I said, "You'd have to be blind not to see what

you see," I was trying to make you happy, Comandante . . . But tell me, now that we've crushed everybody, where the hell is that brewery?

CAPTAIN FUCK DEATH: You really don't see anything?

CORPORAL BONKERS: I really don't see anything.

CAPTAIN FUCK DEATH: The brewery!

CORPORAL BONKERS: The brew . . . But where? I don't see anything . . .

CAPTAIN FUCK DEATH: Over there.

CORPORAL BONKERS: Over there. Where, there?

CAPTAIN FUCK DEATH: There . . . right there . . .

CORPORAL BONKERS: There?

CAPTAIN FUCK DEATH: Yes, there.

CORPORAL BONKERS: I don't see a thing there. It's too dark.

CAPTAIN FUCK DEATH: Right over there, right in front of your nose.

CORPORAL BONKERS: Well you're the one with the binoculars, Comandante . . . Let me take a look . . .

CAPTAIN FUCK DEATH: Stop messing around and turn your searchlight on!

CORPORAL BONKERS: Right, boss, I forgot about that.

He turns his light on and the two of them look straight ahead, mouths agape.

CAPTAIN FUCK DEATH: Is that beautiful or what?

CORPORAL BONKERS: It's . . . it's . . . it's. . . . all this time we've been . . . we've been . . . we've been looking . . . I ended up thinking that maybe . . . maybe . . . maybe . . . it didn't exist . . . maybe it was a dream . . . But that!

CAPTAIN FUCK DEATH: Is that beautiful or what?

CORPORAL BONKERS: Magnificent. One might even say . . . a cathedral in the middle of nowhere.

CAPTAIN FUCK DEATH: Is that beautiful or what?

CORPORAL BONKERS: Boss, do you see what I see?

CAPTAIN FUCK DEATH: If you're seeing something, I've already seen it.

CORPORAL BONKERS: Not a trace of missile damage . . .

CAPTAIN FUCK DEATH: Not even the suspicion of a grenade . . .

CORPORAL BONKERS: No impact from bullets . . .

CAPTAIN FUCK DEATH: Not the slightest machete chop . . .

CORPORAL BONKERS: Or the tiniest knife scratch . . .

CAPTAIN FUCK DEATH: None of this and none of that . . .

CORPORAL BONKERS: Nothing . . .

CAPTAIN FUCK DEATH: A brewery with untouched walls . . .

CORPORAL BONKERS: Perfect, as though the war never happened.

CAPTAIN FUCK DEATH: When I think about all those dirty battles and all those crazy fighters, it's a miracle!

CORPORAL BONKERS: I was just going to say that. Boss, why is it that during all those years of war no one fired on the brewery?

CAPTAIN FUCK DEATH: The mystery of war! Why . . . by what mystery, in every war, even the most barbarous . . . why is it that the world's worst criminals, wherever they come from, all agree without saying so to spare this or that? A secret of humanity. Somewhere I read, or heard, I don't remember any more, maybe I saw it on TV or maybe somebody told me, that during the civil war in Beirut everything was destroyed. All the buildings, all the walls came down; they were crushed, scattered, one by one, until there was only dust. But do you know that some walls never came down in Beirut, never showed the least trace of war, just like the brewery?

CORPORAL BONKERS: Was it the churches and the mosques?

CAPTAIN FUCK DEATH: The stones from the churches and the mosques were crushed and scattered.

CORPORAL BONKERS: The schools?

CAPTAIN FUCK DEATH: The stones from the schools were crushed and scattered.

CORPORAL BONKERS: The hospitals?

CAPTAIN FUCK DEATH: The stones from the hospitals were crushed and scattered.

CORPORAL BONKERS: McDonald's?

CAPTAIN FUCK DEATH: The stones from McDonald's were crushed and scattered.

CORPORAL BONKERS: Was it the theaters?

CAPTAIN FUCK DEATH: You've got to be kidding!

CORPORAL BONKERS: I give up.

CAPTAIN FUCK DEATH: The banks.

CORPORAL BONKERS: The banks? Why the banks?

CAPTAIN FUCK DEATH: The mystery of war, humanity's secret.

CORPORAL BONKERS: If you say so, but it still doesn't explain why the banks . . .

CAPTAIN FUCK DEATH: Your brain should do a little jogging, you big idiot!

CORPORAL BONKERS: I'm trying to think, Comandante, but I just don't get it.

CAPTAIN FUCK DEATH: Well now you'll never know, because you're just too stupid. Talk about casting pearls before swine. I wasn't born smart, but

I worked hard to get there. And I'm not going to waste what I had such a hard time learning on a moron like you. Puzzle it out. Go figure for yourself why only banks were spared during the war in Beirut. I'm not your father or your mother.

CORPORAL BONKERS: Oh yes you are . . . a little bit, anyway . . . You're my comandante . . .

CAPTAIN FUCK DEATH: But I'm not your father or your mother. Think about it; you're a big boy.

CORPORAL BONKERS: When I think too much, I get a headache . . . Right here, and I can feel it coming on . . . But I'll think about it, boss, I will . . .

CAPTAIN FUCK DEATH: Good. In the meantime, let's go see if the vats are as intact as the walls.

CORPORAL BONKERS: And especially if they're full of beer!

CAPTAIN FUCK DEATH: We've got to be careful. In principle, there should only be workers there, but some rebel elements might have snuck in, some sons of bitches who escaped the slaughter, some guys ripe for the hanging . . . Onwards, then: caution, courage, glory, and blood!

CORPORAL BONKERS: I'm ready, boss. Comandante, do you know what I'm thinking?

CAPTAIN FUCK DEATH: Yes. You're thinking that we're stepping into history, that pretty soon we'll be the first ones to have a taste of beer after the war.

CORPORAL BONKERS: You're right, boss! But how did you know?

CAPTAIN FUCK DEATH: That's a boss's secret. The mystery of the Comandante . . . OK, so here's how we approach the factory. *(He whispers something in Bonkers's ear. Bonkers is astonished.)* Now we're ready to face any kind of surprise attack. What do you say, Corporal Bonkers?

CORPORAL BONKERS: In moments like this, Captain Fuck Death, alias El Comandante, I know why you're the boss!

Blackout.

II. THE NEW BABYLON

In the brewery. A man is seated in the middle of the stage. It's Schmeckel. He's in very bad shape. He's obviously been tortured. He's tied up like a salami and attached to a chair. His feet are in a large plastic pan as though he's been given a footbath. But his face, even if covered in blood, is strangely illumined by a smile of intense mockery. Next to Schmeckel is Corporal Bonkers. He's wearing an apron and a surgeon's rubber gloves; they are spotted with blood. He looks like he's been through the ringer and seems exhausted. Not far from them, Captain Fuck Death is drawing on a blackboard something that resembles a cross between a mathematical formula and a sign of the Zodiac.

CORPORAL BONKERS: F . . . f . . . for . . . for . . . the . . . the . . . las . . . last . . . time . . . yo . . . yo . . . your . . . last . . . cha . . . cha . . . cha . . . chance . . . *(He takes a big breath, as if to control his stuttering).* Because if you don't HE'll take over and he's a champion at TORTURE. Latest methods, completely innovative. Studied them. Nobody's resisted yet. Everybody ends up spilling his guts. I'm an old-school kind of guy, but, still, look at the shape you're in! With my boss, you'll think what you've just experienced was a piece of cake. So here's some advice, because I like you. You look like a nice guy . . .

SCHMECKEL: Talk, talk, and more talk . . .

CORPORAL BONKERS: No, it's true, we have to face it, you look like a very nice guy, somebody I could confide in . . . Only you lie, and that's not very nice, because it's really not nice to lie to the representatives of the State. Because from now on, the State is us, since we're the ones who won the war. So no more lies, the other workers are unanimous . . . And stop smiling, it drives me crazy! . . . All your colleagues swore on the Bible that you're the only one who knows how to get the factory going again. So?

SCHMECKEL: It's true, I know which button to push to boot the brewery back into action, but I won't tell you which one it is.

CORPORAL BONKERS: Is that your last word?

SCHMECKEL: It's my last word.

CORPORAL BONKERS: You asked for it! *(He grabs a container.)* You know what this is?

SCHMECKEL: I'm not blind. Sulfuric acid: it says so right on the bottle.

CORPORAL BONKERS: If you don't fess up, I'm going to pour it on your feet . . . Are you going to tell or not?

Schmeckel doesn't answer. He only flashes his unchanging, sardonic smile. Corporal Bonkers empties the whole bottle of acid on his feet, still positioned in the wash basin. Silence. Corporal Bonkers waits for Schmeckel's reaction the way one watches a rat in a laboratory after an injection. But nothing happens. Schmeckel just keeps grinning, flashing his smile of superiority. Disgusted, Cor-

poral Bonkers tears off his gloves and throws them in Schmeckel's face. Then he walks over to Captain Fuck Death who is busy with his formula.

I can't take it . . . I can't take it . . . I can't take it! This guy is fucking with me! He's insolent! He's making an ass out of me. He's having fun. . . . I've tried everything . . . everything there is . . . I don't know what else to do . . .

CAPTAIN FUCK DEATH: Did you really try everything?

CORPORAL BONKERS: I told you, boss. I would've knocked him over the head with the phone book if I had one . . . But these imbeciles don't even have a phone book . . . So I hit him with everything else I had. I started with pinches, like this . . . and this . . . and this. . . .

CAPTAIN FUCK DEATH: Stop that, you big idiot. It hurts!

CORPORAL BONKERS: Sorry, boss . . . And then I pulled his hair, pulled his eyelids, pulled his ears . . . I even pulled his nose . . . Usually Comandante, when it gets to that stage, they crack. But not him. He kept on smiling. . . . He's even smiling now . . . Take a look at him, boss, he's smiling. So I slapped him some, like that . . . And boss, when it comes to a slap, you know I know how to slap . . . But he kept on smiling. That got me nerved up, so I threw a couple of punches in his face until my own hands hurt . . . until he started to piss blood all over me . . . Just look at him, he's covered in blood. He's bloody and he's still smiling!

CAPTAIN FUCK DEATH: What about the sulfuric acid?

CORPORAL BONKERS: Boss, I told you I put him through everything! Look at him: it's demoralizing. He has two feet floating in acid and he's still smiling . . . You'd think he couldn't feel a thing . . . If he were a broad, I'd say he was frigid . . . Just look at him! . . . And I smile, and I smile, and I smile. . . . That piece of shit has tied my nerves in a knot and there's only one thing I'd like to do: smash his head to see his brains trickle out all over the place. God damn mangy dog . . .

CAPTAIN FUCK DEATH: Get a hold of yourself, you big idiot. I'll take care of it.

Captain Fuck Death walks over to Schmeckel. He's very calm. He pulls out his pistol and places the barrel directly on Schmeckel's temple. He's still calm. He pulls the trigger, while smiling. We hear a "click."

Ah, well, no dice this time.

SCHMECKEL: Wasn't even afraid.

CAPTAIN FUCK DEATH: I know. I was watching you earlier . . . You're a brave guy, courageous, tenacious. Those are values our young people sorely lack . . . But we'll do something about it soon, very soon. You're the incarnation of this country . . .

SCHMECKEL: Talk, talk, and more talk . . .

CAPTAIN FUCK DEATH: I mean it. You're the living symbol of this place because, despite what it seems, you don't like yourself right now. What's the point of putting yourself through all this pain when in the end you're going to tell it all, admit everything . . .

SCHMECKEL: I'll never tell.

CAPTAIN FUCK DEATH: Yes you will, and soon. You're courageous, you can stand to have acid eating at your flesh, and you go on smiling like a martyr. All that—because you don't like yourself. Just like the people of this country who've thrown themselves heart and soul into a war that pits brother against brother, sister against sister, even though the gods have given them a country where nobody has to go hungry and where you only have to bend over to gather money, the same way you'd gather fruit from a wild orchard. And all this at a time when everywhere around us, among all the neighboring peoples, the devil is leading the parade . . .

SCHMECKEL: I don't understand a word of any of this, not one word of your bullshit . . .

CAPTAIN FUCK DEATH: This country was the original paradise. But it was a garden of Eden made up of people like you, and me, and him, and all the others—people who can't be satisfied by having enough money and enough food to go around. It's because of love that we began to kill each other. For love, and by love. It's because he didn't feel loved that the brother broke his brother's neck . . . We cut each others' throats in order to love ourselves and be loved. And here we are, unbelievably fulfilled. From now on we too have our wounds. We can show them to the rest of humanity who will love us because they'll pity us. We've become like all the others, we've joined the herd. Leaving behind our arrogant carefreeness, we finally woke up to the world. This country was the original paradise, but there's no love in Eden's heart; if there were, Eve wouldn't have taken a bite out of the apple. So we also brandished our machetes to force open the doors to the New Babylon. And here we are, and here we'll stay for eternity. I'll make sure we do; I swear it before the almighty jungle.

CORPORAL BONKERS: Wow, El Comandante can really speak when he wants to!

SCHMECKEL: What a lot of crap! Not even impressed.

CAPTAIN FUCK DEATH: Untie him!

CORPORAL BONKERS: But boss . . .

CAPTAIN FUCK DEATH: Untie him, it's an order! *(Bonkers unties Schmeckel.)* Wash his face and clean off his feet. *(Bonkers does so.)* You see, young man, to be loved you don't have to knock your head against the wall anymore . . . And by the way, what's your sign?

SCHMECKEL: What do you mean, my sign?

CAPTAIN FUCK DEATH: Of the Zodiac . . . Your horoscope . . . I'm a Scorpion, with Leo rising.

CORPORAL BONKERS: And I'm a Capricorn, with Pisces rising.

CAPTAIN FUCK DEATH: We don't care what you are. *(to Schmeckel)* So, what's your sign? . . . You won't say, huh? You're being coy . . . Well I'll just have to tell you: you're a Taurus, with Libra rising.

SCHMECKEL: You're right! . . . How did you know?

CORPORAL BONKERS: The mystery of bosses, the secret of El Comandante.

CAPTAIN FUCK DEATH: I've been watching you all this time. *(Showing the blackboard where he's drawn several odd forms.)* Look at this, it's you.

SCHMECKEL: That's me?

CAPTAIN FUCK DEATH: Yes, indeed, that's you but in a sectional rendering. See here: it's written Taurus, with Libra rising.

SCHMECKEL: Boy, I'm . . . I have to say I'm . . . It's really . . .

CORPORAL BONKERS: You have to admit El Comandante knows things.

CAPTAIN FUCK DEATH: It's a great sign, the promise of an incredible destiny . . .

SCHMECKEL: But I won't tell you how to reboot the factory . . . because we're not on the same side!

CORPORAL BONKERS: You see how unbelievable he is, boss! Should I tie him up again?

CAPTAIN FUCK DEATH: No, let it go . . . What side are you talking about? There aren't any more sides. We eliminated the foolish rhetoric of all the enemies, on the inside and on the outside. Now our country is clean and pure. Open your eyes, young man. The war is over. I pacified this country. There is no more North, South, East, West. No more Center. One country. Our country. Our homeland. Our territory. There's only silence and emptiness. For everybody. For each of us. All we have to do now is pull together in order to invent democracy . . .

SCHMECKEL: Talk, talk, and more talk . . .

CAPTAIN FUCK DEATH: Democracy! It's what we've been missing! A big fat democracy, well built, with breasts as big as this, and the kind of ass that would give a worn-out horse a hard on. That's what would've kept us from falling into this fratricidal shit. Don't our people have the right to taste the fruits of democracy! Putting the factory back in business, something I want with all my heart, will contribute to building a more homogeneous society. It will enable, substantially and immediately, the least favored among us, the weakest, the losers, the inconsequential, the have-nots, the little guys, to better their situation in life. I have a dream, a very lucid one, of a more brotherly society whose credo is individual initiative, work for everyone, a shared and heartfelt concern for each other, community between young and old, men and women, rich and poor. Yes, the lamb will watch over the pasture and the lion over the lamb. My ambition for our fatherland is a real network of solidarity that will support not just an economic system with a human face, but especially, and unquestionably, culture and the arts. I envisage a playful but vigorous synergy between tradition, modernity, and postmodernity to help construct a unique national identity that will continue to develop, without any kind of push back, thanks to constant dialogue and respect for the law . . .

CORPORAL BONKERS: Boy, El Comandante knows how to speak, when he wants to! You can tell he went to school . . .

SCHMECKEL: Are you sure what you're saying isn't just political bullshit? . . .

CAPTAIN FUCK DEATH: Only the truth, nothing but the truth . . .

SCHMECKEL: You're really pro-democracy?

CAPTAIN FUCK DEATH: On my honor! I swear it! I'm a democrat, a man of tolerance and peace.

SCHMECKEL: And you?

CORPORAL BONKERS: Me, too . . . a democrat just like him, tolerance and everything, just like him, for emotional and spiritual peace . . . the lamb and the lion . . . just like him, a democrat.

SCHMECKEL: Well, since you're both proponents of democracy, I'm going to tell you everything. To get the factory going again, all you have to do is punch button 6 in row 3, counting from right to left, while holding down button 9, counting from left to right, in row 5.

CORPORAL BONKERS: Let me do it . . .

CAPTAIN FUCK DEATH: Get out of the way, you big idiot! This inaugural and historic gesture should only fall to me, the Comandante.

Captain Fuck Death punches the buttons. And suddenly we hear the cantata we heard earlier. Schmeckel falls on the floor laughing. But Fuck Death and Bonkers don't move, listening to the cantata with great concentration.

CORPORAL BONKERS: Boss, the children! It's the children . . .

SCHMECKEL: *(Still overcome with laughter) "Mais c'est une blague! . . . Une blague! Une blague! . . ."*

CORPORAL BONKERS: Great! Now he's speaking French . . .

CAPTAIN FUCK DEATH: *(Concentrated; he seems close to ecstasy, eyes closed, like lovers of Mozart or Wagner or classical music in general . . .)* Be quiet! . . . I'm listening.

CORPORAL BONKERS: I knew I heard what I thought I heard . . . It really was a German song I heard that night . . . I wasn't wrong; I wasn't hallucinating . . . Children's voices rising in the night, carrying with them the sounds of insects and the songs of night birds, forming an aureole above the roof of the jungle . . . Marvelous, magnificent, sublime . . . I wasn't wrong . . .

CAPTAIN FUCK DEATH: Shut up! I'm listening!

Silence. The two of them listen, almost prayerful. Schmeckel stops laughing, visibly rattled by their attitude. He, too, starts to listen to the music, apparently intrigued, as though he had just discovered it, or as if he were trying to understand a dimension of it that had escaped him until now.

SCHMECKEL: I see I haven't upset you . . .

CAPTAIN FUCK DEATH: Shush! . . .

SCHMECKEL: I wanted to relax the atmosphere a little, that's all . . .

CORPORAL BONKERS: Shush! . . .

SCHMECKEL: You like German cantatas?

CAPTAIN FUCK DEATH: I adore them.

CORPORAL BONKERS: We adore them.

CAPTAIN FUCK DEATH: So it was you who played the music a while ago?

SCHMECKEL: Uh huh . . . About an hour or two ago . . . We turned it on . . .

CORPORAL BONKERS: So I really did hear what I heard.

SCHMECKEL: It was a joke . . . *"C'est une blague"* . . . *(He starts to laugh again.) "C'est une blague . . . C'est une blague . . ."*

CORPORAL BONKERS: You speak French?

SCHMECKEL: No, not really, I only know how to say *"C'est une blague."* I think it's *"drôle."*

CORPORAL BONKERS: That's French too. Right, boss, *"drôle"* is French, right?

CAPTAIN FUCK DEATH: There's nothing more French than *"drôle."*

SCHMECKEL: You can say that again . . .

CORPORAL BONKERS: So you can say something else besides: *"C'est une blague?"*

SCHMECKEL: Well, yeah . . .

CAPTAIN FUCK DEATH: You can even make a sentence out of the whole thing: *"C'est une blague est drôle."*

SCHMECKEL: That's true, yeah . . . And if you work on it you can make two or three other sentences. First, like you said: *"C'est une blague est drôle."* But you can even say, more simply, *"La blague est drôle"* or *"Etre drôle est une blague,"* or even, *"Blaguer c'est drôle,"* or *"C'est drôle la blague,"* or *"C'est une drôle blague,"* or just *"C'est."*

CAPTAIN FUCK DEATH: I didn't dare suggest that.

SCHMECKEL: And even more simply: *"Blague, blague, blague."*

CAPTAIN FUCK DEATH: And with that you've said it all . . . You seem like a merry joker, mister. Do you even know who we are?

SCHMECKEL: Of course I do. You are the cruel and famous Captain Fuck Death, alias El Comandante. The legend about what you accomplished during the war, if we can call them accomplishments, is known throughout the country . . . And he's Captain Bonkers, the bloodthirsty clown who does your torturing for you. But you don't impress me really. Nobody ever has . . .

CAPTAIN FUCK DEATH: Do you know why we two managed to get out of the battle alive, untouched, and victorious to go on to conquer the brewery?

SCHMECKEL: No, but I don't lose sleep over it.

CORPORAL BONKERS: Because we're the meanest, meanest, meanest . . . you big idiot!

CAPTAIN FUCK DEATH: Settle down. I had under my command twelve soldiers from the very best recruits, real bad asses. But in the end, who survived the mission?

SCHMECKEL: Just the two of you.

CAPTAIN FUCK DEATH: And why was that . . . Wipe that smile off your face, it's getting old! So why, do you think?

SCHMECKEL: Probably because you two are the cleverest.

CAPTAIN FUCK DEATH: You can do better than that.

SCHMECKEL: Because you're the baddest bad asses?

CORPORAL BONKERS: The baddest bad asses of what?

SCHMECKEL: The baddest bad asses of the baddest bad asses. Everybody's afraid of you because you're ferocious and you have no pity. You kill, rape, and set fire everywhere. They even say you took a mortar and pestle and pounded a bunch of newborns to death.

CAPTAIN FUCK DEATH: Oh we did worse than that.

SCHMECKEL: I know you're famous celebrities today and . . .

CORPORAL BONKERS: Our legend has even crossed the borders . . . Right, boss?

SCHMECKEL: But none of that really makes a dent. I don't give a shit. I won't talk.

CORPORAL BONKERS: But you do know you have in front of you the future President of the Republic and his Minister of Armed Forces?

SCHMECKEL: Who cares?

CAPTAIN FUCK DEATH *(Suddenly pulling down his pants)*: OK, enough of this fooling around. Lower your pants and get on all fours . . . It's time for you to feel the devil's fire between your cheeks! Pants down, on all fours!

SCHMECKEL: No, no, not that . . . Not that; have pity, please . . . I beg you, not that . . . I'll tell you everything . . .

CAPTAIN FUCK DEATH: I thought you'd have talked earlier, but you tried to be smart . . . Too late! On your knees!

SCHMECKEL: Not that, please, it hurts too much . . . I beg you . . . I won't be smart any more . . . I'll tell you everything you want . . . I'll spill the beans: I'm not the one who knows the secret of the brewery! It's a woman! She knows how the factory works!

CAPTAIN FUCK DEATH: A woman?

SCHMECKEL: Yes, yes, it's the whole truth, a woman! I don't understand any of it . . .

CORPORAL BONKERS: Well how about that: a woman! You mean the beer we've been drinking all our lives was made by some woman? . . . A woman like Mom and my sisters?

SCHMECKEL: Yeah, a real woman with tits and ass.

CAPTAIN FUCK DEATH: Holy crap! That's all we needed, a woman. Now things are a complete mess. So a woman managed to keep this whole factory afloat! Are you sure?

SCHMECKEL: She's so really a woman, she's even pregnant!

CORPORAL BONKERS: No kidding!

SCHMECKEL: By me.

CAPTAIN FUCK DEATH: You don't say so!

CORPORAL BONKERS: It's not true. It can't be true! How . . . d . . . d . . . did you . . . d . . . d . . . do it?

CAPTAIN FUCK DEATH: How come? Are you married?

SCHMECKEL: Not really. One morning she said to all of us workers: "Take your pants off!" So we took them off. She looked at us, tested the goods, weighed them, smelled them even, then she chose me: "You're the one who's going to give me a child."

CAPTAIN FUCK DEATH: You mean you let a woman order you to take your pants off in order to . . .

SCHMECKEL: Well she's the boss and we're just the workers . . .

CORPORAL BONKERS: And she chose you?

SCHMECKEL: Yeah she did . . . I have to say I was surprised too, because in terms of . . . I mean there were guys who were dragging their thing between their legs . . . Oh boy! I'd never dreamed that there were such big ones . . . Like this, really like this, I'm telling you. Almost looked like a handicap . . . Mine was the smallest, but she chose me . . . Goes to prove that a woman can be totally off the wall . . . I think she just wanted to have a good time with a nice guy . . . That's the only way I can explain it . . . Not too big nor too . . . A nice guy—and cute . . .

CORPORAL BONKERS: And you ended up being that nice, cute guy, neither too this nor too that . . .

SCHMECKEL: You better believe it. Women have always found me neither too this nor too that. A nice guy and cute too. Anyhow, the two of us really had fun. Every time she had the urge, and sometimes it was seven times a day, she'd come looking for me, even when I was working, drag me into her office, make me stretch out on my back, jump on top of me, and . . .

CAPTAIN FUCK DEATH: That's enough. We get it! Let's cut to the chase!

SCHMECKEL: Well, it's simple. She wanted to have a kid, all to herself. She asked me to make love and so I got her pregnant . . . That's why the other workers think she shared the secret of the brewery with me . . . Because I put a kid in her belly . . . But it's not my kid. It's her kid . . .

CORPORAL BONKERS: Oh boy oh boy oh boy oh boy . . . This is really giving me a headache.

CAPTAIN FUCK DEATH: And what's the name of this crazy woman?

SCHMECKEL: White Magic.

CAPTAIN FUCK DEATH: So she's white?

SCHMECKEL: I don't know. I never looked.

CORPORAL BONKERS: Boss, maybe this guy's more than a little dumb?

SCHMECKEL: I do know something: she speaks German.

CAPTAIN FUCK DEATH: Her name's White Magic?

SCHMECKEL: I'm not really sure. We always called her White Magic. When I started working at the factory, the old guys were already calling her White Magic. So I did what everybody else did, without even wondering how come she was called White Magic.

CAPTAIN FUCK DEATH: Where is she now?

SCHMECKEL: She fled because of the war, but also because of me. She thought I might want access to the kid; but, really, children have never been my cup of tea . . . I don't have anything against them, but I've never thought about it one way or the other . . . But she started to imagine things . . . You know how women are! When they get something in their head . . . If you really want to know, she ran away because she was having more and more trouble staying away from me . . . I'm not trying to be the big shot here, or brag . . . But she was beginning to feel that what I could do for her was becoming a necessity . . . that she was starting to be some kind of slave to me. It's always been like that with women . . . In the beginning, OK . . . But after a while, once they're under my spell, I can't get them to let go . . . Because . . .

CAPTAIN FUCK DEATH: So where is she?

SCHMECKEL: Paris.

CORPORAL BONKERS: Oh shit, a Frenchie.

SCHMECKEL: She's not French. She's German . . .

CORPORAL BONKERS: German? . . . A German! . . . You want me to believe an ugly mug like you was able to mess around with a German?

CAPTAIN FUCK DEATH: What's she doing in Paris?

SCHMECKEL: She's the mistress of ceremonies for a review at the Moulin Rouge. That's what she used to do before the brewery. They say the show's a smash hit. The newspapers in Paris are all over her, because it's the first time the star of a fancy girlie review is pregnant up to her eyeballs . . . It seems her photo is plastered all over Paris.

CORPORAL BONKERS: Ooh la la la la la la. . . . My poor head . . . It's getting more and more complicated . . . God is it complicated! You say you put a kid in her belly, but she abandoned you in the middle of machetes so she could hide out at the Moulin Rouge?

SCHMECKEL: She tells me all that time that I'm pretentious and that I smell.

CORPORAL BONKERS: That part's true. You smell; right, boss?

SCHMECKEL: She also says I have . . . I have . . . She's the one who gave me the nickname "Schmeckel."

CAPTAIN FUCK DEATH: Go get her . . .

SCHMECKEL: From Paris?

CAPTAIN FUCK DEATH: I said, "Go get her!" *(Schmeckel leaves.)* And go right away, because if you're not back in five minutes I'm going to wipe out one of your comrades. And it'll be like that every five minutes until you get back.

III. AND WE'LL GO PLAY AROUND IN LAS VEGAS

CORPORAL BONKERS: How's it possible that a stinkbug like him could land himself a German! I can't get over it! . . . Boss, how'd you know that would make him talk?

CAPTAIN FUCK DEATH *(Indicating the black board)*: A Taurus with Libra rising never likes it up the whazoo.

CORPORAL BONKERS: Ah, I see . . . You really are the boss, El Comandante, sir . . . Boss, doesn't it do something to you to think it was that woman who made the beer the whole country drank?

CAPTAIN FUCK DEATH: Well it's almost over and done with. I'll squeeze the recipe out of her and the secret of rebooting the factory, and then I'll be the King of Beer. We'll sell beer to everyone; we'll bill it as making a patriotic effort to rebuild the nation, so they'll buy and drink with no second thoughts, as though they were participating in a civic action. Money will come rushing back into the coffers . . .

CORPORAL BONKERS: And we'll be billionaires . . .

CAPTAIN FUCK DEATH: We'll establish a tax on national reconciliation . . .

CORPORAL BONKERS: And then we'll take all the beer money and all the tax money, and we'll even repatriate the money the ex-dictator hid outside the country. . . . We'll be super rich and we'll go play around in Las Vegas . . .

CAPTAIN FUCK DEATH: I see you've figured it out.

CORPORAL BONKERS: All the limos as long as anacondas will be ours. And French champagne, Iranian caviar, casinos with the biggest boxing rings, blackjack tables in Nevada where it's great to have a boner when you're losing your money . . . We'll have those giant cushy beds in those fantastic estates where girls with endless legs and clever behinds are waiting for us . . . But boss, what if that toy boy doesn't come back?

CAPTAIN FUCK DEATH: Has to. When you've been threatened with that, you do exactly what you're told; you become a tame little lapdog.

CORPORAL BONKERS: Yeah, that thing really hurts . . . Since you did it to me, I even stutter sometimes . . .

CAPTAIN FUCK DEATH: So you see. He'll come back with his German.

CORPORAL BONKERS: And what will we do with her afterwards, boss?

CAPTAIN FUCK DEATH: As soon as the factory is working full force again, I'll give her to you. You can do what you want with her . . .

CORPORAL BONKERS: Anything, you mean it, anything?

CAPTAIN FUCK DEATH: Really anything. You'll have a completely free hand.

CORPORAL BONKERS: Comandante, you're a real boss. A German! I'm going to mess around with a German!

CAPTAIN FUCK DEATH: But after, you cut her throat . . .

CORPORAL BONKERS: Naturally, boss . . .

CAPTAIN FUCK DEATH: Shush . . . I hear something . . . Maybe it's our gigolo. . . . Or maybe a militiaman who's escaped from the carnage, hate and vengeance filling his heart . . . Let's keep a look out.

IV. SHOWBIZ

CORPORAL BONKERS: Boss, eh eh eh . . . it . . . it . . . it . . . sa . . . sa . . . sa . . . wo . . . wo . . . wo . . . woman. A woman . . . The woman, Boss!

Schmeckel and White Magic enter. She's in a showgirl's costume. The two seem completely out of breath.

WHITE MAGIC: *Immer dasselbe! Unfähig, allein klarzukommen! . . . Was hat sie wieder getan, Magiblanche?*[a] What has White Magic done now? Who did I rape, pillage, steal from this time? Tell me so I can beg forgiveness. I have a show to put on! Who did I enslave now? Who did I colonize this time? Or did I mess up decolonization? I accept the blame for everything, let me expiate for all of it, but let's get it over with. I have a show to put on. *Was hat sie wieder getan, Magiblanche!* Did I launch a new Crusades? Did I bomb some brand-new trains? Did I erect a new set of barbed-wire fences? I'm ready to repent for all of it, but let's get it over with. I have a show to put on. *Was hat sie wieder getan, Magiblanche*! The hole in the ozone layer, the birds covered in sludge, the baby seals. . . . All of it, yes I said all of it. I'm ready to accept the guilt, to make myself sick with *mea culpas*. But let's get it over with. I have a show to put on. It's always White Magic doing this or White Magic doing that! What did I do this time that sent that stinky pretentious little Schmeckel to tear me away from the Moulin Rouge, and right in the middle of my act! What did White Magic do this time?

CORPORAL BONKERS: How beautiful she is! . . .

CAPTAIN FUCK DEATH: Don't get carried away . . .

CORPORAL BONKERS: Frankly, I can't understand how a woman like that could let that hairy spider tickle her thighs!

WHITE MAGIC: So Schmeckel, just where is this pitiless, bloodthirsty guerrilla commando?

SCHMECKEL: They're right here in front of you, Madame!

WHITE MAGIC: These two guys? . . . There are just two of them? . . .

CORPORAL BONKERS: Yeah, but we're really really nasty.

WHITE MAGIC: And you're the ones who squashed all the other militia groups? . . .

CORPORAL BONKERS: Yeah, that's right, it was us . . . But not alone . . . *(Suddenly on the brink of tears)* . . . Not all alone . . . We were thirteen at the outset . . . Real men . . . Men we saw fall right next to us . . . who died in our arms . . . But we won . . . We had to win at any price, for them . . .

CAPTAIN FUCK DEATH: For them and for the fatherland. And in this solemn occasion, let us honor our brothers in arms fallen on the field of battle so that our mother country could live! . . . *(Mozart's Requiem.)* Corporal Bonkers, the moment is portentous, dry your tears and come to attention! . . . Private First Class Heart-On-His-Sleeve . . .

CORPORAL BONKERS: Died for the fatherland!

CAPTAIN FUCK DEATH *(Shooting off a gun salute)*: Private First Class Without Pity . . .

CORPORAL BONKERS: Died for the fatherland!

CAPTAIN FUCK DEATH *(A gun salute)*: Corporal Terminator . . .

CORPORAL BONKERS: Died for the fatherland!

CAPTAIN FUCK DEATH *(A gun salute)*: Corporal Abolê . . .

CORPORAL BONKERS: Died for the fatherland!

CAPTAIN FUCK DEATH *(A gun salute)*: Sergeant Findjougou . . .

CORPORAL BONKERS: Died for the fatherland!

CAPTAIN FUCK DEATH *(A gun salute)*: Sergeant Rape-on-Every-Floor . . .

CORPORAL BONKERS: Died for the fatherland!

CAPTAIN FUCK DEATH *(A gun salute):* Head Sergeant Cemetery . . .

CORPORAL BONKERS: Died for the fatherland!

CAPTAIN FUCK DEATH *(A gun salute)*: Head Sergeant Mass Grave . . .

CORPORAL BONKERS: Died for the fatherland!

CAPTAIN FUCK DEATH *(A gun salute)*: Second-Lieutenant Marcos . . .
CORPORAL BONKERS: Died for the fatherland!
CAPTAIN FUCK DEATH *(A gun salute)*: Second Lieutenant Fisticuffs . . .
CORPORAL BONKERS: Died for the fatherland!
CAPTAIN FUCK DEATH *(A gun salute)*: Lieutenant Yassouaté . . .
CORPORAL BONKERS: Died for the fatherland!

A military salute. Captain Fuck Death and Corporal Bonkers have broken down. The former discreetly wipes away a tear, while the latter cannot manage to hold back his tears and cries like a child.

It . . . it . . . it . . . isn . . . isn . . . isn't . . . isn't . . . fair . . . It's not fair that the best always go first . . . Those guys were real men . . . Always at your side in the worst possible shit . . . They never ran away . . . It's really not fair . . .

WHITE MAGIC: How moving . . . Very moving indeed . . . I share your pain . . . Only I have to tell you, I'm swimming, I'm floating, I'm drowning . . . I don't understand very well, in fact I don't understand at all what I'm doing here . . . Because a few moments ago, right in the middle of my act, at the Moulin Rouge—in Paris, if you please—I heard someone yelling from the audience: "White Magic! White Magic! White Magic! Come! Come quickly! The workers are in danger! They're going to cut all their throats and set the factory on fire!" I realized right away it was that pretentious stinky little Schmeckel . . . The spectators started yelling, screaming, clamoring, destroying their seats, protesting: "This is scandalous! We've never seen such a thing at the Moulin Rouge in Paris! What is that crazy jerk talking about? And why is he calling her White Magic? White Magic! White Magic!" . . . Because you should know that in Paris no one knows me by the name of White Magic. Everyone in Paris calls me the Bavarian Josephine Baker . . . "What does he want with our Bavarian Josephine Baker! This is scandalous! Where's the army! Throw him out! We can't let this happen to the Bavarian Josephine Baker!" I started thinking: These assholes are going to lynch my Schmeckel. So I jumped off the stage, grabbed him, parted the rowdy crowd, and before I knew it, found myself back here, in the middle of the jungle, back again in this country I nursed with my beer like a mother nurses a bunch of children from her milk-heavy breasts, but a country I had to flee when those steely machetes started giving off sparks in the sunshine . . . What did you expect? When all is said and done, I'm not crazy! Do you think I'd wait to be raped, to have my throat slit by those madmen? . . . I left. I took my hard knocks and I left. No more White Magic! White Magic *kaputt*! . . . So tell me, why is White Magic back here, in this jungle where I swore I'd never set foot again? *Warum! Warum! Warum!* . . .

CORPORAL BONKERS: OK Josephine Baker or whatever you call yourself. This circus has gone on long enough . . .

CAPTAIN FUCK DEATH: You big idiot! That's not the way to speak to one of the world's great ladies. You'll have to forgive him, Madame Josephine Baker, but try to understand . . . war, the jungle . . . everything here militates against manners. But I'll put things back in shape, very soon. You have my word as an officer . . .

WHITE MAGIC: If I'm not mistaken, you're the famous Captain Fuck Death? . . .

CORPORAL BONKERS: Alias El Comandante . . .

WHITE MAGIC: Get out of here! . . . You really are the famous Captain Fuck Death? . . .

CAPTAIN FUCK DEATH: Himself.

WHITE MAGIC: I'm standing next to the famous Captain Fuck Death? I can't believe my eyes.

CAPTAIN FUCK DEATH: And yet! . . .

CORPORAL BONKERS: And I'm Corporal Bonkers . . .

WHITE MAGIC: Who cares? Nobody gives a shit about you! . . . *(to Fuck Death)* Can I take a picture?

CAPTAIN FUCK DEATH: Of course.

CORPORAL BONKERS: If it makes you happy . . .

She takes a camera out of her bag while Captain Fuck Death and Corporal Bonkers strike a pose.

WHITE MAGIC: Cheese and . . . *(Click)* Don't move, one more. *(Click)* Now one with me . . . both of you over here . . . Here Schmeckel. *(She hands Schmeckel the camera and stands between the two soldiers.)* Smile. Everybody, cheese! . . . We're good. OK to take it Schmeckel. *(Click)* Take one more! *(Click)* Thank you, thanks very much, El Comandante . . . Oh if you only knew! . . . Paris is bursting with news of your exploits . . . The civilized world . . . The free world has placed its hopes in you . . . You're a huge celebrity in Paris these days.

CAPTAIN FUCK DEATH: I know. I know. . . . But the colossal task that awaits me, that awaits all of us, urges me to remain humble. It's for this country, my country, for these people who have humiliated and martyred themselves. And they're still standing, standing like mythic heroes on the back of the snorting warhorse of their pride. It's for them that I want to become a star. Not because of my exploits as warrior, but because of my untiring commitment to the idea of a gestating democracy for all. I know you have a show to put on, but you see, Madame, the same as we can't live on a ration of rice alone but also need art, we can't live on spectacle alone. We also need our ration of hope. Madame, I implore you, help me. On my knees, I ask you to help me offer a ration of hope to the old people whose dignity has been trampled, to women who've been battered and raped, to children, oh our children, whose dreams have been wrecked by machetes, that, as you said so poetically, give off sparks in the sunshine . . . Help them . . .

WHITE MAGIC: This is getting to me, I must say . . . You're appealing to my emotions and . . . Tell me what I can do to bring even one lone ray of hope to all those unfortunate destinies.

CAPTAIN FUCK DEATH: Get the brewery up and running again.

WHITE MAGIC: *Mein Gott!*

She suddenly realizes that she's in fact in the brewery and that the factory has not been destroyed.

CORPORAL BONKERS: Everything's still in perfect shape, like the banks when . . . By the way, Madame, do you know why the banks were untouched by bombs and missiles in Beirut?

WHITE MAGIC: Of course I do! Any idiot could figure that one out . . . Oh my brewery! . . . I was sure they'd pillaged everything, destroyed all of it . . . set fire to it . . . *Mein Gott!*

CAPTAIN FUCK DEATH: No, you see, everything is intact and the vats are still full of beer, of your beer. As if you'd never left. Everything has been waiting for you.

WHITE MAGIC: I need some time to think . . . This is all so sudden . . . And, then, I've lost my touch . . . I may have forgotten the recipe . . . Showbiz wiped it all out . . . I have to look at the manual again, study all of this . . .

CAPTAIN FUCK DEATH: Hand me the manual. Let me help you study, Josephine Baker . . .

WHITE MAGIC: Really? So you read German?

CAPTAIN FUCK DEATH: It's in German?

WHITE MAGIC: Old, old German.
CAPTAIN FUCK DEATH: Ah hah . . .
WHITE MAGIC: You said it. I'm going to call my agent to have him alert the Moulin Rouge to the change in plans . . . But where did MySweetie go? . . . Ah, there you are! *(She takes her cell phone out of her bag and gives it a kiss.) Hallo Gianfranco? . . . Ich bin's . . . Josephine Baker . . . ja ja Josephine Baker . . . Wo ich bin? . . . Du wirst mir nicht glauben, ich bin mit Captain Fuck Death. . . .* No, I'm not kidding, the real Captain Fuck Death . . . That's right, the one they also call El Comandante . . . *So ist es, der Freund von Corporal Bonkers . . . He? . . . Ja. aber er ist unglaublich dumm . . .* El Comandante, on the other hand, is a perfect gentleman . . . *Ich weiff nicht . . . (to Captain Fuck Death)* Gianfranco, my impresario, wants to know if you already have someone representing you? . . . *Er sagt nein . . . Warum nicht? Es ist in der Tat der richtige Moment . . . He? . . . Hallo Gianfranco . . .* I will never really understand Gianfranco's German. My agent is Italian, from Genoa . . . He only wants to talk to me in German, but, oh *mein Gott!!,* he has one of those accents! . . . *Nein, nein, ich bin noch dran . . .* You've said it, pretty soon every agent on the planet will want to sign him . . . *ja . . . ja . . . ja . . .* So what do you think about having Gianfranco look after your business?[b]

Captain Fuck Death shrugs his shoulders, indecisive.

CORPORAL BONKERS: I think it'd be cool if he was my agent . . .
WHITE MAGIC: You are utterly uninteresting to show-business types . . . *Hallo Gianfranco, Captain Fuck Death würde es sich gerne überlegen . . . Nein, nein, nicht jetzt . . . , weil ich jetzt keine Zeit habe . . . Hör zu, ich rufe dich aus einem anderen Grund an . . .* Tell the Director of the Moulin Rouge that I'm unable to perform tomorrow . . . *genau ich kann die Vorstellung morgen nicht geben . . .* No, not at all, I'm not being held against my will . . . *auf keinen Fall . . . Weder die Polizei, noch die Presse . . . Ich kann auf dich zählen? . . . Ich zähl' auf dich . . . Danke im Voraus . . .* No, no, no ransom . . . *ich hab dir doch gesagt, daff ich nicht entführt worden bin . . . es ist eine Angelegenheit, die bis morgen geregelt sein wird . . .* Exactly, tomorrow I'll be back in Paris . . . *Also, ich umarm' dich . . .* Me too, I kiss you everywhere . . . *Ja überall, überall, überall . . . bis morgen . . .* Oh that Gianfranco! . . . So that's done. *(She kisses MySweetie one more time before putting it back in her bag.)* And now I have to rest a little . . . Everything that's happened, the trip, the time difference . . .

I'm completely worn out . . . *kaputt, kaputt, kaputt* . . . Tomorrow I'll get back to my recipe book . . . Night brings counsel . . . [c]

CAPTAIN FUCK DEATH: We've been waiting for peace and happiness for decades, Madame. I think we can manage one more night. Let night bring wisdom, Josephine Baker of Bavaria.

WHITE MAGIC: And to you as well, Comandante . . . But before we start negotiating, I want you to free all the workers you've taken hostage.

CAPTAIN FUCK DEATH: Your wish is my command.

WHITE MAGIC: That's what I like to hear. Let's go, Schmeckel dear, come massage me a bit.

White Magic and Schmeckel exit.

CORPORAL BONKERS: I really wonder what she sees in him.

CAPTAIN FUCK DEATH: Tomorrow we'll be rich men . . .

CORPORAL BONKERS: Disgustingly rich . . . And we'll go play around in Las Vegas!

CAPTAIN FUCK DEATH: Once the factory's started up again, we'll rub out both of them . . .

CORPORAL BONKERS: But before that . . . You promised me, Comandante, you did . . . Before that, I'm going to bang bang with her . . . if only to get back at her teasing . . . Anyhow, German girls have always made me tingle . . .

CAPTAIN FUCK DEATH: Do what you like. I've promised it: bang bang. Why not? Good night, Mister Corporal Bonkers.

CORPORAL BONKERS: Good night, Mister Captain Fuck Death.

Blackout.

V. THE HOSTAGE

On the blackboard Captain Fuck Death's esoteric figures have been replaced by exotic formulas written in an unrecognizable alphabet.

SCHMECKEL: . . . When it happens, she talks and talks and talks.

CORPORAL BONKERS: She talks? . . . What does she say?

SCHMECKEL: I never know. She speaks in German . . . While she's riding me, she speaks in German. Those are the only times when she speaks German exclusively. Her eyes half closed, her thighs moving on mine, all her body caught up in a fever of pleasure, her lips half open and those . . . those words that come out of her mouth, enchant me. She always starts, systematically, by the same phrase . . . She says, "*Wo bist du, mein Vaterland?*"[31]

WHITE MAGIC *(entering)*: No, no and no!

CAPTAIN FUCK DEATH *(Entering)*: And I say to you, in turn, "No, no, and no."

WHITE MAGIC: Give it back to me!

CAPTAIN FUCK DEATH: Not as long as you refuse to come back to the negotiating table . . .

WHITE MAGIC: What negotiations! You're the one who broke them off.

CAPTAIN FUCK DEATH: That's because you were doing everything you could to make sure they'd fall apart!

WHITE MAGIC: I'm asking you on bended knee: Free MySweetie! You must have seen it's not an ordinary cell phone.

CAPTAIN FUCK DEATH: I'm not blind. It's solid gold and the keyboard is a bunch of diamonds.

WHITE MAGIC: But really what's important, really, it was a present from Pavarotti . . . Pavarotti himself gave it to me in memory of. . . .

CAPTAIN FUCK DEATH: Another good reason . . . Come back to the negotiating table and I'll free your MySweetie.

WHITE MAGIC: In that case, I'm all ears. Let's hear your resolution.

CAPTAIN FUCK DEATH: Thank you . . . thank you . . . I'm happy to see you've adopted a more positive attitude, more conciliatory, in sum more constructive . . . The hour is grave, Madame Josephine Baker of Bavaria . . . Rebooting the brewery, something I want with all my heart, will contribute to building a more homogeneous society, a society that will allow the least favored among us—the weakest, the smallest, the losers, the marginal figures, the have-nots—to better their living conditions in rapid and substantial ways. I have a lucid dream of a more brotherly society whose credo is individual initiative, work shared among all, helping hands between young and old, men and women, poor and rich, their hearts entwined. Yes, the lamb will watch over the pasture, and the lion over the lamb. I want a real system of solidarity in this country that promotes not only an economy with a human face, but especially, and in a complementary fashion, culture and the arts—a playful but vigorous synergy between tradition, modernity, and postmodernity—in order to construct a unique national identity that can develop without hindrance, through dialogue and respect for the law . . . Listen well, Madame, I'm not trying to build a new Eden, but, rather, a new Babylon that will permit everyone to build a garden in the image of his own dream of humanity.

SCHMECKEL *(to Bonkers)*: . . . Suddenly I feel her radiance and I'm happy to see her so happy . . . Little by little the words accumulate, change shape on her lips; her voice gets higher and higher . . . then violently descends to a low register . . . Her words become a familiar song . . . I understand nothing of what she says, but it's beautiful . . . really it's simply splendid . . . Poems, it must be poems . . . For words to come so close to singing, it can only be poetry . . . Then she takes off . . . then we take off, we float on the blossoming words. . . . Until her laughter explodes . . .

CORPORAL BONKERS: White Magic starts to laugh?

SCHMECKEL: Like a crazy person. She always laughs in the fires of satisfaction. Laughter that quiets down with an "*Oh mein Schmeckel*!" and her eyes, rolling towards the back of her head, are turned towards the heavens, like the Virgin's at the foot of the Cross.

WHITE MAGIC *(to Fuck Death)*: You're the one, Sir, who broke off our dialogue and stomped on the most elementary principles of international law.

CAPTAIN FUCK DEATH: Spare me, please, your pointless thoughts on justice. The business at hand, Madame, and you know this very well, is located far above any contingencies or fluctuations of international law. Will you or will you not teach me how to make this fucking brewery work?

WHITE MAGIC: *Nein!*

CAPTAIN FUCK DEATH: And why *nein?*

WHITE MAGIC: Because!

CAPTAIN FUCK DEATH: Because why?

WHITE MAGIC: Because . . . because I've forgotten part of the recipe. Because . . . I haven't been able to study everything . . . Because . . . my feminine instinct does not trust you at all.

CAPTAIN FUCK DEATH: Let me tell you your feminine instinct is off base. I've always inspired confidence. . . . My butcher, my baker, my bus driver have all trusted me. When I was just a little thing, my mother can vouch for it, I inspired confidence. Everyone has always trusted me!

WHITE MAGIC: How can I trust you when not only did you not free the workers, like you promised me, but you also confiscated MySweetie, my cell phone.

SCHMECKEL *(to Bonkers)*: . . . In any event, at the crucial moment she always laughs like a madwoman, with her rolling eyes turned towards the heavens. A laugh that always ends in "Oh Schmeckel!"

CORPORAL BONKERS: Where does that nickname come from?

SCHMECKEL: It means "little prick."

CORPORAL BONKERS: Your German nickname means "little prick?"

SCHMECKEL: That's right. "Schmeckel" means "little prick" in German.

CORPORAL BONKERS: You've got to be kidding?

SCHMECKEL: It's what it means.

CORPORAL BONKERS: "Little prick?" . . . Why? . . . Because you . . .

SCHMECKEL: Well yes, you could say so . . .

CORPORAL BONKERS: How little? . . . Little like this?

SCHMECKEL: More little.

CORPORAL BONKERS: Like this?

SCHMECKEL: Even more.

CORPORAL BONKERS: I don't believe it . . . And all those things you did to her, all those things you told me, it was with that?

SCHMECKEL: You know, I'm like everybody else. I only have one and that's what I use . . .

WHITE MAGIC: *(to Fuck Death)* So if I understand correctly, you're holding me hostage?

CAPTAIN FUCK DEATH: The winds of History have changed, Madame! I therefore demand, in the strongest possible terms, that you show me how the factory works and, crucially, that you hand over the recipe for the beer!

WHITE MAGIC: *Nein!* Call the German Embassy, tell them your conditions, or how much ransom you want. I refuse to speak to you any more.

CAPTAIN FUCK DEATH: Stop acting like a child! Show me immediately . . .

WHITE MAGIC: The whole world, and not just the world of showbiz, not just the free world, but the whole world will never stop talking about the martyrdom of the Bavarian Josephine Baker . . . *Alle Welt wird davon sprechen*![e] . . . You've unmasked yourself, you're no democrat . . . you're only a bloodthirsty brute! . . . A sub-Dictator! . . .

CAPTAIN FUCK DEATH: I invite you to try to control your insults. The wheels of History have turned. Make up your mind, or I'm sending MySweetie to the flames . . .

WHITE MAGIC: No, no, not that . . . not MySweetie . . . Don't throw MySweetie into the fire, for the grace of God . . . I'll negotiate . . . I'm ready to negotiate . . . ready to come to an agreement . . . Just leave me a little time . . . I need a little more time . . . I'm ready to make any concession, just don't throw MySweetie into the flames . . .

CAPTAIN FUCK DEATH: No! Now is the moment to put beer back on the market. It's the perfect time. In a week it'll be too late. The experts are predicting a decline in stock prices . . . And then, fuck it! I just want to know how all this works!! And can you tell me, Madame, you with your subtle knowledge of international law, of democracy, and all that goody-goody humanitarian stuff, how you explain that after so many years in this factory not a single one of your workers has learned how to make those machines function! After all, it's their factory. It belongs to the children of this country! Don't you see, Madame, it's a question of patriotic pride, of national sovereignty! I might be a bloodthirsty brute, a sub-Dictator, but I'm not more stupid that the next guy. Explain this to me, so I can understand . . .

CORPORAL BONKERS *(to Schmeckel)*: You don't mean to tell me it's as small as this?

SCHMECKEL: Now you're going too far . . .

CORPORAL BONKERS: Let me see. *(Schmeckel lowers his pants.)* Hey, it's not as small as you say it is!

SCHMECKEL: You're just saying that to make me feel good . . .

CORPORAL BONKERS: Not at all. I even find it pretty ridiculous to call you "Little Prick."

SCHMECKEL: But coming out of her mouth, it's not so bad, I mean it's more of an endearment . . .

CORPORAL BONKERS: You astonish me.

SCHMECKEL: It's kind of cute. Like she was saying: "My little bunny," "My pickle puss" . . . things like that.

CORPORAL BONKERS: Well . . . In any case, mine isn't any bigger . . .

WHITE MAGIC: Come on now, my Schmeckel, I'm in need of a little massage to help me through all these negotiations.

She starts to pull Schmeckel off stage.

CORPORAL BONKERS: Madame White Magic, do you think you could do me a favor?

WHITE MAGIC: What is it?

He whispers something in her ear. As soon as she hears it, she slaps him.

Oh, you pig! *Grofer fauler Schwanz!*[f]

CORPORAL BONKERS: What did she say?
SCHMECKEL: You big lazy prick!

White Magic and Schmeckel exit.

VI. THE BE-ALL AND END-ALL

CORPORAL BONKERS: She doesn't want to, right boss? . . . She's refusing to reboot the factory?
CAPTAIN FUCK DEATH: She's hard-nosed, tenacious, unyielding.
CORPORAL BONKERS: That's the German in her. Those people are stubborn, opinionated . . . They're like a dog with a bone . . . Unless . . . I could make her go down on all fours in front of you, boss, so you . . .
CAPTAIN FUCK DEATH: No, no, don't even think about it. I'm sure that doesn't scare her, on the contrary . . . She's even the type to ask for it again, like every Pisces . . .
CORPORAL BONKERS: She's a Pisces?
CAPTAIN FUCK DEATH: Rising Scorpio.
CORPORAL BONKERS: You don't say so . . . It's well known that female Pisces . . . when it comes to that . . .
CAPTAIN FUCK DEATH: So we have to find something else . . .

The voice of White Magic reaches them from off stage.

WHITE MAGIC *(off-stage)*:
Nein . . . nein . . . nein . . .
Wo bist du, mein Väterchen!
Ja . . . ja . . . ja . . . nein . . . nein . . . nein . . .
Wo bist du, mein Väterchen!
Komm und hilf mir, Väterchen[g] . . .
CORPORAL BONKERS: Here we go again, that's all we need . . .

White Magic's voice takes on the colors that connote suffering and pleasure: violets, reds, and blacks, until she is screaming . . . Captain Fuck Death, seemingly caught up in the beauty of White Magic's "song," begins to gesture like an orchestra conductor, especially when we start to hear violins, pianos, and clarinets . . .

WHITE MAGIC *(off-stage)*:
. . . Denn ich bin aufs Neue
an der schmackhaften Bisswunde

seines dunklen Schwertes aufgespieft . . .
Ich bin aufs Neue
die Hostie
auf der Spitze seines wütenden Geschlechtes . . . [h]
CORPORAL BONKERS: She has no shame! And in her condition . . .
CAPTAIN FUCK DEATH: Magnificent! . . . It can only be poetry . . .
WHITE MAGIC *(off-stage): . . . wühle,*
wühle in meinem Geschlecht,
wühle in meinem Körper,
wühle jenseits meines Körpers,
wühle jenseits meines Geschlechtes
und töte mich mit deinen geheimen Gelüsten . . . [i]
CORPORAL BONKERS: My God, what does she see in him? . . .
CAPTAIN FUCK DEATH: Shush . . . I'm listening . . . It's sublime . . . Pure poetry . . .
WHITE MAGIC *(off-stage):*
Wo bist du, mein Väterchen?
Komm und hilf mir, Väterchen,
denn er öffnet mich.
Mit seinem dunklen Schwert öffnet er mich,
von Kopf bis Fuf öffnet er mich . . .
Von rechts nach links öffnet er mich . . . [j]
CORPORAL BONKERS: Yeah, it's beautiful, but still . . .
CAPTAIN FUCK DEATH: Shush . . .
WHITE MAGIC *(off-stage):*
Mein Körper, erschöpft von süfen Schmerzen,
liegt auf dem Altar unserer Sünden gevierteilt,
Umgeben von
vier Pferden, deren Nüstern
alle Höllenfeuer schnauben.

Wo bist du, mein Väterchen?
Komm und hilf mir, mein Väterchen,
Denn aus seinem dunklen Schwert
welches aufgerichtet ist
tragen die vier Pferde weg
und stofen und versenken
jedes in seine Windrichtung

meine Teile
in die gesteinigten Freuden des Orients,
in die verbotenen Freuden des Südens,
in die untersagten Freuden des Westens,
in die abgeschafften Freuden des Nordens.

Wo bist du, mein Väterchen?
Komm und hilf mir, Väterchen.
Denn er
vom Altar dem die vier Tiere
mit entflammten Nüstern entschwanden,
das nächtliche Schwert noch immer gegen Himmel gerichtet
lacht
Er lacht,
Er lacht,
berauscht von Überschreitungen die er
mich bereits
aufs Neue saugen lassen will.
Und er lacht,
er lacht,
er lacht . . . [k]

We hear White Magic laugh.

Oh my Schmeckel!

Captain Fuck Death collapses, as though struck by lightning.

CAPTAIN FUCK DEATH: I'm exhausted, emptied out, floored by so much beauty . . .

CORPORAL BONKERS: I think it's disgusting . . . Doing it in the state she's in, it's disgusting. I'm for sending her back to where she came from . . . If she prefers to exhaust herself in this kind of . . . kind of . . . kind of . . . rather than put the factory back to work, she should be sent back home . . . It'll be one less pain in the ass . . . Send her back to where she came from and bring in a French engineer . . .

CAPTAIN FUCK DEATH: No! Not a Frenchman. Certainly not . . . They sacrifice everything to the idols of Patrimony. The French don't understand anything about the future. They only know how to administer the past. And we're looking at the inevitable . . . And besides, the French ask too many questions about everything and the kitchen sink. They complain about every little thing and only think about vacations, and that's just not good for business . . . Anyhow, we don't have time to find a new technician. Now is when we have to get to that beer, because now is when the exchange rate is the best. Let's keep the German, even if she's half loco. She's a sure thing. Only we have to find the way to make her spill the beans as soon as possible . . .

CORPORAL BONKERS: I think I have an idea, boss . . .

CAPTAIN FUCK DEATH: OK! . . . Let's hear it . . . But in my ear . . .

CORPORAL BONKERS *(whispers something in Fuck Death's ear)*: . . . Because, boss, the be-all and end-all is money, and I've never seen anybody turn his nose up when it's a matter of money. And certainly not a mistress of ceremonies who's crazier than a coot and who calls herself the Bavarian Josephine Baker . . .

CAPTAIN FUCK DEATH: You know you're not a complete idiot, right?

CORPORAL BONKERS: Who? Me?

CAPTAIN FUCK DEATH: Yes, you . . . Not an idiot at all.

CORPORAL BONKERS: Thank you, Comandante.

CAPTAIN FUCK DEATH: I tell you what you're proposing isn't idiotic at all. It's even so smart that from now on I'm going to stop being so familiar with you.

CORPORAL BONKERS: No, boss, that's going too far . . .

CAPTAIN FUCK DEATH: And I'll call you: "My Dear Sir."

CORPORAL BONKERS: No, no . . . That's too much, really boss, too much. You're embarrassing me.

CAPTAIN FUCK DEATH: Don't be so pretentiously modest, My Dear Sir, you deserve it . . . It's not idiotic at all . . . Indeed, we should have begun there . . .

CORPORAL BONKERS: Right you are. We tell her everything. Las Vegas and all of it . . . Any way you look at it, there's enough money for everybody . . . And while we're at it, we figure out how to steal the recipe and the secret to rebooting the factory, and once we have control over everything, bang bang, and then I snuff her . . .

CAPTAIN FUCK DEATH: This time, My Dear Sir, I think we've found the right approach. As soon as she's finished monkeying around, I'll put your enlightened proposal in front of her . . . And if she refuses, I'll pull out all the stops: I'll threaten to make a bonfire of MySweetie, her cell phone.

VI. THE DEAL OF THE CENTURY

WHITE MAGIC: We never should have wasted all that time. You could have begun with that. I've always adored Las Vegas.

CAPTAIN FUCK DEATH: We were worried that that kind of proposition would insult your moral values . . .

WHITE MAGIC: Moral values, moral values . . . What moral values? . . . My Dear Friend . . . And may I address you as such?

CAPTAIN FUCK DEATH: Coming from you, Madame, I have to say it's the greatest honor I could hope to receive in life.

WHITE MAGIC: Thank you . . . My Dear Friend, what are moral values at 12%, with a hardship allowance for cultural displacement, with stock options, profit-sharing, and other sorts of golden parachutes just in case. . . .

CAPTAIN FUCK DEATH: Without calculating what this means if everything goes as planned . . .

WHITE MAGIC: And there's no reason why it shouldn't . . .

CAPTAIN FUCK DEATH: And if things really do go as planned, Madame, you will become, in the time it takes to refill the coffers, the first woman Prime Minister of the country.

WHITE MAGIC: The first German woman Prime Minister . . . Especially that: the first German woman. Oh boy, will that have all the households in Germany buzzing. I can see it already: my childhood friends in our little hamlet of Ingolstadt will be green with envy . . . That's enough of a reason to . . .

CORPORAL BONKERS *(to Schmeckel)*: . . . That bloody dictator thought he was being so clever. El Comandante asks him where's the key to the safe where he stashes all the money he's stolen from us. And he goes off—talking, talking, talking: he says that nobody will touch a hair of his fortune, that he's The Great Liberator; that he's going to stay President of the Nation and that a handful of amateur insurrectionaries don't scare him . . . His wife is there, painting her nails, while her dictator husband paces and gestures like the propeller of an antique plane. El Comandante gives us the signal. And with that, Second Lieutenant Marcos and Sergeant Rape-on-Every-Floor throw themselves on the First Lady, tear off her clothes, grab her panties, and we all ravish her, just like that, three by three. . . . Well what do you expect! It's war, isn't it! . . . She cries . . . asks forgiveness for all the crimes committed against the people . . . begs her husband to give us the key to the safe . . . But the President doesn't budge, on the contrary, the more she sobs and sniffles, the more he jokes around; he even says to us: "Rape her! Rape her! That's all she's been waiting for!" . . . Well, it's war, what do you expect? . . . "Rape her! That's all she's been waiting for! She's already cuckolded me with all my cabinet members . . . She even got herself diddled the other day by the guys at the fire station . . . So rape her as much as you like and however you like, you'll never get the key to the safe from me." . . . The more he pontificates, the more ferocious we are with his wife, until we realize she's not crying or sobbing, or even moving anymore, and for the last half hour we've been raping a corpse . . . But that's war, right? . . . And we have some real tough cookies in the squadron . . . Private First Class Without Pity, Corporal Terminator, and Head Sergeant Mass Grave drag the corpse into the next room and keep on raping, keep on raping, keep on raping. . . . That's what war is, always will be . . . The Dictator's in Heaven: "Bravo, my boys, he chortles, thanks for getting rid of that nymphomaniacal hyena!" . . . He laughs some more, "Come over here, boys, come on over so I can pin medals on your chests for service rendered to the highest authority in the State." He jokes again, "to the Great Liberator." . . . All of a sudden, El Comandante has had enough. He says, "I'm putting an end to this circus. Pull his pants down and make him kneel in front of me. It's time he felt the breath of hell in his ass!" . . . So we put him, naked, on all fours in front of El Comandante. And then the President stops joking around, he blubbers like a broad, because the jerk finally understands what's in store. He begs, "Pity, have pity, don't do that, please don't do that to me, nobody does that to his President . . . to the highest authority of the State . . . to the guarantor of our institutions . . . to the Great Liberator . . . Here, here's the key, take all my money . . . I'll even leave you the throne, just let me be without doing that . . ." But the Comandante's torpedo is already planted in his derrière . . . So he's crying even louder . . . He's weeping: "I'm in pain and I've been dishonored forever . . . I'm nothing more than an insect now . . . lower than slime on a toad . . . Kill me, render this last service to the nation, for once and for all put an end to my suffering and my dishonor" . . . El Comandante takes out his pistol and bang! Right in the head. Like a dog . . . That's war, you know! . . . But when we open the safe, there's nothing in it, completely empty. That sissy dictator had already transferred all his money to a private account in an offshore paradise . . .

WHITE MAGIC: *(to Schmeckel)* He just made me an offer I think I can't refuse! . . . Do you have something to perk me up? . . .

SCHMECKEL: What kind of offer?
WHITE MAGIC: The deal of the century!
SCHMECKEL: Really?
WHITE MAGIC: Really. Unbelievable!
SCHMECKEL: Did you already agree to it?
WHITE MAGIC: We're almost there . . . almost . . . The time it takes to adjust another 2% here, 3% there . . . But the end's in sight . . . Don't you have anything . . .
SCHMECKEL: Here. Swallow this before you go back to the battlefield . . . You'll see how well it works . . .
CAPTAIN FUCK DEATH: *(to Bonkers)* Hurry up. I need something to give me some pep! . . .
CORPORAL BONKERS: So what's happening?
CAPTAIN FUCK DEATH: You were right, My Dear Sir . . . So right. Nobody spits on money and celebrity . . .
CORPORAL BONKERS: So she signed?
CAPTAIN FUCK DEATH: Not yet . . . Not yet, but it's almost in the bag . . . She's just about to crack.
CORPORAL BONKERS: Did you tell her about the Moulin Rouge?
CAPTAIN FUCK DEATH: I'm saving it for the coup de grâce . . . These negotiations have worn me out; don't you have anything to . . . Because right now I'm about to get her to sign the agreement . . .
CORPORAL BONKERS: Here. Take this before you go on the attack . . . But be careful, it's pretty strong . . .
SCHMECKEL *(to Bonkers)*: She goes crazy . . . She's over the moon, it's as simple as that, but without any effort on my part.
CORPORAL BONKERS: But you do some weird and crazy shit, right?
SCHMECKEL: She's the one who does those things.
CORPORAL BONKERS: But you make up those honeyed words for her, you give her flowers all the time? . . .
SCHMECKEL: Nope. Not even. She's the one who grovels at my feet . . .
CORPORAL BONKERS: So you have a magic charm . . .
SCHMECKEL: I don't need one . . .
CORPORAL BONKERS: Of course you have a magic charm, come on . . .
SCHMECKEL: I have no need of a *gri-gri* . . .
CORPORAL BONKERS: Don't lie to me, you have a magic charm! You've put a spell on her! . . . Tell me who concocted the spell for you . . .
SCHMECKEL: I'm telling you, I have no magic charm, no *gri-gri* . . .
CORPORAL BONKERS: You don't give her flowers, you don't say pretty things,

you don't have a magic charm, and I bet you don't even know why only the banks were spared when Beirut was bombed? . . .

SCHMECKEL: The dumbest moron knows why that happened.

CORPORAL BONKERS: So you know?

SCHMECKEL: Like everybody else.

CORPORAL BONKERS: Then you can tell me?

SCHMECKEL: Sure. It's as obvious as the nose on your face . . .

CORPORAL BONKERS: So? . . .

CAPTAIN FUCK DEATH *(to White Magic)*: Mink coats . . . sable stoles . . . whatever you can dream of . . . of course if everything goes as planned . . .

WHITE MAGIC: And why wouldn't it? . . .

CAPTAIN FUCK DEATH: The Moulin Rouge, an exact replica, built just for you in Las Vegas . . . For you, alone . . .

WHITE MAGIC: On my, that's really too much, too much, too much . . .

CAPTAIN FUCK DEATH: Nothing will ever be too much for the Bavarian Josephine Baker, the greatest singer the world has ever known.

WHITE MAGIC: Your flatter me, My Dear Friend . . .

CAPTAIN FUCK DEATH: Why should I flatter you, Madame! It's the truth, nothing but the truth.

WHITE MAGIC: The Moulin Rouge! For me. For me alone. In Las Vegas . . . Las Vegas!

CAPTAIN FUCK DEATH: Where you can sing morning, noon, and night . . .

WHITE MAGIC: And also after midnight . . .

CAPTAIN FUCK DEATH: That goes without saying. After midnight . . . and even at 3:00 a.m., 4:00 a.m., 4:33 a.m., even 5:17 in the morning . . .

WHITE MAGIC: I'll sign . . .

CAPTAIN FUCK DEATH: White Magic is signing! *(She signs the accord.)* White Magic has signed! Glory and riches to White Magic!

To celebrate this milestone, White Magic grabs a megaphone and strikes up an aria that is obviously from an opera. But as soon as she begins to sing, something becomes as clear as day. Despite the best will in the world, White Magic is a terrible singer. But even so, the three others congratulate her heartily: "Bravo!" Her aria is followed by a Johann Strauss polka, "Eljen a Magyar," No. 332, to which the four characters dance with reckless abandon.

WHITE MAGIC: Schmeckel, go get the camera . . . We must immortalize this moment . . .

He leaves.

CORPORAL BONKERS: And just as important, Madame Josephine Baker, we must find a father for your child . . .

WHITE MAGIC: Don't be ridiculous . . .

Schmeckel returns with the camera and sets it on a tripod. He focuses it, then joins the three others.

CORPORAL BONKERS: . . . It's not so great for our scenario that the Prime Minister is pregnant.

WHITE MAGIC: Shut up and smile!

CORPORAL BONKERS: . . . With a child of, shall we say, an unknown father . . .

WHITE MAGIC: Give me a break and smile!

CORPORAL BONKERS: . . . People will talk . . .

WHITE MAGIC: *(in the megaphone)* I don't give a shit! *(The camera goes "click," on its own, automatically.)* Well, that's done . . .

CORPORAL BONKERS: . . . I could be that father, because . . .

WHITE MAGIC: *(in the megaphone)* No one will stick me with a father for my child! Or I'll blow up this agreement . . .

CAPTAIN FUCK DEATH: Let's calm down here! Nobody will force you to have a father for your child . . . We'll explain to the people that an angel appeared one day, etc., etc., etc. . . . There's a precedent for it, and it didn't change a hair on anyone's head, on the contrary. And think about how this will add a certain *People* magazine aura to the power structure . . . You'll be the sole mother and sole father of your baby . . . And the rest of you, get a hold of yourselves! We're almost at the finish, and this is not the moment to lose control! And I won't say that again! At ease!

Blackout.

VII. THE CHOSEN

White Magic enters, humming the aria from the last scene.

CAPTAIN FUCK DEATH: Congratulations again for your last performance. You were splendid.

CORPORAL BONKERS: Splendiferous . . . Splen-di-fer-ous . . .

CAPTAIN FUCK DEATH: Splen-di-fer-ous! Bravo again!

WHITE MAGIC: In the old days, every time there was a lag in production, I put on a symphony, a cantata, a sonata . . . Mozart, Wagner, Beethoven, the Brothers Haydn, Strauss . . . all the Strauss family. Or I sang, of course . . . You like German music?

CAPTAIN FUCK DEATH: I can't get enough of it.

CORPORAL BONKERS: We can't get enough of it.

WHITE MAGIC: The workers adore it. As soon as production slowed, I broadcast it to the whole factory, or I grabbed the megaphone and sang, just like that, and everything started up again; my voice intoxicated the workers . . .

She sings.

CAPTAIN FUCK DEATH: It's gorgeous . . . I've got the feeling that the workers are going to hear a lot of your fantastic music. Because we need a lot of money and as soon as possible.

CORPORAL BONKERS: So now we have an agreement, when do we start up the factory? . . .

WHITE MAGIC: Now. Right away. But before that I'd like to submit one last proposal to the assembly . . .

CORPORAL BONKERS: I thought we'd sewn up everything?

WHITE MAGIC: But this last proposal will cement the group we've just formed.

CAPTAIN FUCK DEATH: Out with it then.

WHITE MAGIC: Instead of handing over to only one person everything about the recipe and how the factory functions, I propose we divide up the information . . .

CAPTAIN FUCK DEATH: I don't understand . . .

CORPORAL BONKERS: I get it! . . . I get it! . . . It's . . . It's . . . It's . . . I mean . . . I mean . . . it's like a puzzle . . . In order for the factory to start up and the beer to flow, all the pieces have to fit into each other . . . That's what they do in pirate films . . .

WHITE MAGIC: You have indeed understood everything.

CORPORAL BONKERS: I don't think this is idiotic at all.

CAPTAIN FUCK DEATH: Not idiotic. . . . not idiotic . . . But, My Dear Sir, don't you see this doesn't cement the group but rather chains us to each other . . .

WHITE MAGIC: This is the very best way to protect every one of us . . . until we get to Las Vegas . . .

SCHMECKEL: A sort of I got you by the short hairs, you got me by mine . . .

CORPORAL BONKERS *(to Schmeckel)*: Now that is idiotic.

WHITE MAGIC: We're only human . . .

CAPTAIN FUCK DEATH: No! Never! I'm totally opposed to it. This is a kind of Mafia logic, nothing to do with democracy . . .

WHITE MAGIC: If that's the case, let's vote. Who's for?

Corporal Bonkers, Schmeckel and White Magic raise their hands.

CAPTAIN FUCK DEATH: I see there's no other choice than for me to bend to the popular will! So be it. And so, Madame, assign . . . assign . . .

WHITE MAGIC: I'd like to propose that 50% of the information goes to El Comandante because he is, after all, the brains of this operation, the President, the Holiest of Holies . . .

CAPTAIN FUCK DEATH: Let's not get carried away . . .

WHITE MAGIC: 35% to Corporal Bonkers, 5% for me, symbolically, and the last 10% to Schmeckel . . .

CORPORAL BONKERS: What! 10% for him! No! Never! That's scandalous! He shouldn't even get 1%, even 0%! I didn't fight against the Red Ninjas, the Crazy G.I.'s, the Warrior-Gravediggers, and the terrible Fire-Breathing Rambos . . . I didn't watch all my brothers in arms get killed in order to hand the brewery over on a silver tray to a playboy who lacks the goods! He'll never be part of our group! . . .

CAPTAIN FUCK DEATH: Oh yes he will, My Dear Sir. Given what's happened—negotiations, deliberations, the signing of the agreement—he is perfectly apprised of our plans. We have to consider him, de facto, an integral part of the group. The 10% he's being offered doesn't even begin to count as a scandal.

WHITE MAGIC: Motion adopted?

THE OTHER THREE: Here. Here.

CORPORAL BONKERS: But he'll never be a Minister . . . Not even Minister of Culture!

WHITE MAGIC: Of course not, because while we're in the Capital facing the weighty responsibilities of the Presidency and the Cabinet, Schmeckel will . . . Well I think he should be C.E.O. of the Brewery.

CAPTAIN FUCK DEATH: Excellent idea.

CORPORAL BONKERS: Best one yet. That way I won't have him underfoot all the time . . . *(to Schmeckel)* So what do you think about that, you lucky shit!

CAPTAIN FUCK DEATH: When do we get on with transferring the information?

WHITE MAGIC: Now.

She whispers his 50% into Captain Fuck Death's ears.

CAPTAIN FUCK DEATH: You don't say so!

WHITE MAGIC: Oh yes indeed.

CAPTAIN FUCK DEATH: That's 50% of it?

WHITE MAGIC: That's 50%.

CAPTAIN FUCK DEATH: It's unbelievably simple . . . Never, ever, ever would I have imagined such a thing! . . . Something so simple . . .

WHITE MAGIC: But there it is! . . . . Your turn.

She whispers his 35% into the ear of Corporal Bonkers.

CORPORAL BONKERS: It's . . . it's . . . it's . . . it's not possible. It's marvelous, just marvelous, as marvelous as light! . . . It's as if I've just seen the light . . .

WHITE MAGIC: But Mister Minister of the Armed Forces, you have just seen the light . . .

CAPTAIN FUCK DEATH: Let's not go that far.

WHITE MAGIC: Now your turn, Schmeckel.

She whispers his 10% in his ear.

SCHMECKEL: I wondered about that . . . I wondered about that . . . I always wondered if that could be it . . . But I never dared go there . . .

WHITE MAGIC: Think, Schmeckel, think. Dare to think. Don't ever get lazy about thinking.

SCHMECKEL: Thank you . . . Thank you for everything . . . I don't know how to thank you enough . . .

WHITE MAGIC: Of course you know how to thank me . . . In a little bit, when we're finally alone, you'll know how to thank White Magic just fine, you little tease . . . Comandante, now that we've dotted the *i*'s and crossed the *t*'s, might you find it possible to liberate MySweetie?

While White Magic and Captain Fuck Death discuss, Schmeckel suggests something to Corporal Bonkers who leaves the room immediately.

CAPTAIN FUCK DEATH: Not now and not here.

WHITE MAGIC: But why? . . . And when? . . . And where? . . .

CAPTAIN FUCK DEATH: I'll liberate MySweetie one day; you have my word as President of the Republic. But for the moment, and following your own example, Madame, MySweetie will remain a hostage until we all get to Las Vegas. To protect us from each other. Think of it as an automatic, maybe even natural, extension of how we control human interactions, if you see what I mean. We're only human, Madame.

WHITE MAGIC: Oh poor MySweetie . . . I swear to you, I'll free you soon from this shameful captivity . . . Come, Schmeckel . . .

Just when White Magic and Schmeckel are getting ready to leave, Corporal Bonkers returns with a bouquet of flowers.

CORPORAL BONKERS: I know you find me a little vulgar, Madame, but I can't contain myself any longer . . . I feel as though I'm burning up inside . . . I'm choking . . . I'm suffocating . . . Endless love for you is roiling my heart, you are the sunshine of my life . . . I know, I know too well that I don't deserve you and that it's an insult for a low-life nothing such as me to speak about your beauty, your gracefulness, your glow, but if I don't tell you what I feel, I'll die . . . Madame, I love you with a seismic love that is churning and churning and churning in me, until I have no breath left . . .

WHITE MAGIC: *Ich bin* . . . I am . . . I am . . . I don't know what to say . . . *Ich bin* . . .

CORPORAL BONKERS: Have you noticed? . . . Have you noticed that since I saw you, I've stopped stuttering? . . .

WHITE MAGIC: To be honest, I've heard you stutter once or twice, but what does it matter . . . It's so charming to hear you now . . . And, then, there's so much spontaneity, freshness . . . real feeling in your confession, I'm at a loss for words . . . *Ich bin* . . . *Ich bin* . . .

CORPORAL BONKERS: Accept at least these flowers, Madame, flowers I've gathered with my own two hands, my ten fingers, while thinking of you, every single minute . . .

WHITE MAGIC: They're for me?

CORPORAL BONKERS: Everything in me, about me is for you! What do I care about power, about vaults overflowing with bank notes, what do I care about the insolent luxury of American palaces, the sophisticated carefreeness of Nevada casinos, what does Las Vegas matter if you refuse this jewel box of flowers in which my anxious heart trembles as I lay it at your feet . . . You are so beautiful, Madame, so gracious that you are, all by yourself, the quintessential reason to live . . .

WHITE MAGIC: Wow, how about that . . . You . . . My God . . . It's so sudden . . . I'm so stunned that. . . *(She takes the flowers.)* Thank you . . .

CORPORAL BONKERS: OK, so now can I . . . your breasts!

She slaps him.

WHITE MAGIC: You pig!

CORPORAL BONKERS: Oh no, that's not fair, how come I get it every time!

SCHMECKEL *(cracking up with laughter)*: *"C'est une blague! C'est une blague! C'est une blague! . . ."*

White Magic leaves, followed by Schmeckel.

CAPTAIN FUCK DEATH: And yet, Dear Sir, you were . . . I never thought you capable of expressing yourself with so much . . . No, really I'm still . . . You've just, as they say, to be trivial, knocked the wind out of my ass.

CORPORAL BONKERS: I was . . . I was nearly . . . I felt her on the brink, breathless, ready to give in . . . ready to melt in my arms, and then, poof! . . . I must have missed a step . . . I don't know where or when . . . But that has to be it . . . I can't think of anything else . . . I must've fucked up somewhere . . .

Blackout.

VIII. WHERE ARE YOU, DEAR FATHER?

Noises of a working factory. Captain Fuck Death and Corporal Bonkers each have a giant stein of beer in their hands. Their eyes are closed. They are in ecstasy. It's hard to know if it's because of the beer in their hands or the "music" of the brewery at work.

CAPTAIN FUCK DEATH: This time, My Dear Sir, we've finally extricated ourselves from a fratricidal tragedy.

CORPORAL BONKERS: It's finally our turn! . . . I feel the wind in our sails . . . Las Vegas . . . Las Vegas . . .

CAPTAIN FUCK DEATH: We've finally closed the doors of Eden behind us . . . And we're on the way to building the foundations of a new Babylon . . .

CORPORAL BONKERS: A miracle . . . It's a miracle . . . This beer . . . This music . . . this moment . . . Everything's a miracle . . .

CAPTAIN FUCK DEATH: In the forest's silence, I hear the call of the people, our people . . . My Dear Sir, listen to them begin to sing our praises . . . I see in the night of the jungle our people kneeling in prayer . . . My Dear Sir, do you hear our people beg us come open the doors of the rebuilt Babylon . . . We're coming . . . We'll get there . . . I'm coming, my people . . .

CORPORAL BONKERS: Comandante . . .

CAPTAIN FUCK DEATH: What?

CORPORAL BONKERS: Ummm . . . out there . . . the shadows . . . what do we do with them? . . . We're not just going to abandon them, are we? . . .

CAPTAIN FUCK DEATH: Don't you worry about them, My Dear Sir. They're already waiting for us in Las Vegas.

CORPORAL BONKERS: How do you know?

CAPTAIN FUCK DEATH: Secret of the shadows. Mystery of the world's people . . .

White Magic's voice can be heard from backstage.

WHITE MAGIC *(off-stage)*: *Nein . . . nein . . . nein . . .*
Wo bist du, mein Väterchen? . . .
Ja . . . ja . . . ja . . . nein . . . nein . . . nein . . .
Wo bist du, mein Väterchen!
Komm und hilf mir, Väterchen . . .

The cantata beings to play again. The voice of White Magic and the "music" of the machines are replaced by the voices of the singing children. Captain Fuck Death and Corporal Bonkers close their eyes. Ecstasy.

CORPORAL BONKERS: Children! . . . Oh the children! . . . Do you hear them, Comandante? . . . It's the children . . .

CAPTAIN FUCK DEATH: Shush! . . .

Blackout.

END OF PLAY

Melancholy of Barbarians, directed by Sébastien Bournac at Scène Nationale d'Albi, France, 2013. Photo by François Passerini.

Melancholy of Barbarians

2008

TRANSLATED BY CHANTAL BILODEAU

INTRODUCTION TO MELANCHOLY OF BARBARIANS

It's always night, or we wouldn't need light.
—Thelonious Monk

Melancholy of Barbarians projects us into the fantastical and cartoonish world of a tough working-class suburb in an urban site. (Kwahulé, in fact, wrote this play at the behest of a cultural and social committee in Rodez, France, as a way of giving form to some of the community's concerns about internal racism, drugs, unemployment, and misogyny.) He imagines a revenge fantasy in which the character Baby Mo turns the dominant and tyrannical patriarchy on its head by destroying both policeman-husband, the Komisari—old enough to be her father—and the man-child, Zac, who spurns her.

Such a straightforward summary is far too simple to capture the several recurring motifs and bravado that hide the deep melancholia of the play. For Baby Mo, Zac, and even the Komisari are lost and hence destructive characters, covering themselves or being covered by an ideological mask, sanctioned by various forms of fundamentalism and Hollywood hype. Thus, the Komisari, standing in for all the absent fathers, rants about Golgotha and Jezebel like a hellfire and brimstone preacher, citing Old Testament verse and veiling his wife, taking her to church to keep her out of the hands and gaze of the immigrants he and the community fear. Brought in by the town authorities to restore law and order, the Komisari's idea of punishment is to drag offenders behind a pickup truck. (Here Kwahulé takes a poke at some of America's worst vigilante excesses.) Zac hides behind the posture of gang leader and drug dealer, attempting unsuccessfully to fill the shoes of his dead father, unable to rise to the challenge posed by his rebellious sister Lulu or to respond to either his "passing fancy," Judikael, the boy who loves him, or to Baby Mo, the girl who desires him and who works as his mule, connecting him to a more important drug lord.

Coming under the sway of the Komisari, who offers him manhood in the form of a gun, Zac continues, nonetheless, to identify with "Scarface," the cult movie antihero who destroys himself in his effort to take over the criminal world. Baby Mo (née "Monique"), rechristened after her recent marriage to the Komisari, is remaking herself in accordance with her new name: "Mo" homophonically suggesting wrongdoings (*maux*), or pain (*maux*), or words (*mots*), or all three. She fabricates stories that are both entrapping and freeing, leading finally to the slaughter of those she thought she loved. Her gang of girlfriends teases her about her hypocritical choices, riffing in the funniest tableau of the play on the strange similarities between pigs and human beings. There is resistance in their inventiveness and in girlfriend Lulu's clear-sightedness about the oppressive "Law of the Father," that has, in any case, run amok in the smoke and mirrors environment in which they live. But even Lulu's relative lucidity does not allow her to take her distance from wanting to join a corporation that would both control the world's economy and set up its employees as victims meant to be violently attacked.

These characters have no real boundaries, no strong sense of who they are. They do not know, as we hear in Baby Mo's parable at the end of the play, that the scent of the most beautiful perfume in the world comes from within. Yearning for transcendence, as seen in Zac's lyrical meditation on fireflies, they often resort to perverse empowerment through porn fantasies (Zac's gang), through harassment and belittling (the Komisari, the Recruiter), or by playing the dangerous adolescent games that equate eros with death and destruction (Baby Mo). As is frequent in Kwahulé's work, the signs of hope are found in the music of the words, here projected in the rap image of a metamorphosing Zac, who in death becomes a wondrous condor, the greatest of all birds, soaring on high to merge with the "red eye of the sky."

Notes for reading and for production:

1. The translation of this play moves into interpretive grounds by assigning lines to characters' names where there are no names in the original. Kwahulé again puts unassigned voices into play with other voices. It would surely be possible for a director to rethink how the lines are assigned according to how many actors he or she would want to use in a production.

2. Kwahulé always chooses characters' names for their musicality and often for their symbolic referentiality. Zachariah (Zac) is the name of a minor prophet from the Bible who foresaw a Messianic kingdom to come. Judikael is an old Breton name that can be loosely understood as meaning "kingly and generous." The Komisari evokes different Eastern European language terms, as well as a Baoulé word for a police officer.

3. *Scarface* is a 1983 Brian de Palma remake of a classic 1932 Hollywood film. Scarface (Al Pacino) takes over the drug territory of his boss in Miami, only to have his own business swept up by a rival Colombian gang in an excessively violent gun battle.

4. Golgotha is the site at which the crucifixion of Jesus is said to have taken place.

5. Jezebel was the power behind the throne in an ancient Hebrew kingdom, as recorded in the Old Testament. The Jezebel figure has come to be associated popularly with wicked "painted" women.

SETTING

A small town.

CHARACTERS

THE KOMISARI: Old enough to be Baby Mo's father.
ZAC: In his early twenties.
BABY MO: A teenage girl.
GIRL 1: A teenage girl.
GIRL 2: A teenage girl.
GIRL 3: A teenage girl.
THE MOTHER: In her late forties.
LULU: A teenage girl.
THE JOB RECRUITER: In his forties.
THE WOMAN: In her thirties.
JUDIKAEL: In his early twenties.
GUY 1: In his early twenties.
GUY 2: In his early twenties.
GUY 3: In his early twenties.
THE JURY MASTER: In his fifties or sixties.

TRANSLATOR'S NOTE

In its original French version, this play is written as pure dialogue—there are no character names and no stage directions. To facilitate the reading of the English translation, I have done the work of assigning lines to specific characters based on clues found in the text. But this distribution should be seen as only one possible interpretation; actors and directors are free to rethink the character breakdown and to assign lines differently. Passages in italics are drawn from the Bible.

IN THE NAME OF THE FATHER

THE KOMISARI: Baby Mo, you haven't seen her? . . . My wife? . . . I was told she was with you . . . But I see that's not the case. . . . Do you think that this, here, is a place for a gathering? That this is a time and place for such turbulent behavior? . . . I was appointed in this town so justice and equity make it their home again . . . And believe me, they will. . . . The Town Square is everybody's square. It's the core of the town. As its name indicates, it belongs to the town. To everybody. But with your behavior, with all this racket, you've driven all the respectable people away . . . See for yourselves, the terraces of the cafés are deserted . . . The Jury Council could sentence you to be dragged by the feet behind a pickup truck, you know that? . . . Let me see your IDs . . . Don't rush, I have all the time in the world. . . . Everybody in one line. . . . A straight line. . . . That's not a straight line. I want an impeccable straight line. You've never seen GIs on TV? There you go. . . . You see, with a little good will. . . . Show me your IDs. . . . All right, it will do for this time. Now get out of here, go back to your families. . . . Except you, Zac. . . . All of you, get lost. . . . Pay attention to the sound of my words, Zac. I'm talking to you in the name of your father. Your father who I never had the good fortune to meet but who, the whole town agrees, always lived in fear of the law, away from the pleasures of evil. An upstanding man. *Blessed is the man who does not walk in the counsel of the wicked, or stand in the way of sinners, or sit in the seat of mockers.* But I always find you, Zac, hanging around those young people . . . Do you know that some of them have already strayed far from the path of the law? You're like a lamb among jackals. You're not one of them, Zac. They live in hatred of the world because they haven't grabbed hold of the hope that the world offers. You're not one of them, Zac. Not of the same flesh, not of the same mind. Beyond your outrageous outfit and behavior, I see a pure soul. You're not one of them, Zac. Those people's minds are filled with malice and bile, with iniquities against the innocence of the world. That's why I pulled Baby Mo away from them. When I came to this town three months ago, Baby Mo was running with her back to the light, running without a goal, like a boat without a rudder, on paths strewn with thorns and shrouded in darkness. She was falling into impiety. She was getting lost. I pulled her away from them and I loved her and she was saved. She was saved not because I loved her but because she, herself, felt love. I simply gave her the gift of love. It's the only thing that can save us, Zac. To love. But for those people, it's too late; there's a point of no return in everything. They have nothing but loathing in their hearts. That's why I made Baby Mo dress the way she does now. That's why I made her cover herself. It's up to me to protect her. And all those people who recently washed up on our shores, having left women and children behind. Left women behind. Left everything behind. They are the parents of some of your partners in foolishness. What do they think? That on top of work, housing and food we also provide women? . . . I don't like that sex-starved look in their eyes. The idea that those eyes rest on Baby Mo makes me writhe in agony. And it's my duty to protect her. . . . At first, Baby Mo would only do as she pleased. She would strike rebellious poses, playing some unlikely warrior in army shoes, her navel sparkling with fake jewels. Like Lulu, your sister . . . Lulu, that's her name, right? . . . Watch your sister, Zac. It's up to us to protect our women. But at that age, they're extremely ungrateful. So it's with the same caution the mongoose uses to lure the cobra out of its lair that I slipped Baby Mo's body into those clothes and under that veil. Those people don't respect anything, except that. It's a mystery but it's the one thing, I noticed, that they respect. Any other woman is a harlot who must be punished with rape. But a woman dressed like Baby Mo, veiled like Baby Mo, they respect that. Their penises limply lower their heads in a sign of respect. If not surrender. Like the beast being crushed under the heel of the Saint on the façade of the cathedral. A mystery. So I'm asking you to direct your footsteps away from theirs. It's a request. Because be aware, Zac, that the day you let temptation rule over you, the day you stray from the garden of innocence, the day you move away from the light of the Spirit, the hand of justice will strike heavily. All the more so now that you've been warned. I'm telling you this in the name of your father whom I never met but who always lived, everybody here agrees, within the confines of the law. You can go now. . . . In the footsteps opposite theirs. . . . And if by chance you see my wife, tell her, Your husband is looking for you everywhere, Baby Mo.

MY MAN

BABY MO: I've always hoped something would happen to me. I called for love and love came. Not Prince Charming but a husband. Maniac and jealous so in a word, depressive. Finally, something's happening.

GIRL 1: Cops are often depressive.

GIRL 2: People are not objects. You can't do what you want with them. As you please. Even those who don't have enough to buy a cigarette, even those who have nothing but the sky and the stars for a roof, even the weak, those we can wipe our feet on with impunity, they resist, they always find a way to resist, through passivity, inertia, or resignation if they have to.

GIRL 3: A maniac can't understand when things are not how he thinks they should be.

BABY MO: He wants to keep me in a cage.

GIRL 1: That's all cops ever think about, keeping people in cages.

BABY MO: He's not a cop, he's a komisari.

GIRL 2: She's right, you know. 'Cause a komisari, that's not a cop.

GIRL 1: But it's still a policeman.

BABY MO: A policeman, yes, but not a cop.

GIRL 3: He scares the shit out of me your husband with his new laws. To drag someone by the feet behind a pickup truck, that just makes my blood run cold.

GIRL 1: I'd say he's a cop but not a policeman.

GIRL 3: Anyway your husband, well, he scares the shit out of me when he starts talking like a priest.

BABY MO: All the time, he's asking about this or that person . . . Who's who? . . . Who does what? . . . About Zac and his gang . . . And that just drives me bonkers.

GIRL 1: That's 'cause he's a cop. Cops always ask a lot of questions.

BABY MO: But I behave, I dress the way he wants, on Sundays, you saw me, I go to mass on his arm. But for him that's not enough, I'd have to stop breathing.

GIRL 2: The veil, it's him?

BABY MO: Yes, but I like it. It makes me different, it gives me a style. And I mean, if that's all it takes to make him happy . . . You know what? He buys my underwear now . . .

GIRL 1: Shut up!

GIRL 2: Does he have good taste?

BABY MO: It depends. It's kind of "sex shop" what he wants me to wear . . .

GIRL 3: So under your veil and everything, it's kind of Sodom and Gomorrah? . . .

BABY MO: I'd say more Sodom than Gomorrah.

GIRL 1: Oh, the dirty pig!

BABY MO: Hey, he's still my husband!

GIRL 2: Can you show us?

GIRL 3: You resisted, I hope?

BABY MO: So he'd start hitting me?

GIRL 1: Look, here comes Zac's mother.

GIRL 2: I find that sweet, a guy who'd be so crazy about me that he'd have me followed, that he'd put me in a cage like a cute little bird, that he'd hang himself on a butcher's hook out of jealousy, and that he'd choose my panties himself . . . It'd be like his fingers were imprinted on the panties and all the time he was . . . touching me . . . with his big manly fingers . . . I mean, can you imagine? . . . Just thinking about it, it makes me all—

BABY MO: What, you're getting wet?

GIRL 3: He beats you?

BABY MO: I never said that.

GIRL 3: Yes, you did.

GIRL 1: She must be looking for him again.

GIRL 3: No, I mean, it's true, you said it.

GIRL 2: Can you show us?

GIRL 3: Besides, cops are always quick to hit. It's their job.

THE MOTHER: Monique, you haven't seen my son by any chance?

BABY MO: No, Ma'am. Maybe you should look at the bar Le Grand Café on the Town Square. He goes there sometimes to play pool.

THE MOTHER: The Town Square . . . Thank you, Monique.

BABY MO: Ma'am, I'm not Monique. I'm Baby Mo.

. . .

GIRL 2: Poor woman. Running after her son like that all the time.

GIRL 3: Why does she ask you about her son?

BABY MO: I don't know . . . We went to the same high school. We're old friends from school, that's all. We dropped school at the same time. I'm mainly friends with his sister Lulu. But we see each other often . . . Maybe that's why.

GIRL 1: So it's true? . . . It's true or it's not true?

BABY MO: What?

GIRL 1: About Zac . . . I heard rumors.

BABY MO: In a small town with nothing to do, you can't prevent people from gossiping. That's all they have to fight boredom.

GIRL 3: It's true that in small towns, talking behind people's back helps kill time.

BABY MO: Except I've got a jealous depressive husband at home. How can people see me with Zac? He's too tormented, too tortured, too in his head for me. And anyway, I'm married.

GIRL 2: He scares me, that guy. In school, we used to call him Zac-the-Wacko.

GIRL 1: He's always been a bit cracked.

GIRL 2: Not just a bit. I say he's downright crazy.

GIRL 1: I have a hard time with the whole family. His sister Lulu with her Doc Martens, and even their mother. Since the father died, the family's been a mess . . . And you know me, men are not exactly— . . . 'Cause the thing about your cop is that—

BABY MO: He's not a cop, he's a komisari.

GIRL 3: You said he'd start hitting you?

GIRL 1: Your cop . . . Your policeman . . . Your husband. He hits you, you said.

GIRL 2: Come on, show us.

BABY MO: Wait, where did you get that idea? . . . I just said it like that . . . OK, a slap. Once. I wouldn't call that beating me. He didn't throw himself at me. He didn't punch me. I wasn't covered in bruises . . . And I have to admit, I had kind of pushed him to the limit.

GIRL 3: Still! He has no reason to hit you. It's obvious that he's stronger than you so he doesn't have to hit you.

BABY MO: But I keep telling you, he didn't hit me!

GIRL 1: Daddy just spanked his sweet little girl, is that it?

BABY MO: One slap. I didn't even get a bruise.

GIRL 3: He'll do it again, it's inevitable.

BABY MO: Not him. He grabbed his hand afterwards like he was hurt. He was crying and kept repeating, Forgive me Baby Mo . . .

GIRL 2: It's true that since your wedding he's been calling you Baby Mo.
BABY MO: He doesn't like Monique. He says it's a corny name good for country folks. He says it sounds old.
GIRL 2: Now everyone calls you Baby Mo.
GIRL 1: I have a hard time imagining a cop crying.
BABY MO: Forgive me Baby Mo, I didn't mean it, I didn't mean it, I didn't mean it, he was crying. I won't do it again, he was crying . . .
GIRL 3: He'll do it again.
BABY MO: He didn't beat me, just one slap. Then he went downstairs and came back with flowers. Madagascar jasmine. In a pot. He put it at my feet, knelt in front of me and asked me to forgive him. He kept repeating, I didn't mean it, I didn't mean it, I didn't mean it . . . And crying. 'Cause deep down, he's a good man. In a way, he's even sweet. Not tender but sweet. Like an angel. Well, the way we imagine angels to be. So I call him sweet husband.
GIRL 1: Mine too is a good man. But you and your cop—
GIRL 3: It's true that— . . . Has anyone told you? You look kind of strange together.
GIRL 1: It's the age difference, you know what I mean?
GIRL 3: It's too obvious.
GIRL 1: It's all we see: a girl and her father.
GIRL 3: No, I mean, it's true, look at us, we're the same age, we're not teenagers anymore but I don't feel like a woman yet . . .
GIRL 1: Not woman enough to lose myself in a marriage . . .
BABY MO: Here's Zac's mother again.
GIRL 1: And with a cop who's not—
GIRL 2: Leave her alone, it's her life, she can do whatever she wants.
GIRL 1: So as I was saying, mine too is a good man. And we're the same age. He washes dishes at the restaurant where I wait tables. La Taverne . . . Have you ever seen us together? . . . Always calling me sugar . . . cupcake . . . creamy peachy pie . . . sweet banana love . . .
GIRL 2: Mine calls me the honey nut muffin of his heart.
GIRL 1: But when he gets the urge—
BABY MO: The last time I saw you together, I thought he looked blasé.
GIRL 1: It's a front, it's just a front. Deep down, he's a sensitive soul; smart, passionate and he can be really funny when he wants to . . .
GIRL 2: And you'd have to be blind not to see he's got a lot of charm.
GIRL 1: He's drop dead gorgeous, you mean?

GIRL 2: If on top of that, in bed he's— . . . That sure doesn't hurt. I mean, if I can believe what you told me the last time . . .

GIRL 1: It's true that in that department, I've got nothing to complain about. And on top of that, he's a romantic, a dreamer, an artist . . .

GIRL 3: An artist? Watch out, he'll end up unemployed. Artists are all unemployed. Even the very rich and famous. Deep down, they're always unemployed. They were born that way.

GIRL 1: Yes, but he's only an artist on the side. He's got a job washing dishes. And in his spare time, he writes poems and songs about plants and flowers. He's convinced that we can stop the North Pole from melting with songs about flowers.

GIRL 3: I don't see how we can patch up the ozone layer with flowers.

BABY MO: Only love can save us.

GIRL 1: My man's got a lot of love! He's got so much love that he gives it to cactuses, his place is full of cactuses. But even a guy like that, who writes songs about flowers to stop the ice from melting, who's bursting with love for cactuses, well, the other day he didn't hesitate to— . . . 'Cause what I'm trying to say is—

GIRL 2: Come on, don't be a bore. Show us.

BABY MO: What?

GIRL 2: Your underwear. You said it was kind of "sex shop."

GIRL 1: Baby Mo, your husband.

THE KOMISARI: *Stay away from a foolish man,*
for you will not find knowledge on his lips.

Baby Mo, I came to get you. We're going home.

JUST LIKE IF DAD WERE HERE

ZAC: What do you expect, Ma? . . . You really want me to tell you where I get my money?

. . .

THE MOTHER: No, it's OK . . . We can't afford to open our eyes these days . . . I don't want to know. I don't want to know anymore. I would rather not know . . . Opening my eyes is a luxury I can't afford . . . Let's change the subject.

ZAC: I met Baby Mo's husband. He's a good guy. He too thinks it's my duty to protect you. Since Dad's not here anymore, it's up to me to make sure you've got everything you need. I do what I can, Ma. It's just that I don't have the strength to run from interview to interview like Lulu. 'Cause there isn't a single job around here. Maybe she tells herself, You never know. Maybe it keeps her busy. But me, I have to protect you, to make sure you've got everything you need. Just like if Dad were here.

THE MOTHER: It smells good. . . . You should stop seeing Baby Mo.

ZAC: She's the one chasing after me.

THE MOTHER: It's strange the way she dresses since she got married . . .

ZAC: I wish Lulu would dress like her . . .

THE MOTHER: She's like an image from the desert. But it suits her. It makes her, how can I describe it, not more woman but less girl . . . You wish what?

ZAC: That Lulu would wear the veil too.

THE MOTHER: Lulu?

ZAC: Yes, Lulu.

THE MOTHER: My daughter wear the veil?

ZAC: It'd protect her.

THE MOTHER: From what?

ZAC: I don't know . . . From all kinds of things . . . From certain people . . . All those people who took over our town . . . Who have that look in their eyes . . .

THE MOTHER: What's this thing about a veil all of a sudden? . . . Listen to me, Zachariah, you will never make your sister wear the veil.

ZAC: But I'm telling you, it'd protect her . . .

THE MOTHER: You will never make your sister wear the veil.

ZAC: Baby Mo wears it.

THE MOTHER: So? Monique is Monique and Lulu is Lulu . . . Where did you get that idea, Zachariah? . . . You will never force your sister to wear the veil.

ZAC: I just said it like that . . .

THE MOTHER: You will never subject your sister to the veil!

ZAC: What did you think, Ma, that I really wanted to deck Lulu out in that thing?

THE MOTHER: Swear it!

ZAC: On Dad's head.

THE MOTHER: For Monique, I don't want to judge . . . She's a married woman now, Zachariah.

ZAC: I told you she's the one chasing after me.

THE MOTHER: She's not chasing after you, she loves you. She's a married woman and she loves you. She's a troubled woman. A woman that the slightest thing can break. So go easy on her.

ZAC: I met her husband. The cop. He says he wishes he'd met Dad . . . He talked to me like a father . . .

THE MOTHER: It smells so good!

ZAC: You like it?

THE MOTHER: It must have cost you a fortune.

ZAC: It's just a bottle of perfume, Ma. It's not like I gave you a Ferrari. . . . You like it?

THE MOTHER: It smells good.

ZAC: You'll have everything you need, Ma. I'll protect you. Just like if Dad were here.

. . .

THE MOTHER: No, Zachariah . . . Zachariah, stop . . . I said stop!

. . .

LULU: Can you believe the new police guy those idiots hired? I just bumped into him, Baby Mo's husband, he was prowling around the building again.

THE MOTHER: How did it go?

LULU: It could've gone better. Bad. They only talked about my bandana and my shoes . . .

THE MOTHER: You were wearing those shoes?

LULU: What else do you want me to wear, Mom? Stilettos? Fuck them, my shoes don't need a job, I do. Anyway they don't fucking care nobody fucking cares they talk and talk and talk but it's all bullshit they don't fucking care. What they want is to see us die without a word among ourselves die in silence maybe even die saying thank you thank you for everything as if all of this were normal. That's why they sent us that new police guy.

ZAC: It's what this town needed . . .

LULU: I'm talking to Mom.

ZAC: A man with a firm hand. Who's got balls and uses them.

LULU: That's just smoke and mirrors it's their own smoke and mirrors. The truth is that everything's dead it's all dead. But they dumped that guy on us Baby Mo's husband so they can keep the illusion that they're still capable of a few erections like those old farts who watch porn obsessively in the hope that they'll get it up again. But it's dead it's all dead and I wasn't talking to you.

ZAC: Someone who can't be messed with when it comes to order. 'Cause we'll need order with all these miseries coming at us.

LULU: Moron! When things blow up those like you those like me will be crushed first. So keep acting like a big shot keep pretending you're one of them instead of looking for a job.

ZAC: The law. Someone who still remembers the law. We only need one person to remember it and the air in this country will start smelling human again. All those people who are piling up around our walls . . . Having left women and children behind. Left women behind . . . All those people with dubious morals.

LULU: Mom tell him to leave us alone! Here I don't want your bandana anymore!

ZAC: We've got our miseries too. There's no shortage of poor people around here. But we don't ask anyone to feel sorry for us. We don't flaunt it for the world to see. Out of decency. And pride. These people have no pride. And you can't achieve greatness without pride.

THE MOTHER: Don't be unnecessarily mean, it's not like you.

ZAC: I'm trying to say out loud what everyone's thinking quietly, Ma.

THE MOTHER: It may be that what's being thought quietly shouldn't be said out loud. Maybe not all thoughts are meant to be said out loud.

ZAC: You really don't want this bandana?

LULU: I don't want it anymore.

ZAC: Dad wouldn't be happy with that.

LULU: Leave Dad where he is. You think he's happy with you?

ZAC: It looked good on your head. Looked really good, sis.

LULU: I'm not sis. I'm Lulu.

ZAC: You really don't want my gift anymore, Lulu?

LULU: Or anything else from you.

ZAC: Then these clothes, Lulu, why don't you take them off? Since they were a gift from me.

LULU: I'll give them to you after dinner.

ZAC: I want them right here, right this minute.

LULU: Don't start again Zac. You're dying to see me strip naked right here in front of you?

THE MOTHER: Lulu!

ZAC: Who asked for such a thing? Did I imply such heresy, Ma? You're dreaming, sis, you're dreaming dangerously.

LULU: Be careful Zac be very careful. I'm not Mom.

. . .

THE MOTHER: You should go easy on your brother . . .

LULU: Of course we always have to go easy on him! But does he go easy on us? Since Dad's been gone you've been waiting on him hand and foot. Like he's become Dad . . . Even Baby Mo's at his feet . . . But me— . . .'Cause I told him . . . I told him Zac you've gotta stop talking to me like that. This way he has of talking to me like I'm a five-year-old a pile of shit with no ears. I told him You've gotta stop behaving that way. 'Cause it could all end very badly. It could end very very badly. And believe me Mom these are not empty words. I'm not his thing. He needs to understand that. You need to make him understand that. I'm not his girlfriend. I'm not you. 'Cause he's dying to see me spread wide open . . .

THE MOTHER: Lulu!

LULU: Everybody bends over backwards for him what's Zac doing what's Zac drinking what's Zac eating did Zac poop did Zac pee did Zac sleep oh poor Zac! No, poor Baby Mo! A smart girl who could've gone to college and beyond if she'd wanted to but instead crawls at his feet all tears and apologies. He's the one who should be kneeling in front of her covering her feet with kisses and thanking everything worth thanking on earth and in Heaven for the love of a girl like Baby Mo . . . Christ what does she see in him? What else is she gonna come up with to make a fool of herself? And the other one too Judikael whom he calls his passing fancy . . . Everyone wants the best for him. But what does he do for others? What does he do for himself?

THE MOTHER: Zachariah! . . . Zachariah, are you coming to eat? . . . Zachariah! . . .

LULU: Leave him if he doesn't wanna eat he doesn't have to.

THE MOTHER: Your interview was that bad?

LULU: I'd rather not talk about it. I have another interview anyway. A connection of Baby Mo's.

THE MOTHER: You want to tell me about it?

LULU: No. I want it to be a surprise. Baby Mo told him about me. I know Dad would be proud. I want you to be proud.

THE MOTHER: This time, think about not wearing these things you call shoes. I'll buy you shoes, real women's shoes. During the interview, don't talk like a whirlwind or let yourself get carried away—

LULU: I don't get carried away it's my way of talking in my head I have the right rhythm.

THE MOTHER: Speak calmly and watch the rhythm of your breath. The rhythm of your heart. Watch the rhythm of your heart. Be confident without being arrogant. Watch your language. And if by chance one of them says something unkind, tell yourself it's not about you personally, tell yourself he's playing a role, tell yourself the circumstances require he talk to you that way, to test your cool. So pretend you don't hear the hurtful words, keep your fist in your pocket. And smile. No smile ever cracked a jaw. And most importantly, don't speak fast. Take your time, chose your words and align them with the rhythm of your breath. And most, most importantly, watch the rhythm of your heart.

LULU: I'll remember that, Mom.

THE MOTHER: Earlier when you were talking to your brother, you said, I'm not Mom, and to me you said, I'm not you. What does that mean, I'm not you?

LULU: It's clear, I'm not you, I'm not you, I'm not you, it's clear.

THE MOTHER: When you said to your brother, I'm not Mom—

LULU: Mom!

THE MOTHER: You said, when you were talking to your brother—

LULU: You know exactly what that means. There are certain things you shouldn't allow him to do. To rub against you. It's like you're both spitting on Dad's grave.

THE MOTHER: You should be ashamed of yourself for thinking that!

LULU: Talk to him, Mom. Tell him he's gotta stop rubbing against you. Tell him he can't do that. 'Cause people are talking. In the building, gossip is spreading. From top floor to bottom floor. I've talked to him. Several times. I've told him, Zac, you've gotta stop rubbing against Mom. You've gotta get those ideas out of your head. Get that out of your head. Get that out of your head. Get that out of your head, I've told him, and told him, and told him, and told him. Otherwise, I'll have to do something. What Dad would've done. Yes, Mom, it could end very badly. It could all end very very badly. Believe me Mom, these are not empty words. People are talking, you know?

THE MOTHER: People are talking . . .

LULU: It's up to you to explain that to him. You're the mother.

WE'RE FIREFLIES WHO HAVE NOT YET LOVED

BABY MO: Give me some light! . . . *Scarface* again? . . . How can you hole up in the dark and watch this ridiculous film when outside it's so beautiful you want to dance out of sheer gratitude for being alive? . . . Lulu and your mother are out? . . . Here's a new package. . . . You don't say thank you? . . . A kiss on the forehead, that's all? . . . Kiss me. . . . This is the last package. I'm not proud of myself. I'm a married woman. So I could tomorrow become the mother of one of the children you sell this thing to . . . No, not proud of myself at all. I feel dirty, can you understand that, Zac? Not dirty like— . . . No, dirty like I've raped myself. . . . Can you stop the film? . . . Thank you. . . . Mr. Africa wants a lot more now . . .

ZAC: Fuck Mr. Africa.

BABY MO: He wants you to raise the price of the doses. He says you need to cut it to create more volume. Basically, he wants a lot more money. . . . This is my last trip, Zac.

ZAC: You always say that.

BABY MO: Maybe but this time it really is the last one . . . You should think about looking for work. Real work . . . I could help you. There must be a job somewhere in this town. I'll fight for you. I'll find you a real job. We just have to get ready for war, Zac. 'Cause real life is war. I'll fight for you. Talk about it to my husband maybe. He knows people and he likes you, you know. . . . You're not alone, Zac, I'll hold your hand. . . . When are Lulu and your mother coming back?

ZAC: No idea.

BABY MO: I'm right here in front of you . . .

ZAC: I'm thinking about striking out on my own.

BABY MO: And we're alone . . .

ZAC: So Mr. Africa can go fuck himself.

BABY MO: Hold me in your arms, Zac. . . . Just hold me. . . . Thank you. . . . Simply in each other's arms.

. . .

ZAC: They say that fireflies . . . The other night, I was with your husband . . . On the right bank of the river . . . He had asked me to go with him. He said he wanted to show me something amazing that happens there . . . Every night, on the right bank of the river, there's a dazzling performance: a ballet of fireflies. Not thirty, not fifty like you see from time to time but thousands and thousands and thousands of fireflies. They appear out of nowhere and sparkle, and sparkle, and sparkle . . . And then, in the midst of the fireflies' dance, I felt streams of luminous love wash over me. Yes, Baby Mo, love. A crushing love 'cause it wasn't attached to anything. To anything at all 'cause the fireflies were sparkling with love. Your husband explained to me, like to a son, that love is what makes fireflies sparkle; that we too, if we reach a certain degree of love, will become luminous; others will see love shine through us, exactly like the fireflies, 'cause we're fireflies who have not yet loved. And that night, on the right bank of the river, in the blink of an eye, I felt cleansed, yes, Baby Mo, cleansed of all the iniquities of my life. And filled with love. . . . The males will stop sparkling first. The females will sparkle a few hours more in order to ensure a lineage. Within a few days, the fireflies will have fulfilled the law: to love. And since there's nothing after love, they'll be able to return to the source of all things. On my way back from the right bank of the river, I wanted to die for you, Baby Mo. I so wish I could sparkle for you but I'm only me . . . I'm only Zac . . . And I can't . . . I can't . . . I can't . . .

. . .

BABY MO: Tell me about the fireflies again.

ZAC: I'm done talking about the fireflies.

BABY MO: Earlier, when you were talking about the fireflies, it seemed like your desire was swelling under my hand . . .

ZAC: I'm done talking about the fireflies.

. . .

BABY MO: When are Lulu and your mother coming back?

ZAC: I told you, no idea . . . No, no . . . No . . . Don't take your clothes off. Just stay how you are . . . Even like this, you're— . . . You're so beautiful, Baby Mo, so beautiful I could collapse into blissful sobs. You're beautiful 'cause you're gentle. And I wish I could die for you. But—

BABY MO: Give me your hand . . . Let me guide you. Let yourself go . . .

ZAC: No, no, not that . . . Not that . . . I just— . . . Just wanna suckle . . . I just wanna suckle, Baby Mo.

BABY MO: What have you done to me, Zac? . . . Here's my breast . . . .

ZAC: Stroke my hair . . .

BABY MO: Many times I've told myself, What are you doing with your life, Baby Mo?

ZAC: Like I'm your child . . .

BABY MO: You're not dumb and they say you're beautiful . . .

ZAC: Give birth to me, Baby Mo . . .

BABY MO: You're a married woman. Your husband loves you and you love your husband. Your husband is the komisari of this town; you're welcomed into the homes of the Procurator, the Senator, the Mayor, the Jury Master . . . into the homes of everyone who matters in this town. You're on friendly terms with their wives. You have connections. What you've always dreamed of, you've achieved. Whatever the cost was. You, who came from nowhere, you matter in this town. You're someone. You're happy. Or at least you should be, Baby Mo. But here you are, crawling at the feet of a child who's afraid to become a man. . . . Zac, I want to feel on my nipple not the bitter tongue of a brat but the fierce desire of a man. . . . Tell me about the fireflies again . . .

ZAC: No . . . No . . . I don't want that . . . I just wanna suckle . . . Baby Mo, stop! . . .

BABY MO: Let's try one more time . . .

ZAC: Just suckle.

BABY MO: I beg you Zac, don't humiliate me again.

ZAC: I'm not ready . . . It's my head . . . It's all in my head . . .

BABY MO: Give yourself a chance . . .

ZAC: Since my father died, my head hasn't been right.

BABY MO: Give us a chance. At the very least tell me, I love you. Tell me once. Just once. Tell me, I love you, and I'll believe you. . . . Please tell me something, Zac, tell me that you love me, I know it's not true, I know you're not willing to die for me but tell me and I'll believe you. . . . It's your mother, isn't it? . . . You really don't want to talk to me anymore? . . .

ZAC: I wish I could love you, Baby Mo. . . . Don't judge me too harshly 'cause you have a lot of luck . . . It's lucky to love the way you love.

BABY MO: Talk about luck! . . . You need to face a fact or two: You're not a child and I have no desire to be your mother. Sorry Zac, I'll never be your mother.

STONING

GIRL 3: What the fuck do you want, Monique? What do you think? That you're now important 'cause you get on all fours in front of the head cop?

I saw him the other day, your man, he looks beat up, already worn out by life and his line of work. 'Cause that job's not for the faint of heart. Sooner or later, it wears you out. Whether you want it or not, it wears you out, it makes you old before your time. And you, Monique, you're still a child. You have everything in front of you . . .

GIRL 2: I saw a pig eat a spoon. The other day. A tablespoon. I was at a farm and I saw a pig eat a spoon. Crushed, swallowed and digested. I got to that farm by chance. A friend with only half a brain had asked me to go to a pigpen with her; she wanted to drink pig's milk. We don't think about it but pigs are more than just Chinese spareribs, Frankfort sausages, Bayonne ham, dry Auvergne sausages and American bacon. Among other things. 'Cause everything's good in a pig . . .

GIRL 3: You don't even know the guy, in fact nobody knows him. He hasn't been here three months, you've already married him. We don't know what's trailing after him. And the little we know doesn't smell very good . . .

GIRL 1: 'Cause basically, the pervert, it's not him, Monique. It's you . . .

GIRL 2: Like all mammals, pigs have udders that produce milk but we don't think about it. In any case, I saw that pig, actually that sow, eat a spoon. Immediately I thought, it's exaggerated to say that man is a pig on the basis that, like the animal, he's omnivorous, which means he eats everything. Man eats everything, yes, but I have yet to see someone eat a spoon, even a very small one. Like a teaspoon. Razor blade swallowers, diamond crunchers, sword swallowers, OK, but tablespoon eaters, that remains to be seen . . .

GIRL 1: I mean fuck, why do you dress like this, Monique? Indulge him as much as you want in the name of what you believe to be a burning passion but for God's sake, get rid of this ridiculous outfit! 'Cause I don't buy it, you look costumed, I'm telling you as a friend, you look ready for carnival. And it's all of us, women of this town, you're allowing him to insult, you're exposing us to the sarcasm of the nearby towns . . .

GIRL 2: Granted, some people are born with a silver spoon in their mouth but they don't eat it. It's an image. Those people don't come out of their mother's belly with a silver spoon between their teeth. It's just an expression so we can't take the thing literally. Someone who's got money coming out of his ass is not necessarily pulling wads of cash out of his behind, and snake swallowers— . . . Well, no need to harp on it, it makes sense. Like those who shoot themselves in the foot or put their foot in their mouth. Like those who split hairs or cut off their nose to spite their face. Like those who are bone-lazy or twirl their thumbs. Like those who shit bricks or have a broomstick up their ass . . .

GIRL 3: If at least he were handsome, Monique. 'Cause even among old guys, there are handsome ones. But even the handsome ones don't do it for me. I can't imagine myself with them, skin to skin. It's physical. The rancid smell maybe. Or the stench of mothballs. So other than a big rod, I don't see what he's got. 'Cause it's no secret, Monique, you've always had a weakness for uniforms. You used to talk about it all the time at school. Cops, gendarmes, soldiers, even firemen . . . But turns out, he doesn't wear a uniform. Then what? If it's not the uniform, there's gotta be something that makes up for it . . .

GIRL 2: Those who pay on the nail. Those who have scales falling from their eyes. Those who pull the rug from under people's feet. Those who lie through their teeth. Those who wear their heart on their sleeve. Those who talk out of their ass. Those who speak with a forked tongue. Those who are wet behind the ears . . .

GIRL 3: Big rods must turn you on, Monique. 'Cause I'm wracking my brain and I can't find any other explanation. He's old, he's ugly . . . Yes, I think he's ugly, he's just a cop . . . OK, a komisari but fuck, a komisari, it's not like you scored the top prize!

GIRL 1: No, I mean, it's true, a komisari, it's not like it's America!

GIRL 3: I'm sure it's his big thing that turns you on. Does he at least let you touch it? . . .'Cause I can't lie, I'd love to know what it feels like to have one in my hand. To grab it, like this, really tight. Just to see . . .

GIRL 2: Or who have a frog in their throat. Or who wait to see which way the cat jumps. Or who beard the lion in his own den. Or who drink like fish. Or who put the cart before the horse. Or who throw pearls before swine. Or who count their chickens before they're hatched. Or who have the constitution of an ox. Or who lead a cat and dog life. Or who have a bee in their bonnet. Or who don't let sleeping dogs lie . . .

GIRL 3: OK, so you've stroked and stroked his big thing. Day and night stroked it. Hundreds of times stroked it. OK . . . It may be time to move on now, don't you think?

GIRL 1: Who are you trying to kid with your outfit, Monique? You, the school pinup, the shameless flirt, the tease who used to get fondled in every school corner! And always wanted more! Unless you've suddenly gone nuts? That's all I can think of, you've completely lost your marbles . . .

GIRL 3: I mean really, what's this bullshit, Monique? You believe in God now? You? You worship every Sunday! You, Monique, well behaved, hands clasped, listening to a flood of religiosity like a doddering old fool! I find that staggering. Unless you've had a revelation?

GIRL 1: While stroking his thing maybe . . .

GIRL 3: How far are you going to take this? What's next? The convent? A retreat in the desert eating crickets and roots? I know you Monique, you've never believed in God, not even in baby Jesus. The only thing you've ever believed in is the size of your ass. No frankly, I don't buy it . . .

GIRL 2: Anyway, the whole thing's ridiculous. Man eats everything but not spoons. Pigs, on the other hand, do. Conclusion, man, contrary to a commonly held belief, is not a pig. 'Cause pigs eat everything while man eats of everything. Subtle difference. Which explains why everything's good in a pig while with man, you've got to separate the wheat from the chaff. Man, though not restricted in any way, refuses to indulge with as much abandon as pigs. But you, Monique, you wallow in the mud and expose this honorable and pretty town to the sarcasm of the entire region. You're barely out of puberty and you've already thrown yourself, against father and mother, against a whole town, in an improbable union. And in doing so, you're undermining the fight of countless generations of women. Look at your outfit. The Middle Ages are over, Monique. If at least you were doing it in the name of some religious sacrifice! You're lowering us to the rank of pigs. You're a pig! You're a swine! Shame on your house! Shame on you who've turned this town into a prostitute! . . . Here's a spoon, stuff yourself!

BABY MO: I admit that I'm a pig, and even, let's not beat around the word, a swine, a dirty swine who has, through her actions, dragged the town's honor into the mud in which fat pigs and fat swine like to frolic. And that's not good. I admit that I crossed a line when I married this man older than my father, a man with an uncertain past who forced me to put my life under the authority of the veil and to do a number of other things you far from suspect. I admit that through this act, I've covered all the women of this town with shame. And that's not good. I admit that on Sundays, when he drags me to our place of worship and during the sermon I hear the call of boredom, I like to slip my hand under his coat, and with the tips of my fingers, stroke his big thing without moving the rest of my body, my face as solemn as the face of the Virgin standing by her son's blood. And that's not good. Now that you've proved how much you know what's just and good for me, what's honorable for this town, now that I've agreed with all of you, that I've recognized my faults, now that you've established that you're the world's shining light, leave me the fuck alone with my swine's life. And another thing: Stick this once and for all in the roomiest part of your brain. I'm not Monique, I'm Baby Mo. Not Monique. Baby Mo.

THE RECRUITER

LULU: Good morning, Sir . . . I read your ad . . .

. . .

THE WOMAN: I waited for you yesterday.

LULU: Good morning . . . Two days ago, I talked to your— . . . Well, to someone from here . . . On the phone . . . He told me I could stop by . . .

THE WOMAN: What's going on? . . . How come you didn't show up? . . . I'm not leaving until you give me an answer.

THE RECRUITER: Can't you see I'm working?

LULU: It's about the ad . . . Lulu . . . My name's Lulu . . . I'm Lulu . . . The girl on the phone . . . Lulu . . . Baby Mo must have told you about me . . .

THE WOMAN: Who is she?

THE RECRUITER: Can't you see? She's looking for work.

LULU: I talked to someone here on the phone . . . And then I received the notification . . . It's for the position . . . Baby Mo told me to come see you. She's a friend.

THE RECRUITER: The komisari's wife. I know.

THE WOMAN: How come you didn't show up last night?

LULU: I might as well say it now, as Baby Mo must have explained, I don't have a diploma. Just a driver's license. After what happened to my father, I lost my taste for everything. Starting with school. So I quit.

THE WOMAN: You don't want to answer?

LULU: I've filled out an application. Everything's on my application. Name, date and place of birth, level of education . . . Well, I didn't really get an education . . . Anyway, everything's on the application. But I don't mind talking about it, I think that's how you say it, face to face.

THE WOMAN: Your silence is beneath contempt.

THE RECRUITER: I told you, it's over.

THE WOMAN: What's over?
LULU: I need this work.
THE WOMAN: What's over?
LULU: My family and I need it . . .
THE WOMAN: What is it that's over?
LULU: Plus, I like the work. I'd even say it's a vocation. I think that's how you say it, a vocation. Thanks to my father. Since I was little—
THE WOMAN: What are you willing to do?
LULU: I beg your pardon, Ma'am?
THE WOMAN: For the position, are you willing to do anything?
LULU: Yes . . . Of course . . .
THE RECRUITER: Mind your own business! This is not a game, I'm working!
THE WOMAN: You don't want to answer me?
THE RECRUITER: Go on, Miss.
LULU: It's a vocation and I don't have a diploma. But I guess you don't need one for this type of work. It's my brother who should be here in front you but my brother doesn't have the vocation. And he's got other things on his mind. Or maybe he's got nothing in his mind.
THE WOMAN: You could have called, could have warned me . . . To stand me up like that, in that hotel room . . . It shows such contempt! . . . Don't you think I deserve more consideration? . . .
LULU: Maybe I'm wrong. Maybe I'm not expressing myself well. Maybe vocation's not the right word; I sometimes mistake a word for another. But that doesn't change the fact that I need this work. For my mother and my brother, and in the name of the father. In the name of the father. That's why I talked about my brother earlier. He should be here in front of you but he doesn't even have a driver's license. And he doesn't have the vocation. My father worked here until what happened. The newspapers talked about it. Even on TV, they talked about it. But you must know.
THE RECRUITER: You know, Lulu, this is a big firm. A huge firm. It's a world unto itself. So if we had to stay abreast of every little incident . . . But anyway . . . Go on.
LULU: An hour before, on the day it happened, just before leaving for work, Dad said, 'cause Mom was begging him to change jobs as she'd been doing since that car bomb attack, it was in the news a lot, where the van and obviously the entire team, people Dad knew, were completely blown to pieces, so just before leaving for work, Dad said, It's my life. The van's my whole life.

THE WOMAN: Tell me at least what I did to you.

THE RECRUITER: Nothing, you did nothing . . . Go on, Miss.

LULU: It was a normal run done dozens of times before. Nothing unusual. A shopping mall. It happened in the parking lot of a shopping mall.

THE WOMAN: Have I asked if you were willing to do anything?

THE RECRUITER: For God's sake! . . . Would you leave her alone? I'm working!

THE WOMAN: OK, I get it . . . I get it . . . I'm leaving.

. . .

LULU: The guy with the machine gun showed up as they were coming back with the money. He shouted at them to drop the bags on the ground and they wouldn't be killed. It was in the middle of the parking lot. The guy was shouting but he wasn't moving. So Dad and the messenger drew their guns and pointed them at the guy. Without shooting either 'cause the guy wasn't moving. They were just holding him at bay. Like in a Tarantino movie. As for the driver, he couldn't take off 'cause the money wasn't in the van. We don't know how long the machine gun and the two revolvers would've stayed like that, looking daggers at each other in the middle of the parking lot, if the other one hadn't fired . . .'Cause there were two more criminals hidden behind a car. One with a shotgun and the other with a machine gun. The guy with the shotgun fired first. Then everybody started screaming and shooting in every direction. The three criminals were killed. Just like the messenger, Dad's co-worker. The driver came out fine 'cause he stayed in the armored van. Dad too would've come out fine if it weren't for that bullet in his neck . . . One bullet in his neck and Dad fell flat on his face . . .

. . .

THE RECRUITER: And you think that's a job for a young woman?

LULU: For this job, you need a weapon and courage, that's what Dad used to say, and courage knows no gender.

THE RECRUITER: Maybe your dad also told you about abnegation, about unwavering loyalty to the firm?

LULU: Yes, and much more. He told me about a sense of sacrifice, that my life has to be the shield that ensures the firm's survival. And I'm willing. My blood for the firm, that's something I'd do.

THE RECRUITER: Let's say the criminals had taken your father hostage after the money was safely dropped in the van. What would you have done if you had been the driver?

LULU: Take off. Leave since the money's in the van.

THE RECRUITER: You abandon your father?

LULU: . . . Dad always told me, What matters is the money. Money's the raison d'être of the firm. So in principle, the van has to go. And Dad has to stay. That's how it is. Those are the orders. As soon as the money's in the van, Dad's of no use anymore . . . No, that's not it, that's not what I mean . . . What I mean is as soon as the money's gone, as soon as the van's left with it, Dad's of no use to the thugs . . . There, that's what I mean: as a hostage, Dad's of no use to the criminals. In theory.

. . .

THE RECRUITER: I'm listening.

LULU: In theory 'cause, as you know, things are not that simple. But it's clear, that's what Dad used to say, that what matters is the money or in other words, the survival of the firm. 'Cause without the firm, there are no more superstores, no more ATMs, no more economy, no more Treasury, no more banks, no more stock market, no more government . . . Money's the world's blood and blood, even fresh in a bowl, is no longer life, blood in the ground is just a grave. For life to be sustained, blood needs to move, needs to circulate, be carried around, and in the world, what carries blood from one organ to another is the firm. Without the firm, everything would stop and that's in no one's best interest.

THE RECRUITER: Courage, as you rightly say, Miss, knows no gender. What are you willing to do to show your complete dedication to the firm other than, of course, give up your life?

LULU: Anything.

THE RECRUITER: Anything meaning what?

LULU: Well, anything.

. . .

THE RECRUITER: What if, Lulu, the firm were to ask you to take off your scarf?

LULU: . . . This? It's not a scarf, it's a bandana. My brother gave it to me . . .

THE RECRUITER: Is it your brother, Lulu, who insists that you wear it?

LULU: No . . . I wouldn't say that. I wear it— . . . I like wearing it, that's all . . . I threw it in his face after we had a fight the other day . . . Then he apologized and— . . . I don't know why I'm telling you this . . . It's just family stuff . . . I can take off the bandana if—

THE RECRUITER: No, Lulu, it looks lovely on you . . . The shoes, it's also him?

LULU: No, the shoes it's my mother. She says they make me stand straight.

THE RECRUITER: Those stilettos deliciously accentuate your beautiful legs, Lulu. . . .

LULU: Thank you, Sir.

THE RECRUITER: Now Lulu, the firm asks that you take off your clothes . . .

LULU: That I take off my clothes?

THE RECRUITER: Yes, for the job.

LULU: That I get undressed?

. . .

Really get undressed?

. . .

I'm sorry, I don't think I heard you right.

. . .

You asked me to . . .

. . .

THE RECRUITER: All your clothes.

. . .

LULU: Well . . .

. . .

THE RECRUITER: Absolutely everything, Lulu . . . Your panties too.

. . .

LULU: There.

. . .

THE RECRUITER: You're infinitely prettier like this, Lulu.

. . .

THE WOMAN: It can't end like this! It can't be over just because you snapped your fingers! You can't treat me with so much contempt! . . . What is she doing naked? . . . You're planning on screwing her too?

THE RECRUITER: Put your clothes back on, Lulu, we'll contact you . . . Would you leave me alone? I didn't go to that hotel because it was the only way to make you understand that for me, this affair—

THE WOMAN: Because to you, this is only an affair?

THE RECRUITER: What else did you expect? You're married, I'm married. You have kids, I have kids. Did you expect me to just cross my wife and kids out of my life? I've never asked you for that so don't expect it from me . . . Put your clothes back on, Lulu, we'll contact you . . .

THE WOMAN: I was such a fool . . .

THE RECRUITER: Be realistic . . .

THE WOMAN: Because— . . . Because— . . . The day before yesterday, I filed for divorce. He didn't put up any resistance . . . You hear me? I said the hell with everything . . . Husband and kids . . . I screwed it all up . . . Broke it all up . . . To give myself over to love . . .

THE RECRUITER: But I've never asked for that!

THE WOMAN: I found love . . . And it's you . . . You're a part of me . . . I've made you a part of me . . . I've made you the cornerstone of my life . . . The source of all my joy . . . You inhabit every corner of every moment of my life . . .

THE RECRUITER: Here we go, deep into melodrama again. Let's stay adult about this. Responsible. We both had, at the same time, on opposite ends of the town, what we could call a need to escape. This little jaunt has been a beautiful adventure . . . A beautiful story. With neither your loved ones nor mine having to suffer from it . . . At least not until the day before yesterday . . . Now let's draw the curtain . . . Put your clothes back on, Lulu. You can go, we'll contact you . . . Let's draw the curtain before disgust takes root in us, before the recriminations and the drama start . . .

LULU: You know all I want is to work for my mother my brother and in the name of our father just to work . . .

THE RECRUITER: Let's draw the curtain to preserve the innocence of our passion. I'll remember this all my life, I've lived wonderful moments in your arms during those few days and I hope you had a good time in my arms too. But there comes a time when we must have the strength to say stop before we hurt other people . . .

THE WOMAN: A good time . . .

THE RECRUITER: Don't leave like that . . . We can't part on that note . . . Wait, I'll walk you out . . . Would you put your clothes back on, Lulu, we'll contact you . . .

. . .

LULU: The job
Our father often told me about it
Our father instilled it in me
Our father taught me to love it and I love it
If only in the name of the father
I have the vocation
Maybe it's not the right word
I sometimes mistake a word for another
But it's something like that
Something that says that I'd do anything to
Join the firm
'Cause
Like Dad used to say
I can feel it
It's my life
The van
Is my whole life
I beg you
Give me a bit of a chance at last
I wanna join the firm
'Cause
I need to dedicate my life
To something great
Something highly human
'Cause
I want blood to keep circulating and circulating
In the world's veins
'Cause I don't want everything to
Suddenly stop
'Cause it's my vocation
'Cause
'Cause
'Cause . . .

ABSOLUTION

THE KOMISARI: I'm happy you've once again answered my call, Zac. I brought you here, to the right bank of the river, away from the town, to tell you this story . . . Too bad the fireflies have disappeared. . . . The story of a man. That man was a recruiter by trade. And incidentally, the nephew of the Jury Master. The story of the recruiter is also the story of a young man. One morning, the young man's sister, unemployed by trade, if I can put it that way, goes to the office of the recruiter. The recruiter sees that the beauty of the young woman standing in front of him is a manifestation of the glory of the One who sits in Heaven. The young woman is beautiful, beautiful like Lulu, your sister, Zac. And so the man, consumed with desire for the young man's sister, takes advantage of his position and covers her with shame. In tears, the young woman crosses the entire town all the way to her brother's feet, recounts in detail the humiliation she has just suffered and demands revenge. The brother promises to avenge his sister on the condition that from now on she wears the veil. Because there would have been no infamy if the sister had been veiled when she met the recruiter . . . Really too bad the fireflies have returned to the source of all things . . . Three days ago, we found on the railroad tracks, between the Avenue de la Gineste and Impasse Carnus, along the viaduct, the remains of a body. Or at least what looked like something that had once been a human body. A few hours later, we found the head in Saint-Félix, by the side of the tracks. Intact. Neatly severed from the rest of the body by a train wheel. The head belonged to the Jury Master's nephew. Without the shadow of a doubt. Yet the investigation, which I quickly wrapped up, concluded it was an accident. The recruiter, probably drunk, got lost on the railroad tracks and didn't see the train coming. So the case is closed. Laid to rest. There won't be a prosecution, Zac, even though it was effectively a murder. I arrived first at the scene of the crime so I was able to conceal the clues that could have led directly to the murderer. And do you know why I concealed those clues from the police, Zac? In the name of the law. Because I asked myself, Why was the recruiter tied to the railroad tracks? I didn't ask myself who tied him but why did that person commit such a crime? Why? . . . Baby Mo told me, the day before the head and strips of flesh turned up, that she had asked the recruiter to look favorably upon your sister Lulu's job application. Baby Mo told me that the interview had gone very badly. Baby Mo told me that Lulu was humiliated, sullied. Baby Mo told me that Lulu begged you to reclaim her honor. That, Zac, was what I knew when I found what was left of the recruiter on the railroad tracks. Right now, I don't know who killed the recruiter but I suspect one thing: Baby Mo, your sister Lulu, myself and you wouldn't need more than a brief moment of reflection to uncover the perpetrator. But is this what's most important? No, Zac. What matters is not who broke the law of blood but why it was broken. Why? The recruiter was a despicable man. An unfit father who neglected wife and children to indulge in shameless fornication. A notorious sodomite who has subjected more than half of the women in this town to the worst abominations of the flesh. We must protect and sanctify our women. He deserved more than anyone to be dragged behind a pickup truck until death followed, in accordance with the law. And so it was just that he be thrown into the grave he had himself dug. *All who sin apart from the law will also perish apart from the law.* The perpetrator was right, a thousand times right to reduce the house of the recruiter to a torrent of wails and tears. Because if this is how we treat our women, how do we expect others will treat them? We must protect and sanctify our women. How do we expect these people, who have been vomited by the ocean at the foot of our walls after crossing forests, savannahs, steppes and deserts in the most complete abnegation, because you need a lot of abnegation to reach our gates of mercy, how do we expect these people, who left children, wives and fiancées behind, will look at our women if we treat them like this? The brother was right to make this confrontation a personal matter, a private matter, between men, far from the eyes of the law. Didn't the man cover his sister with shame? I, too, asked myself the question, Would you, for the same reason, have sent that man to the dwelling of the dead? And I answered, I would have sent that man to the dwelling of the dead if he had sullied Baby Mo. In all conscience, Zac. It's the law. So in his own way, the man who destroyed the life of the recruiter is a man of law. We must protect and sanctify our women. . . . What you did was good, Zac . . . I saw your sister Lulu this morning . . . It's good that you've finally convinced her to wear the veil. . . . You don't say anything, Zac? . . . Good, certain things are better left unsaid . . . When I saw her covered like that, I had the feeling Lulu was born to wear the veil . . . You did your duty. . . . I've often told you, Zac, you can commit any crime as long as it's in the name of values and now, you have values. And that's what's most important . . . You know Zac, Baby Mo told me about your mother, your sister, about how your family lives in adversity. She told me about your efforts, the small jobs you take so your mother and Lulu can keep their heads high and stare life straight in the eye. . . . I thought about you for a job. The militia. Welcome to the House of the Law, Zac. I told the Commander of the Militia about you. I told him that an entire family depends on you, and most importantly, that you have a sense of duty and law. He agreed to hire you. He's hiring you. You're a militiaman, Zac. From now on, you have a job, like any honest citizen. Tomorrow, go to Town Hall, to the Department of the Municipal Militia. There's a uniform waiting for you, with a militia hat. And a gun, Zac.

0.9

JUDIKAEL: I like it when you look at me with those eyes. . . . I've never been as happy as I am now, here, next to you. Just the two of us. The back of your hand brushing my cheek. . . . I bought this shirt yesterday. I spent a fortune. An impulse. A whim. Linen is like a caress. . . . Can I stop the movie? . . . Or at least mute it? . . . Feel . . . I thought you'd like it. . . . You like it? . . . Let me guide your hand. . . . Lately, I've been feeling like my presence is weighing on you . . .

ZAC: Where the hell's Baby Mo!

JUDIKAEL: So that's it, I'm a burden? . . . Here. This is for you . . . I had your name engraved on it . . . You like it? . . . Let me put it on your wrist. I bought it near the cathedral . . . on rue Fraysinnous . . . which turns into rue Terral and ends at the Town Square . . . Earlier. On my way here. I saw it and I immediately thought of you. I went in and said to the lady, without even asking for the price, I'd like to have that name engraved on it. Zac. Let me put it on your wrist . . . Why are you so tense? . . . Relax . . . Look at me. . . . Who do you see? . . . You have here, in front of you, the friend your thoughts haven't caressed in weeks. Not since you got brainwashed by Baby Mo's husband . . . What does he want from you? . . . I spent the last few days beside you, outside of you. While this guy was making his way between you and me. . . . No, don't touch me . . . You know how I am. Just look at me. I mean, talk to me. Tell me yes, tell me no. Tell me it's raining, tell me it's sunny. Talk to me. 'Cause every time, your silence sends me into throes of despair and many times I've come this close to—

ZAC: The others are coming up . . .

JUDIKAEL: Zac, let's talk about us. Again. A little. Again a little talk about us. The two of us. You and me, what are we doing together? . . . Who am I, what am I to you? I beg you, let's talk a little about us before darkness completely swallows me . . .

. . .

GUY 1: It's true, right, Zac, that when girls say no, it means— . . . What's up, Judikael?

JUDIKAEL: Why should something be up?

GUY 1: You look all weird . . .

GUY 2: What's the movie?

GUY 1: Zac, you too, you look a little weird.

GUY 2: There's no sound?

GUY 3: Zac always looks a little weird. But Judikael—

GUY 1: I can't get used to the idea that you've become a cop.

ZAC: Well, you're just gonna have to.

GUY 2: What's this stupid movie?

GUY 1: You two look like you just had a fight.

GUY 3: I'd be surprised, Zac doesn't easily lose his cool. But Judikael—

JUDIKAEL: For fuck's sake, I'm telling you, everything's fine!

GUY 3: Whoa, easy. Don't bare your teeth at me! We're just asking, that's all. Have you seen yourself? You're all upset. So don't vomit your hatred on me, Judikael. OK, to a certain extent, your business is your business and nobody else's business. But we're friends, right? So if we find you in a state, it makes sense that we'd—

GUY 1: Hey, Zac, when women say no, it actually means yes, right? 'Cause this dickhead—

GUY 3: Asshole!

GUY 1: Son of a bitch!

JUDIKAEL: How do you know?

GUY 1: What?

JUDIKAEL: That his mother is a bitch?

GUY 1: I'm just saying. Just messing around, that's all. You're not gonna get on my case with your stupid questions, Judikael?

GUY 3: You're the cocksucking bastard son of a bitch.

GUY 1: Go fuck yourself on the Internet, you prick. It's true, right, Zac, that girls say no to mean yes? 'Cause he's been dicked around by a chick for a whole week now. She keeps saying, no, no, no. All the time, no. No to everything. And I'm telling him he needs to hurry and fuck her 'cause if she keeps saying yes, yes, yes and he doesn't bang her against the wall . . . You see it all the time in porn movies, it's what girls are waiting for. Right Zac, it's true that's what they're waiting for, for us to come in their face? That girl, if you don't show her you're a stud, she'll think you're a fag and she'll move on. So stop fucking around, girls hate it when we fuck around. Next time she says no, you pin her against the wall, she'll struggle, it's normal, it's part of the thing but you don't let that faze you and you rip off her clothes. They love it when we rip off their clothes. The Tarzan thing, I guess. And then, even naked, her hands stuck behind her back, she'll start to wriggle again, to twist and turn like an eel on a fishhook and, of course, to say no, no, no. So then, you smack her, they take that as a sign of love, don't try to understand, girls are really twisted. After that, you'll see, she'll look at you with the eyes of a doe and know you're a stud. Then she's ready, you open her up and you fuck her, you fuck her, you fuck her, inside and out you fuck her and you shoot your load all over her. Well, I swear on my mother's head, a girl like that, right Zac, a girl like that will never forget you. You can ask her to work the streets, she'll do it, happy as a clam. It's the only thing that works with them: to keep them on a tight leash. You hold the leash very tight, she'll cry, bawl, beg, then you give her some slack, and just when she thinks the storm has passed, you tighten the leash again, for no reason you tighten, until she starts to beg, on her knees, bawling her eyes out and covering your feet with kisses. Then you give her some slack again—

JUDIKAEL: What kind of girls do you hang out with?

GUY 1: Shut up, Judikael!

JUDIKAEL: Girls are not like your cactuses, airhead!

GUY 1: Well, that's where you've got it wrong, asshole! They're the same. Exactly the same. Girls are born with lots of thorns, like cactuses. And those thorns have to be pulled out one by one otherwise you get pricked in the soul. And that fucking hurts! Worse than a fish bone in your throat . . . It's like that Japanese fish, the *fugu*, apparently it's a real delicacy but if it's not prepared right, you're fucked. 'Cause the *fugu*'s full of shit. Same with chicks, they must be prepared right . . . And you know what, fuck you! . . . I'm gonna rip your guts out . . . I'm gonna gouge your eyes out with a fork . . . I'm gonna eat your mother's pussy out of a trash can . . . Her pussy and her ass . . . And I'm gonna fuck you dry with a cactus, Judikael.

JUDIKAEL: Blah, blah, blah . . . What else? You're gonna buy yourself a brain?
GUY 1: Judikael, you're fucking pissing me off!
GUY 2: Weird, this film . . . For a porn movie, I find it's really low on action . . .
GUY 1: So
you tighten you let go
you tighten you let go
you tighten you let go
you tighten you let go
you tighten you let go
you tighten you let go
you tighten you tighten you tighten
the more she thrashes around the more you tighten
the more she cries the more you tighten
the more she begs the more you tighten
you tighten until you forget
the reason why you tightened in the first place
until you feel
the warmth of your come crawl down your thighs . . .
'Cause it's crazy how good the whole thing feels. And then suddenly, you stop. All of a sudden, for no apparent reason, you don't tighten anymore. One morning, stop. Right when she expects you to tighten, don't. And you watch her . . . That's a trick I stole from scientists. On TV. You often see them do that with mice; they tear off the tail, a leg, an eye . . . But careful, it's not cruelty, they do it to save humanity . . .
GUY 2: What's this bullshit, Zac? . . . I mean I'm not kidding, I've been watching this silent porn and I haven't seen a single cock or pussy . . . Not even a pair of tits . . . For a porn movie, it's really fucking dull.
ZAC: Are you high? It's not a porn movie, it's *Scarface*.
GUY 2: Oh, that's *Scarface*? My brother's seen it . . .
GUY 1: So your chick, all of a sudden, you stop tightening and you observe her. And you'll see, 'cause girls are really twisted, she'll want you to mess her up again. 'Cause she's used to it, like to a song stuck in her head. The following days, you still don't tighten despite her nagging. Just the opposite, you take her to the movies, you buy her cookies, chocolate, flowers, and if you've got some cash, a diamond or sapphire or something. You go all out. Despite all this, she's gonna push you to smack her again, so knock yourself out and let her have it. Like a vaccine booster. You have

to understand her, the poor girl, it's become her dope; it's seized her flesh and her mind. In a way, it's screwed up her genetic code. She's become addicted to being whacked, you know what I mean? So you're doing her a favor.

JUDIKAEL: Zac, can you tell him to shut his bitch ass trap?

GUY 1: Judikael, the day you grow cactuses and show up with a girlfriend will be the day you can tell me what goes on in a woman's head . . . OK, so after this treatment, you'll have a chick like this, perfectly straight. Without thorns and ripe for the street. And whores bring in as much as dope, right, Zac? . . . She'll never be on your case again and, most of all, she won't say no to mean yes and yes to mean no. She'll say yes, yes, yes, all the time. Strictly yes. Right, Zac?

ZAC: Stop running off at the mouth! The merchandise should've been here a while ago and all you do is drive everyone bonkers with your bullshit.

GUY 1: Baby Mo's not here yet?

JUDIKAEL: As you can see.

ZAC: It's the last time I deal with her. I'm gonna strike out on my on. Go right to the source.

GUY 2: You wanna be the chief.

ZAC: The boss. I'm sick of being a middleman. And you too, you're gonna climb up a notch. You'll go from street dealers to middlemen. My middlemen. Everyone will have a piece of the territory. No more mom and pop business. We gotta flood the whole region. With pure shit.

JUDIKAEL: You always say that, that you're gonna strike out on your own, and then—

ZAC: But this time, I've got the means to do it.

JUDIKAEL: And Mr. Africa?

ZAC: Mr. Africa can go fuck himself. He's getting greedier and greedier. While we're out on the street taking all the risks. If we have to deal directly with the head honchos from the other side of the world, I'll deal directly with the head honchos from the other side of the world. The network in this town is me and no one else. So from now on, Mr. Africa can go suck his own dick.

JUDIKAEL: You're not afraid that he'll—

ZAC: And what's this, decoration? . . . Who should I be afraid of? What should I be afraid of with this? I'm a militiaman.

GUY 2: Can I touch it, Zac? . . . It's true that with that in your hand, it changes everything.

GUY 3: Yeah, when you're a cop, 'cause a militiaman that's also a cop, you're not afraid anymore, everyone else has to be afraid. When you have a piece on your belt, you're on the right side of the law. And on top of that, it's a legal rod. An official rod. You can waste anybody with it, legally. No matter how we look at it, you're the boss now, Zac.

ZAC: I'll be the boss and people will call me Scarface.

GUY 2: Whoa! Scarface! That's so cool!

GUY 3: And me, Cherokee!

GUY 1: And I'll be Cactus-man!

GUY 2: Scarface! I'd love to work for a boss named Scarface. While Mr. Africa— . . . By the way, Zac, who's Mr. Africa?

ZAC: Only Baby Mo's seen him in person . . .

. . .

It's Baby Mo. Stop the film . . . Go open the door, Judikael.

. . .

BABY MO: Hi.

GUY 1: What's up, Baby Mo?

BABY MO: Why should something be up? . . . Zac, here's your package.

ZAC: How come you're not on time?

BABY MO: This is my last delivery. I'm not proud of myself . . .

ZAC: You always say that, Baby Mo, but you always come back with the merchandise.

BABY MO: Can we be alone, Zac, just the two of us?

ZAC: These are my friends, I've got nothing to hide from them.

BABY MO: I've got nothing to hide either, Zac, but I still think you and I—

GUY 3: For fuck's sake, get off his back! Can't you see he's never loved you?

. . .

BABY MO: Zac?

ZAC: This is the only thing that connects us, you and me . . . That brings us together. But I'm done dealing. I'm stopping this shit. I have a job. A hell of a job! I'm a policeman . . . Well, a militiaman. I'm the law, Baby Mo. The example. And I wanna make my life a less tortuous path. A straight path. You know what I mean, from now on I wanna go through life without averting or lowering my eyes. To live and make a living through destructive means is not healthy for the soul. On the Day of Judgment, I wanna show up in the Valley of Jehosaphat with a clean soul.

BABY MO: Where did you get these words, Zac?

ZAC: Your husband's a father to me, Baby Mo. He's making me into a man. A real man. If I'm a cop today, me, the most abject of all beings, it's thanks to him. It's through his grace that I've crossed over to the light. He's my redemption . . .

GUY 2: Whoa! Listen to you, Zac!

ZAC: And I don't want the affection he has for me to be tainted by a suspicion that has no reason to be . . .

BABY MO: In other words, Zac?

GUY 3: I think what Zac's saying is clear.

BABY MO: In other words, Zac?

GUY 1: When a guy says no, it's no, period.

BABY MO: In other words, Zac?

ZAC: I don't wanna see you in this bedroom anymore.

GUY 3: Crystal clear.

ZAC: And I don't want our paths to ever cross again. Here or anywhere else in the world . . .

GUY 3: Couldn't be any clearer.

ZAC: I don't know you, you don't know me.

GUY 3: Do you get it now?

BABY MO: You've never loved me?

ZAC: I don't wanna see you anymore, Baby Mo.

BABY MO: You didn't answer.

ZAC: I owe everything to your husband. I'm his son.

GUY 2: So you're his stepmother . . . Trippy, huh?

BABY MO: I'll come back once the crows and spiders have left your head.

ZAC: I won't let you in.

GUY 3: He doesn't wanna see you anymore so fuck off!

BABY MO: I'll come back . . .

GUY 1: Jesus Christ, would you stop harassing him!

ZAC: I won't let you in.

GUY 3: That's enough, get out!

JUDIKAEL: Don't push her! . . . You can't let them talk to her like that . . . Zac, it's Baby Mo.

BABY MO: It's OK, Judikael . . . It doesn't matter.

GUY 3: OK, now, out! Come on, get the fuck out!

. . .

ZAC: By the way Baby Mo, who's Mr. Africa? . . . How is he?
BABY MO: I'll tell you next time . . .
ZAC: I won't let you in . . .
BABY MO: . . . when I come back.

COME INSIDE ME

THE KOMISARI: I'm listening.

BABY MO: You're listening, you're listening . . . I've already told you everything, sweet husband.

THE KOMISARI: Tell me again, I'm listening.

BABY MO: You're driving me bonkers.

THE KOMISARI: Don't talk to me like that, Baby Mo, do not talk to me like that! You don't talk to your husband like that. I don't like it when you talk to me like that, with those words, You're driving me bonkers, you know that. You may still be a child but you're also a married woman, Baby Mo. So talk with the words of a married woman. You're bothering me, you're annoying me, you're irritating me, you're getting on my nerves, those are the words of a married woman, maybe even you're pissing me off, fine. But not, You're driving me bonkers. You need to understand that, Baby Mo, to get that in your head, you're a married woman and a married woman has duties, rights too, of course, but first of all duties.

BABY MO: And you? What are your duties?

THE KOMISARI: To sanctify and protect you. That's why it is written: *He who loves his wife loves himself. After all, no one ever hated his own flesh.*

BABY MO: I love you and protect you too. In my own way, not the way it is written perhaps but I love you and protect you, sweet husband.

THE KOMISARI: Don't be insolent, Baby Mo. It's up to men to protect women, not the other way around. You owe me obedience and respect, and I sanctify you and provide for you. I protect you. That's why it is written: *For man did not come from woman, but woman from man; neither was man created from woman. For this reason, the woman ought to—*

BABY MO: You're driving me bonkers! Do I spend my time asking what you do with your day?

THE KOMISARI: You don't need to.

BABY MO: Lower this gun from my temple.

THE KOMISARI: I get up.

BABY MO: Lower this gun from my temple.
THE KOMISARI: I wash myself.
BABY MO: Lower this gun from my temple.
THE KOMISARI: I eat breakfast.
BABY MO: Lower this gun from my temple.
THE KOMISARI: I kiss you.
BABY MO: Lower this gun from my temple.
THE KOMISARI: I go to work.
BABY MO: Lower this gun from my temple.
THE KOMISARI: So I can provide for you.
BABY MO: Lower this gun from my temple.
THE KOMISARI: A man's responsibility is to feed his family.
BABY MO: Lower this gun from my temple.
THE KOMISARI: Then I come home.
BABY MO: Lower this gun from my temple.
THE KOMISARI: That's what I do with my day. Nothing wrong. But you, what do you do when I'm not looking, when I'm at work sweating blood and tears? I'm listening.
BABY MO: I've already told you.
THE KOMISARI: Tell me again.
BABY MO: First, lower this gun from my temple.
THE KOMISARI: I won't lower anything and you're going to talk . . . I intend to soon make you a mother, Baby Mo. You hear, a mother. An offspring. Your flesh and my flesh. A family. But first, I want to see through you, to measure the width and depth of the dross that still tarnishes your soul.
BABY MO: I did nothing wrong. Like you, I do nothing wrong. I was with my girlfriends. Alone at home, when you're not here, I get bored. I miss you. So I go out to see my friends. We spent the day in the park. Talking. Laughing. Talking about our men as usual. Girl talk. I talked about you. About my sweet husband. That you're a good man. That you even cry sometimes. It made my friends laugh. Then I came home. So I would be here when you got back from work. I know that makes you happy.
THE KOMISARI: That's it?
BABY MO: That's it. We also ate roasted chestnuts. Nothing wrong.
THE KOMISARI: You're lying, you unworthy woman.
BABY MO: It's the truth.
THE KOMISARI: You were at his place.
BABY MO: You're not going to start with that again.

THE KOMISARI: You're lying shamelessly, you woman of little faith. I had you followed.

BABY MO: You're having me followed?

THE KOMISARI: I couldn't help it. I'm a cop.

BABY MO: You're not a cop, you're a komisari. . . . Then why are you driving me bonkers with all of this? All right, I was with him . . .

THE KOMISARI: At his place.

BABY MO: I was with him at his place, are you happy? . . . I went to see Lulu, his sister. We're friends, that's not news, I hope. Lulu wasn't there . . . He told me she would be back soon and he invited me to have a Coke and watch TV in his bedroom while I was waiting for her. But it's not what you think . . . In fact, we were not alone . . . He was with his friend Judikael, the one who's always with him and whom he calls his passing fancy, and with other friends I've seen before but whose names I don't know . . . So there's no need to get so upset . . . We were not alone. And even if we had been, I'm your wife, everyone knows that . . . We talked about things from when we were in school. Nothing wrong . . . How can you even imagine such things?

THE KOMISARI: Don't take your husband for a fool, Baby Mo. You want me to believe you crossed the entire town, all the way into his bed, to talk about the weather?

BABY MO: That's right. I just wanted to look into his eyes.

THE KOMISARI: You persist on being disrespectful? . . . A man who sees a girl like you, Baby Mo, enter his bedroom . . . Even if he's not in the mood . . . If only out of male pride . . . A girl like you . . . A man is only a man, Baby Mo . . .

BABY MO: I'm telling you that nothing happened so lower this gun from my temple.

THE KOMISARI: Tell me about this nothing that didn't happen.

BABY MO: There's nothing to tell.

THE KOMISARI: In any case, you have no business being in a man's bedroom while your husband is not looking. Tell me what he did to you!

BABY MO: Nothing.

THE KOMISARI: Nothing?

BABY MO: Nothing.

THE KOMISARI: Absolutely nothing?

BABY MO: Nothing at all.

THE KOMISARI: Do you regret it? . . . That he did nothing to you?

BABY MO: You're driving me bonkers.

THE KOMISARI: The next time you say, You're driving me bonkers, you'll hear the bark of this weapon one millisecond too late. What did he do to you?

. . .

BABY MO: Forgive me . . . Forgive me, sweet husband . . . I'm ashamed of myself . . . Forgive me . . . You're right, something did happen . . . But I'd rather not talk about it . . .

THE KOMISARI: Tell me.

BABY MO: Not talk about it and forget . . .

THE KOMISARI: Tell me.

BABY MO: To protect you from yourself . . .

THE KOMISARI: Tell me.

BABY MO: Things . . . Oh God! . . . I disgust myself . . . You really want to hear?

THE KOMISARI: My job is to lend an ear to all the disgrace of this world.

BABY MO: I don't want you to be hurt.

THE KOMISARI: Tell me.

BABY MO: I didn't go to see Lulu but to see him. Not for what you think. I just feel like seeing him sometimes. To find out how he's doing, nothing more. . . . Since school, he's had that effect on me. I don't know why . . . Lower the gun from my temple. . . . And promise to forgive me. . . . He was with Judikael, the one he calls his passing fancy, and other guys. . . . They were horsing around and watching football on TV. They were smoking . . . When I came in, his friends stopped watching TV and turned toward me, staring at me in silence like they were seeing me for the first time, and one of the guys went, Wow, you're kind of hot without the rag on your head, and the one he calls his passing fancy added, I like your haircut. It really suits you. You're beautiful like that, Baby Mo! You've always been beautiful. . . . I got my hair cut and you didn't even notice . . .

THE KOMISARI: Oh my God! . . . You're not wearing your— . . . And you got your hair cut? . . . You crossed the entire town against what is written? . . . Keep going, we'll talk about that later . . .

BABY MO: The one he calls his passing fancy and the other guys said all kinds of nice things about my hair, that I was pretty, that I was beautiful . . . Really nice things. . . . But he didn't say a word; he barely turned around when I walked in. Then I heard his back ask, What do you want? To say hi, as usual, I said. You're here to stuff my share of the apple down my throat, Baby Mo? I got scared 'cause he suddenly started talking like you, like a church. He turned toward me and he talked about man sitting quietly in the garden, following the ways of the law. He talked about woman, ridden by the Prince of this world, who shows up with her winks, her ass, her breasts. And he talked about the Fruit of Knowledge. And he talked about darkness . . . He was telling me these things with his eyes glued to my breasts . . . Eyes like I'd never seen before, on fire in his head . . . I started thinking that I was having quite an effect on him and that he was making this stuff up so he didn't have to listen to the whispers of his flesh when he said, You're here to lose your way, Baby Mo. And to make me lose mine. You're here to get fucked and to throw my soul into the Tempter's fire . . . That knocked the wind out of me. That word . . . That's when I should've— . . . But I didn't know what to say . . . what to do . . . All my strength suddenly left me . . . Since school, he's always had that effect on me . . . Now I tell myself I should've— . . . When those filthy words escaped his mouth like a pack of rats, I should've— . . . His hand slipped between my breasts and I felt his fingers pinch my nipple.

. . .

THE KOMISARI: He sullied you?

BABY MO: He withdrew his hand. He opened the door and said, Now get the fuck out, daughter of Jezebel! But I didn't move. I couldn't figure out what was going on inside me. 'Cause normally, after his crude remarks and his fingers on my nipple, I should've— . . . But all my strength left me . . . I was petrified . . . There was a silence, which seemed very long. The only sound was coming from the football game on TV. Then he said to me, If this is how it's gonna be, then strip down. I said, Tell your friends to leave us alone. He gave a slight smile from the corner of his lips and told me to hurry and that his friends were not going to leave—

THE KOMISARI: What did they do to you?

BABY MO:—and that if I wasn't happy, I was free to go. But I didn't move. I couldn't move . . . I still don't understand why . . . Then he told the guys to strip me down. They took off my clothes . . . I was paralyzed . . . Since school, he's always had that effect on me . . . And then— . . . Oh God!

THE KOMISARI: What did he do to you?

BABY MO: I'd rather not . . .

THE KOMISARI: What did he do to you?

BABY MO: I don't want to hurt you.

THE KOMISARI: What did he do to you?

BABY MO: Forgive me . . . I should've— . . . Forgive me . . .

THE KOMISARI: He sullied you?

BABY MO: It's my fault . . . Forgive me . . . All my fault . . .

THE KOMISARI: He sullied you, is that it, he sullied you?

BABY MO: Things I was far from imagining . . .

THE KOMISARI: What? What things?

BABY MO: Only beasts in the depths of the jungle are capable of such abomination . . .

THE KOMISARI: He sullied you.

BABY MO: Then he said to his friends, Now your turn . . . I'd rather not say any more. I don't have the strength to tell you what happened next . . .

THE KOMISARI: Tell me. I want to gauge the depth of the well of ignominy in which you were thrown.

BABY MO: Judikael, the one he calls his passing fancy, didn't move. He looked like a little boy frightened by what he was seeing. The others hesitated for a moment then one of them, the one who now calls himself Cherokee, ripped off his clothes and told me to get on all fours and— . . . They all threw themselves at me, all at once. The one he calls his passing fancy was curled up in a corner, his knees folded up under his chin, crying like a child lost in a field of desolation. He was mumbling, Stop. Don't do that. Don't do that to her. Guys, it's Baby Mo. Zac, tell them to stop . . . But he didn't lift a finger; he was leaning against the door, naked, his arms crossed, watching me beg him with my eyes to tell them to stop doing these things that were making my flesh flinch with horror. And pain . . .

THE KOMISARI: *I pursue my enemies and overtake them;*
I do not turn back till they are destroyed.
I crush them so that they cannot rise;
They fall beneath my feet.

BABY MO: What are you going to do with Zac, sweet husband?

THE KOMISARI: I have enough to convince the seventy-one members of the Jury Council to sentence him to be dragged by the feet behind a pickup truck until death ensues. . . . Oh, my little angel, how you must have suffered! . . . He must pay for sullying you.

BABY MO: I'm counting on it . . . But I know Zac, he's as clever as the devil . . . If the case is presented to the Jury Council, Zac won't have any qualms about being wicked to escape the law. He'll invent anything. And he'll twist things around so much that in the end, I'll be guilty. Plus, even if he ends up being dragged by a pickup truck, you never come out clean from that kind of public display; people will see me as a woman who's been humiliated, I'll be guilty of being sullied. And that view of myself, I don't like it. I'll be debased in the eyes of the town . . . They'll say that there's no fire without smoke . . . But I'm still your wife.

THE KOMISARI: I never considered summoning him before the Jury Council, my little angel, and sentencing him to the pickup truck even less. This is a man's business. Between men. Him and me. Nothing official. Simply man to man.

BABY MO: That's it, a man's business . . . Corner him in an alley one night and give him a good beating. . . . Or even, while you're at it . . . Since it's night . . . Since it's in an alley where no one goes . . . Since it's man-to-man business . . . while you're at it . . . 'Cause he's as clever as the devil, that Zac . . . Oh no, what is my mind whispering to me? . . . I'm ashamed to let myself have that thought . . .

THE KOMISARI: Yet I'm thinking the same thing, Baby Mo . . .

BABY MO: No! . . . No, sweet husband . . . Not that . . . That's completely different . . . That's too much!

THE KOMISARI: And what he did to you wasn't too much? He did everything to you so everything will be done to him.

BABY MO: Blood?

THE KOMISARI: Can only be washed with blood.

BABY MO: Oh, sweet husband . . . Well, if that's your will . . . But be very careful, these things can backfire like a ton of bricks.

THE KOMISARI: Not with me. An arrest that goes wrong, a refusal to cooperate, a scuffle, the shot goes off. An accident. Or the classic scenario: he brutally charged me with a knife, the shot went off. Self-defense. I have a whole panoply of these. I'm a cop . . .

BABY MO: You're not a cop, you're a komisari.

THE KOMISARI: Your Golgotha won't be thrown to the lions of this town, and his blood won't be shed behind a pickup truck but by my own hands. This is a personal matter. A private matter. Man to man.

BABY MO: You're doing this for me?

THE KOMISARI: I must sanctify and protect you . . . Tell me, Baby Mo . . .

When Zac forced you on all fours . . . When he thrust his flesh into your flesh . . . Did you feel— . . . Was it at all— . . . Did you experience—

BABY MO: Pleasure? . . . You really want to know?

. . .

THE KOMISARI: No. Actually, no. Forget it. Let's move on.

BABY MO: That's the best thing to do: to move on . . . Sweet husband, earlier, your gun, was it loaded?

THE KOMISARI: It's always loaded.

BABY MO: Fully loaded.

THE KOMISARI: It can't be any more loaded.

BABY MO: Then press it against my temple . . . And kiss me. . . . Come inside me . . . Oh, sweet husband . . .

. . .

THE KOMISARI: *If you find honey, eat just enough;*
too much of it, and you will vomit.

BABY MO: You're driving me bonkers . . . Come inside me . . .

THE KOMISARI: I love you Baby Mo . . . I love you to death . . .

BABY MO: Lose yourself inside me . . . All the way in . . . Inside me, come . . . All the way in . . . All the way in . . . All the way inside . . . Until your flesh rests within the folds of my soul . . . Until, the gun against my temple, your flesh licks my soul, sweet husband.

GUNSHOT

ZAC: I'm telling you these are lies! . . . Don't shoot, I beg you, don't shoot . . . I never did these things to Baby Mo. Never . . . Don't shoot . . . Baby Mo often comes to our house, it's true, but my mother and Lulu and all my friends can attest that there's never been anything between us . . .

JUDIKAEL: I'm glad you agreed to meet me, Baby Mo.

BABY MO: Time is running out, Judikael, I came to tell you that—

JUDIKAEL: Me first. Let it go, Baby Mo. Turn your back on Zac, he doesn't love you, he's never loved you. I'm sorry to tell you this so brutally—

BABY MO: My husband has dragged Zac to the edge of the river.

JUDIKAEL: His mother, Lulu, our friends, you, me, your husband—

BABY MO: Zac and my husband are standing on the right bank of the river.

ZAC: We've known each other since high school, that's all . . . I don't know why Baby Mo told you those horrible things . . . I didn't do anything to her . . . Trust me . . . Don't kill me . . . You can't kill the lamb you brought back from the Kingdom of the Seducer . . . Remember, I was a young man reveling in debauchery, far from the light, and it was you— . . . Don't shoot, I beg you . . . I'm too young to die . . . To die so stupidly . . . You rescued me from perdition and showed me the way of the Spirit . . . You rekindled my desire for life . . . I don't wanna die . . . You gave meaning to my life . . . Don't shoot . . . I didn't do any of the things Baby Mo said I did to her . . . You gave me back to the world . . . You gave birth to me . . .

JUDIKAEL: Everyone loves Zac but Zac loves no one. He pretended to love you 'cause you were the ideal runner. He took advantage of you, Baby Mo, like he takes advantage of everyone who loves him. Who would think of looking under the clothes of the Chief of Police's young wife? Nobody. You were the perfect mule. You carried his dope like one carries a child. And you only mattered for that. He doesn't love me either. I've realized and accepted it. Believe me, it's not a bitter and unhappy lover who's talking to you, Baby Mo, it's a friend. Zac uses all of us as a cover. To pretend. He's covering himself. But why the hell does he need that cover?

ZAC: The last time she came to our house, I told her I didn't wanna see her anymore . . . I didn't wanna— . . . Nothing like that ever happened. Ever . . . So for her to tell you these things . . . Believe me, I've always conducted myself properly with her . . . You have to trust me . . . I'm too young . . . I've barely started to live . . . I'd like to be here, on the right bank of the river next year, to see the ballet of fireflies . . . In your footsteps . . . And the year after, and the year after the year after, and all the years to come . . . Remember the fireflies . . .

JUDIKAEL: If you're bored with your marriage, find yourself another lover, Baby Mo. 'Cause your husband and he are getting closer and closer, like father and son. Eventually he'll find out. I've never been crazy about the guy but you chose him, he's your husband and I respect that. I respect him for that. Even if I don't understand . . . I'll never understand . . . But I respect it . . .'Cause it's you, Baby Mo, and everything you do is beautiful . . .

BABY MO: Every one of us has a Promised Land, Judikael, a secret America. I've always dreamed of meeting those people, of being one of them.

Their cars, their houses, the outfits of their women, the way they drink their tea, the way they laugh softly, like they don't want to frighten anyone, the notes trickling from their pianos . . . Even the lazy casualness of their teenagers . . . I envy everything about them. And now I'm one of them, me, who came from nowhere. You realize, Judikael, I'm there! Shit, I'm there! Maybe it's stupid but those people are my America. And he was the key to my America . . .

ZAC: Please, don't shoot . . . I'm gonna leave . . . Gonna turn around . . . I'm gonna turn my back to you and leave . . .

JUDIKAEL: By the way, Baby Mo . . . I've always wondered . . . Who's Mr. Africa? . . . Zac says you're the only one who knows him.

ZAC: Here's what happened . . . The truth . . . What I first saw, 'cause I was lying down, was her red stilettos and her bare legs. She said to me, You see, I came back. She was wearing a yellow tank top . . . She didn't have a bra on and her green skirt barely covered her ass. From where I was, I could see she had no panties. She wasn't wearing her veil either and she'd just gotten her hair cut. I stood up and said to her, my soul filled with repulsion, 'cause Baby Mo's entire person was a provocation against the One Who Probes our Minds and Hearts, I said to her, thinking of the affliction that would be yours when you saw her all decked out like that, and without a veil, I said to her, You won't use me to disturb the peace of his soul, and I made her understand that even if she had no bad intentions, she was a married woman and it's not proper for a married woman to— . . . I made her understand that every one of her visits subjects me to temptation . . .'Cause I'm only a man . . . And you're my father . . . That's what I made her understand . . . Then I told her to leave but she smiled and kissed the corner of my lips and her kiss was ice like the kiss Judas Iscariot placed on the forehead of the Lamb. And I was seized with vomiting. I vomited. I vomited and said to her, For the last time, slave of the Tempter, get out of my house, it's an order! But she threw herself at my feet, pleading, and begged me to stop talking with words that were burning her inside, that this wasn't like me, that someone was speaking through me and that she'd come to free me from you . . . And more unbearable words . . . So I did what you would've done; I grabbed her by what was left of her hair, dragged her out of my bedroom, dragged her out of the living room past Lulu and my mother, they can testify . . . dragged her out of the apartment and threw her into the dark of the stairs . . . And, in the name of the Comforter, I prayed for you because of the burden that will be yours . . . That's the truth, nothing but the truth, other than that, nothing happened . . . Any other truth is a lie . . . I know it's your wife's word against mine . . . But I beg you, you must believe my word the way I always have, and still do, in this very moment, believe yours . . . I can face any adversity but not your doubts . . . Don't doubt me, in the name of the right hand which you have laid on my person . . . I'm leaving now . . . I'm gonna turn my back to you . . . The law forbids you to shoot someone with his back turned . . . You don't shoot someone in the back . . . A father doesn't shoot his son in the back . . . I'm turning around now and I'm leaving . . . Don't ever doubt me.

. . .

And gunshot! . . .
I saw, my back turned,
the mouth of the barrel spit
a dark streak of light.
I saw it slice
through my neck.
I saw it come out
of my forehead . . .
And I heard a rumble
Birds taking flight over the river . . .
You're gonna die Zac . . .
Die without having been Scarface . . .
A gunshot and
Scarface loads another cartridge in his gun . . .
A war weapon,
black, heavy, hideous.
From another war . . .
On the screens
all around him,
attackers
enter the house by the dozens . . .

BABY MO: My husband is about to kill Zac.

JUDIKAEL: Your husband . . . Zac?

BABY MO: That's what I came to tell you, Judikael. On the right bank of the river . . . He got it into his head that Zac and I have committed a sin.

Fornicated many times. The words he uses sometimes! I've already warned the authorities of the town: the Procurator, the Senator, the Mayor, the Jury Council . . . Everyone is heading to the river. I came to tell you, Judikael, that Zac is dead.

ZAC: In Scarface's back,
for some time already,
a man, dark glasses, is approaching,
gun in hand . . .
You're dying Zac . . .
And the music has the color of blood.
And the stairs have the color of blood.
And the house has the color of blood.
Alone against all, Scarface.
The more he kills, the more he has to kill.
Dust . . .
The screen is dust . . .
The screen is smoke . . .
The screen is flames . . .
The screen is blind . . .
And gunshot!
Scarface is hit.
His body pierced.
All of a sudden.
Through and through.
Fuck Zac, you're dying . . .
In Scarface's back,
the man,
eyes hidden behind glasses,
keeps approaching,
gun in hand . . .
We can only see the gun now
draw nearer to Scarface . . .
The man was blurred a long time ago
by dust,
by smoke,
by flames . . .
Scarface is standing,
his body riddled with death . . .

He curses his enemies . . .
Insults them . . .
The screen only shows the double barrel of
the gun draw closer,
draw within an inch,
of Scarface's back . . .
You can't die
like this,
alone,
like this,
by the river,
like this, Zac? . . .
And gunshot! . . .
Propelled forward by the bark of the gun,
Scarface is thrown into the pool.
Vermillion on blue . . .
From where Scarface fell,
the camera looks.
In the middle of the vermillion on blue
Scarface floats,
face in the water . . .
You're dying, Zac . . .
He shot you in the back
Through and through
Didn't even hurt
You stumbled
While thinking
I'd like to ask my mother to forgive me
And I'd like to tell her I love her
I'd like to ask Lulu to forgive me
And I'd like to tell her I love her
I'd like to ask Baby Mo to forgive me
I'd like to tell her that I forgive her
And that I love her
I'd like to tell everybody
Forgive me
Forgive me
Forgive me

For failing to
Fulfill the law
I'd like to be in a place where
The hand of man hasn't spoiled anything yet
I'd like to see the fireflies one last time
And you looked around you
Panoramic without moving your head
Your vision already gone
But two suns in your eyes
The fireflies appeared
Myriads of them
You stumbled for a moment
In the middle of the fireflies' dance
Then the body sank into the river
Then the fireflies sank into the river
Then the trees sank into the river
Then the river banks sank into the river
Then the town sank into the river
Then the world sank into the river
Then the river sank into the river
Everything sank
And then
Like a condor I emerged from the water
And
I disappeared into the red eye of the sky.

. . .

THE JURY MASTER: Drop your weapon at your feet.
THE KOMISARI: It was self-defense.
THE JURY MASTER: At your feet.
THE KOMISARI: It was him or the komisari.
THE JURY MASTER: Take three steps back.
THE KOMISARI: I didn't have a choice.
THE JURY MASTER: Three steps.
THE KOMISARI: I'm telling you, self-defense!
THE JURY MASTER: Hands behind your head.
BABY MO: They heard and saw everything, sweet husband.
THE KOMISARI: Baby Mo? . . . What are you doing here, among them?

. . . And without your veil again! . . . You continue to disobey me? . . . What is that rope you're wearing as a necklace?

BABY MO: It's the rope that will soon drag you by the feet behind a pickup truck, sweet husband.

THE KOMISARI: Drag me?

THE JURY MASTER: You shot someone with his back turned and that's against the law of this town.

THE KOMISARI: But this bastard dared to raise his manhood against my wife! . . . Tell them, Baby Mo . . . Tell them how he defiled you.

BABY MO: I told them. What I told you: there's never been anything between Zac and me. But you only heard what you wanted to hear, sweet husband. You've let hate dominate you and took the life of an innocent.

THE KOMISARI: An innocent? . . . Zac?

BABY MO: You got all fired up over nothing and you murdered Zac. Aggravating circumstance, you used, sweet husband, your service weapon to settle a personal matter. A private matter. Man to man.

THE KOMISARI: Salome! . . . Jezebel! . . . Trollop! . . . Twat! . . . Scum! . . . Swine! . . . Slut! . . . Filthy bitch! . . . Piece of shit! . . . Tart!

THE JURY MASTER: Our ears have heard enough, take him away!

THE KOMISARI: I have the right to defend my case before the Jury Council!

THE JURY MASTER: Take him away!

THE KOMISARI: No one can deprive me of that right! . . . This snake whom I fed from my own hand, to whom I've given everything, whom I brought back from the Kingdom of Dead Souls, has dared to cover my house with ignominy . . .

BABY MO: You keep getting worked up over the same stupidities, sweet husband.

THE KOMISARI: May you be cursed! . . . May you be devoured alive by the dogs of this town, daughter of Jezebel! . . . May you be plagued with adversity forever, in this eternity and the next!

BABY MO: It's no longer up to you to judge and call down curses, sweet husband.

THE KOMISARI: Oh, the slut! . . . The slut! . . . The slut! . . . Deep down, you're nothing but a slut!

BABY MO: And you have no idea to what extent, sweet husband.

THE KOMISARI: Stop calling me sweet husband, bitch!

THE JURY MASTER: Take him away!

THE KOMISARI: My death will be nothing compared to the days of plague awaiting you around every corner of your life!

BABY MO: I doubt there is a worse suppurating canker than you, sweet husband.

THE KOMISARI: I'm going to kill you, you stupid cow! . . . Stupid cow! . . . Stupid cow!

THE JURY MASTER: Take him away and tie him behind the pickup truck!

THE KOMISARI: Don't push me! . . . Why? . . . Why all this, Baby Mo? . . . This disaster? . . . Why? . . .

. . .

THE MOTHER: Have you seen my son, Monique?

BABY MO: At the bottom of the river.

THE MOTHER: Oh . . . What's all this noise in the distance, Monique?

BABY MO: It's my sweet husband . . . He's being dragged by the feet behind a pickup truck.

THE MOTHER: Behind a pickup truck . . . But why, Monique?

BABY MO: Personal matter. Private matter. Woman to man.

THE MOTHER: And my son? . . . You haven't seen my son, Monique?

BABY MO: In the steppes of Asia, or perhaps in the forests of Europe, or the plains of America, or the savannahs of Africa, or perhaps in the pampas, or the tundra, there's a six-legged beast that spends its life chasing after a smell said to be the most exhilarating of all perfumes. As soon as the first ray of life dazzles it, the beast's nose is overwhelmed by that perfume. From then on, its entire life is framed by a wild quest: to discover the source of that mysterious perfume. Quest in the farthest reaches of the heavens 'cause in addition to its six legs, the beast also has six wings. Quest in the unfathomable depths of the seas 'cause in addition to its six legs and its six wings, the beast also has six flippers. Hysterical, helter-skelter quest. But vain. Then one day, at the end of its tether, the end of its life, the beast collapses in agony. And just before its soul deserts its body, the beast discovers that the perfume was coming from its own navel. The man who's being dragged behind a pickup truck through the streets of the town told me this story.

THE MOTHER: Do you know where my son is, Monique?

BABY MO: At the bottom of the river, a bullet in his neck.

THE MOTHER: At the bottom of a river behind a pickup truck a bullet . . . What is he doing at the bottom of the river?

BABY MO: The bullet came out the forehead.

. . .

THE MOTHER: Have you seen my son, Monique? . . .
BABY MO: I'm not Monique!
I'm Baby Mo!
Baby Mo!
Baby Mo!
Baby Mo!

END OF PLAY